European Union and United States Foreign Policy

A STUDY IN SOCIOLOGICAL JURISPRUDENCE

F. S. C. Northrop

Sterling Professor of Philosophy and Law

in

The Law School of Yale University

"The difference between men is in their principle of association."—Emerson.

New York · 1954

THE MACMILLAN COMPANY

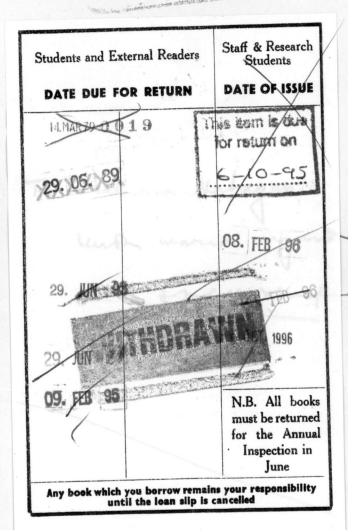

European Union and
United States Foreign Policy

Books by

F. S. C. NORTHROP

THE MEETING OF EAST AND WEST
SCIENCE AND FIRST PRINCIPLES
THE LOGIC OF THE SCIENCES AND THE HUMANITIES
THE TAMING OF THE NATIONS
EUROPEAN UNION AND UNITED STATES FOREIGN POLICY

To

UNDERHILL MOORE

Preface

In judging the book from the standpoint of its title, it is to be noted that its historical account of the relation between European Union and United States foreign policy begins roughly with the Hague Congress of the European Movement in May, 1948, and ends when the manuscript of this book went to the publisher during the Geneva Conference in April of 1954. This period of six years is sufficient, however, to indicate the manner in which the Truman-Acheson-Kennan policy of containing Communism, the Eisenhower-Dulles rollback crusade against Communism, and the movement toward European Union affected one another.

The subtitle of this book is to be taken seriously; otherwise the reader will misjudge what this inquiry is trying to do and may expect of it more than it pretends to, or can, do. Sociological jurisprudence is the science which studies the relation between (a) the positive legal constitutions, institutions and procedures, and (b) the underlying living habits, associations and beliefs of the people to whom the positive legal institutions are applied. The sociologist of law, Ehrlich, referred to the former as "the positive law" and to the latter as "the living law." The terminology of this book follows his usage. The movement toward European Union, which exhibits itself in the Council of Europe and in the Continental European Community, is an experiment in sociological jurisprudence because it attempts to put a single, new supranational positive law upon the diverse living associations of fourteen European peoples. The degree to which this aim is achieved turns out to be much greater in the case of the six peoples and nations in the Continental European Community than is the case with the fourteen nations of the larger community of the Council of Europe. Nevertheless, different types of success are attained in both instances. The cause of these different degrees and kinds of success throws novel and permanent light on the factors upon which the creation of a more effective international law depend. Hence, this inquiry has a lasting significance transcending the events of contemporary interest, important as they are, upon which it is based.

Because sociological jurisprudence takes the living law for granted, this book cannot pass judgment on the validity of the living law itself. There is a very important sense, however, in which this limitation is an asset rather than a liability. It means that any principles for creating an effective international law, discovered by this inquiry, are principles which can succeed with the de facto living beliefs, assocations and practices of the peoples and nations of the world as they are. In other words, our findings will not be utopian; the existing ideological beliefs and practices of peoples will not have to be transformed by decades or centuries of education in order that an international law, reared on such foundations, be effective.

Evidence for the statements made in this book is to be found for the most part in the references. Much more than this, however, lies behind its statements and its conclusions. At the suggestion of Dr. Paul Fejos, the Director of Research of the Wenner-Gren Foundation for Anthropological Research, the writer spent the last four months of 1952 in the Netherlands, Austria, Greece, Turkey, Italy, Portugal, France, Belgium, West Germany and Luxembourg investigating European Union at first hand. Representative leaders of the major political parties, national governments, and religious and other social groups in these nations were interviewed with respect to the factors upon which its success or failure depend. The statements and conclusions of this book reflect also the results of these interviews. Grateful acknowledgment is given to Dr. Fejos, the Wenner-Gren Foundation for Anthropological Research, and Yale University for making this possible.

This volume is dedicated to the man who introduced me to sociological jurisprudence, my friend and former colleague in the Yale Law School, the late Professor Underhill Moore. He made students of this subject aware of the need for an objective method in determining the living law of any society. The method used in this book lacks the rigor for which he sought. It does, however, have the lesser merit of avoiding the prevalent error, against which Underhill Moore inveighed, of identifying the norms of the living law of the society being investigated with those of the social group or the pet social reforms of the investigator. To this extent, at least, it is hoped that he would approve.

Tables II, III and IV have been gathered and computed by Miss Helen H. Livingston. The production of the manuscript and the index are also her accomplishments. I am indebted to the editors of the Macmillan Company for valuable suggestions which improved the text.

F. S. C. Northrop

The Law School
Yale University
New Haven, Connecticut
May 26, 1954

Contents

Contents

A Remarkable Phenomenon

The three major wars of the last hundred years have arisen in Europe. In all three Germany invaded Luxembourg, Belgium and France. The last invasion produced a quick defeat which for the French was especially humiliating. In World War I Germany and Italy were on opposite sides; in World War II they started on the same side. In the latter instance, Germany also invaded the Netherlands, reducing Rotterdam to rubble in the world's first mass bombing attack. Nothing would seem to be more unlikely, therefore, than a rapprochement between Germany and the other five nations and particularly between the Germans and the French. Nevertheless, World War II was hardly over before Frenchmen, Belgians, Netherlanders, Luxembourgers and Italians, and very soon the Germans also, began to work out such a rapprochement. Its economic implementation—the European Coal and Steel Community—is already in effect, and its military and political institutions—the European Defense Community and the European Political Community—have been officially authorized by the respective foreign ministers and voted by at least two of the six parliaments, with a vote by at least two more likely. The name of this rapprochement is Continental European Union.

Consider what the existence of the European Coal and Steel Community means. The sovereign parliaments of Belgium, France, Italy, Luxembourg, the Netherlands and West Germany have already actually transferred portions of their traditional, unilateral national

1

control of their own respective national economies to a supranational federal government at Luxembourg. Since August 10, 1952, its High Authority, composed of Frenchmen, Germans, Belgians, Netherlanders, Luxembourgers and Italians working collaboratively in the status of Europeans, rather than nationalists, has been transforming the six previously independent national economies into a single Continental European economy. This economy has resources greater than those of Great Britain and rivaling those of the United States. Furthermore, its supranational European executive body possesses specified sovereign powers to make decisions which the member nations cannot withdraw or veto for a period of fifty years.

To be sure, the particular transfer of sovereignty from the national to the supranational community affects only coal and steel. In an industrial age, however, coal and steel are the basis and backbone of any effective society. Here is the first reversal of the trend away from European universalism to greater and greater nationalism that has occurred in Western history since the breakdown of the Roman and the Holy Roman Empires. Whatever the future may bring forth, this is truly a remarkable phenomenon.

The European Defense Community of Continental European Union is equally remarkable. It envisages taking the national uniforms off French, German, Dutch, Belgian, Luxembourg and Italian soldiers to clothe them instead in a European military tunic. Instead of having one's own sons ordered to battle and directed in battle by the President and General Staff of one's own nation, it prescribes that they be under a command in which the authority will be that of five other nations as well as one's own. Already the treaty transferring such sovereign power to a supranational military authority, with no chance of veto by the participating nations for fifty years, has been signed by the six foreign ministers and approved by four of the six parliaments. Furthermore, military experts of the five member nations, including even Germans in a civilian status, have been meeting at the Palais de Chaillot in Paris to formulate the plans for such a military authority and to devise its single European strategy. The German civilian members will be official members when and if

EDC is approved by the legislative bodies of the six participating states. In October 1952, an American military observer at the Palais de Chaillot told me that there was less friction between these military executives from the different nations than there is often between rival military services in any one nation.

Nor is this all. The Foreign Ministers of the six Continental European nations have authorized the creation of the European Political Community with a lower house of parliament whose members are elected, not by the parliaments or citizens of the individual member nations, but by the 157,000,000 people of the Community voting as Europeans, rather than as French, German, Netherlands, Belgian, Luxembourg or Italian citizens. In fact reference to the Treaty of Paris of May 27, 1952, constituting the European Defense Community, brings out that it calls for the institution of this supra-national European Political Community.

What this means in terms of dollars and cents, or francs, lire, guilders and marks, has not received the attention it deserves. The French budget is typical. An examination of that part of it which is concerned with coal and steel and the military shows that the concrete, practical effect of French membership in the Coal and Steel Community and the European Defense Community will be to transfer the decision about how and where approximately one-third of the present French budget is spent from the French Parliament to two supranational bodies—the one located permanently in Luxembourg, the other situated temporarily at the Palais de Chaillot in Paris. In terms of the total national economy—i.e., the total production of goods and services—this removes roughly 20 per cent of the national economy from control by the individual nation for fifty years and places it under the control of a European executive and parliament in which the national membership will be approximately one in six, or the ratio of the population of the particular nation to that of the population of the Continental European Community as a whole.

Can one imagine Secretary of State Dulles, who so bluntly urged the French National Assembly to ratify EDC "or else," recommending to the Republican party and the Congress of the United States such a transfer of national sovereignty for fifty years? To talk about international collaboration in international congresses is commonplace; to implement it in the finance committee and the subsequent vote of one's own national legislature is indeed remarkable.

What makes Continental European Union even more notable is that its practical institutions for bringing Germans and Frenchmen and other Continental Europeans into supranational collaboration were proposed and designed initially by Frenchmen. M. Pleven—former Premier, the leader of the underground wing of France's oldest political party in World War II and the Minister of Defense in the 1953–1954 government of Premier Laniel—was the first to propose the rearming of the Germans inside this supranational community. This is why in Europe EDC is known as the Pleven Plan. Jean Monnet, a career member of the French civil service, and Robert Schuman, Christian Democratic (Mouvement Républicain Populaire) Premier or Foreign Minister of every French government from the end of World War II to January of 1953, conceived and led in the establishment of the European Coal and Steel Community. This is why M. Monnet is the first and present President of its High Authority and why the Community is called the Schuman Plan.

Furthermore Léon Blum, former Socialist Premier of France; Guy Mollet, present head of France's largest liberal democratic party; François de Menthon, former Christian Democratic Minister of Justice and 1954 President of the Consultative Assembly of the Council of Europe; and Pierre-Henri Teitgen, former Minister of Armed Forces, head of France's Christian Democratic party—a Frenchman arrested and tortured by Germans in 1944—were prime movers in the wider movement toward European Union of the Council of Europe at Strasbourg and in the establishment of the smaller Continental European Community. In short, the major political leaders of every French liberal political party contributed to the initiation and construction of a rapprochement between the German and French peoples within a supranational economic, military and political community with sovereign powers.

Belgian, Luxembourg, Netherlands and Italian leaders, fresh from the heels of German soldiers, have done the same thing. And as soon as they were allowed, German statesmen supported by the votes of the majority of the German people joined them. The list of builders of the Continental European Community is impressive. It includes: M. Spaak, former Socialist party Premier of Belgium and present President of the Common Assembly of the European Coal and Steel Community; former Christian Democratic Premiers van Zeeland and Eyskens of Belgium; Queen Juliana and Premier Drees of the Netherlands; President Heuss, Chancellor Adenauer, Free Democratic Vice Chancellor Blücher, Dr. Hallstein, Secretary of State for Foreign Affairs, and Dr. von Brentano, Chairman of the Constitutional Committee for the European Political Community, of Germany; President Dupong and Foreign Minister Beck of Luxembourg; and former Premiers de Gasperi and Pella and former Ministers Croce and Sforza of Italy.

The list becomes even larger when one notes that the Continental European Community, composed of the six Continental European free nations, is part of a larger European Community called the Council of Europe which is made up of eight additional members. The latter members are: Great Britain, Ireland, Iceland, Denmark, Norway, Sweden, Greece and Turkey.

The movement toward this larger European community was launched at the Hague on May 8, 1948, by an International Congress of some eight hundred outstanding Europeans representing practically every nationality and every significant political party, religious group and economic section of the whole of free Europe. The keynote speech at the opening session was delivered by its President of Honour, Winston Churchill, in the presence of Princess Juliana and Prince Bernhard of the Netherlands and Dr. Louis J. M. Beel, Prime Minister of the Netherlands. Elsewhere Mr. Churchill put in one succinct sentence the essence of what he said: "My counsel to Europe can be given in a single word: 'Unite!' " [1] Two days later this Hague Congress of European citizens adopted by acclamation a "Message to Europeans" expressing the desire for a united

Europe, a Charter of Human Rights, a Court of Justice and a European Assembly and pledged its members in their home, public, political and religious life and in their "professional and trade union circles" to support all persons and governments working for European Union.[2]

To this end, on October 25, 1948, a new organization called the European Movement was formulated to coordinate all existing groups and bring their recommendations to bear upon the member governments. The first Presidents of Honour of this European Movement were Léon Blum, former Socialist Premier of France; Mr. Winston S. Churchill, leader of the Conservative party of Great Britain; Premier Alcide de Gasperi, leader of the Christian Democratic party of Italy; and Paul-Henri Spaak, Socialist Premier of Belgium.

At the Hague Congress of May 1948, a Political Committee under the chairmanship of Paul Ramadier, former Premier and Socialist party leader of France, brought in a political report. This report contained the following:

The European nations of the Marshall Group alone comprise some 250,000,000 of the most civilised and intelligent people in the world. Their soil is fertile. Their combined resources . . . are rich and varied. Their productive potential is as great as that of the United States of America. Yet all these immense possibilities cannot be realised so long as Europe allows herself to remain enfeebled by internal division . . . Judged from any standpoint—political, economic or cultural—it is only by uniting herself that Europe can overcome her immediate difficulties and go forward to fulfill her mission for the future. . . . It is impossible to keep problems of economic collaboration and defence separate from those of general political policy. Economic and defence plans having been made, political power is required to implement them. The processes of industrial and military integration, even in the early stages, inevitably give rise to conflicts of national interests. These difficulties can only be resolved and the necessary compromises accepted when the problem is viewed in the light of wider political considerations. If therefore the policy of mutual aid [i.e., the Marshall Plan] . . . is to bear any substantial fruit, it must be accompanied step by step with a parallel policy of closer political union.

Sooner or later this must involve the renunciation or, to be more accurate, the joint exercise of certain sovereign powers.[3]

Thus from the very outset this French leader and the 300 members of the political section of the Hague Congress saw that economic aid for, and the military unification of, Europe cannot succeed without political unification.

M. Ramadier's Political Committee saw also that the basis for the success of the Marshall Plan and of the European Defense Community cannot be merely its practical utility in stopping Communism. For, they added, "An association resting solely on such negative foundations would possess no guiding principle nor power of endurance. The forces which alone can provide a solid and lasting basis for unity are moral and spiritual—our common belief[s]. . . ."[4] In short, there cannot be a common effective economic, military or political community without common living law norms in the majority of the people to whom the community is applied. At this point European Union connects with sociological jurisprudence and, as the sequel will show in detail, its study becomes a study in sociological jurisprudence.

All these recommendations of the Hague conference were more than merely verbal, pious hopes. The leaders of the Congress were men of such standing and influence that they could bring their recommendations to bear upon every free government in Europe. Two months later Premier Spaak spoke in the Belgian Senate in favor of the creation of the European Assembly and asked the European Movement to submit to his government detailed recommendations which he would bring officially to the attention of other governments to the end of achieving their agreement. About the same time the French government issued an official communiqué expressing its support of European Union and its intention to "initiate all necessary action" to bring it into being.[5] Forthwith the French and Belgian governments combined to press for the establishment of the Council of Europe, and the governments of the Netherlands and Luxembourg gave a favorable response.

At this point an opposition to implementation of European Union appeared from a source as remarkable as the European Union movement itself. It came, of all places, from the very country, Great Britain, whose distinguished war-time Prime Minister and European citizen had launched the European Movement, but three months before, at the Hague. In August of 1948, Britain's Labor government Prime Minister Attlee wrote: "If an Assembly is to be convened this must . . . be done by governments. On the other hand I think that this is not the right time for governments to take this major initiative, when their hands are so full already with urgent and difficult problems." [6] In other words, the approach must be piece-by-piece and inductive; European Union must come after the solution of Europe's specific problems; it is not the sole, practical instrument for their solution. A few weeks later, speaking in the House of Commons, Ernest Bevin, the British Foreign Minister, concurred, when he said that to build the Council of Europe at this stage would be like "putting on the roof before building the house." [7]

Even so, the other statesmen of Europe were not to be daunted. One month later the Foreign Ministers of France, Great Britain, Belgium, the Netherlands and Luxembourg met in Paris and appointed a commission of eighteen members to study both the European Movement's proposal for the Council of Europe and the British Labor government's alternative proposal for merely a European Committee of Ministers. This Commission included, among others, Hugh Dalton, former Minister of Economic Warfare, and Sir Gladwyn Jebb of the Foreign Office of Great Britain, and former Premiers Blum and Reynaud of France, with Edouard Herriot, the dean of French statesmen, former Premier and the senior leader of France's Radical Socialist party, as Chairman. Paul Reynaud's name adds one more liberal French party to the list of those supporting European Union. M. Reynaud is the leader of the French Independent party. Again with respect to the wider Council of Europe, as well as the narrower Continental European Community, French leadership showed itself. Nor was the selection of M. Herriot as the Chairman of the Commission accidental. Years before World War II, in 1930, he had published a book entitled *The United States of Europe*.[8]

M. Herriot's Commission immediately invited the European Movement to submit its specific recommendations for the unification of Europe. The European Movement recommended the creation of both the European Assembly and the European Committee of Ministers, making each, together with a European Court, a part of the Council of Europe. M. Herriot's Commission, with the British delegates reserving their judgment, adopted these proposals and recommended them to the Foreign Ministers of France, Great Britain, Belgium, the Netherlands and Luxembourg, who met in London in January 1949. There the five Foreign Ministers approved the creation of a "Council of Europe." Forthwith it was decided to call a "Conference of Ambassadors" in London to authorize the establishment of the Council of Europe and to include Denmark, Ireland, Italy, Norway and Sweden.[9] On May 5, 1949, less than twelve months after the Hague Congress, this Conference of Ambassadors created the Statute of the Council of Europe. It was signed by the Foreign Ministers of all ten nations and became effective August 3, 1949. One week later, on August 10, the Council of Europe held its first meeting at Strasbourg with M. Herriot its provisional President.[10] Within two years Turkey, Greece, the Federal Republic of Germany, Iceland and the Saar joined as members.

Immediately, the Continental European leaders made every effort to secure a real transfer of national sovereignty in the economic, military, political and judicial fields, from the fourteen member nations (fifteen if the Saar is counted as a separate nation) to the supranational community of the Council of Europe. Very soon, however, a serious cleavage began to appear which had suggested itself before the Council of Europe was created. We have already noted the lack of interest of the British Labor government in European Union. Before the Council was set up a difference of opinion appeared between the point of view represented by France and Belgium and the point of view of the British Labor government. As a result, the Council of Europe, which was authorized at the London meeting of

January 1949, was a compromise composed of a legislative body that was merely consultative, with no power, and the Council of Ministers from which all initiative came and which had all the power. On October 26, 1951, when Mr. Churchill became Great Britain's Prime Minister it was hoped that all this would change. Instead, the conflict became sharper and more serious. M. Paul-Henri Spaak, later President of the European Consultative Assembly, has described the situation as follows: "It was plain that if the Laborites were holding fast to their positions, the Conservatives had simply joined them." [11] The British, and the Irish, Scandinavians, Greeks and Turks who followed them, were simply unwilling to transfer any national sovereignty to the supranational community. They were for "solving single, isolated problems one at a time." [12] "Suddenly it became plain," M. Spaak continues, "that nothing would be achieved if one accepted British collaboration as an indispensable condition of European unity." [13]

The Continental European nations had no alternative, therefore, to setting up a supranational community of their own. Thus, Continental European Union arose. On April 18, 1951, the Foreign Ministers of Belgium, France, Italy, Luxembourg, the Netherlands and West Germany signed the Treaty Constituting the European Coal and Steel Community. On May 26, 1952, the Convention on Relations Between the Three Powers and the Federal Republic of Germany, which gave the portion of Germany occupied by Great Britain, France and the United States its own government and the right to rearm, provided that it become a member of the European Defense Community, was signed in Bonn. The next day in Paris the Treaty Constituting the European Defense Community was signed by the Foreign Ministers of the six Continental European nations. On September 10, 1952, these Foreign Ministers, meeting in Luxembourg, authorized the Consultative Assembly of the Coal and Steel Community to construct an Ad Hoc Assembly to bring into being the Political Community of Continental European Union as specified in Article 38 of the Paris Treaty of May 27th which set up the European Defense Community. Five days later in Strasbourg this

Ad Hoc Assembly was created, and a committee of twenty-six members, with Dr. von Brentano of West Germany as its Chairman, was appointed to draft the Constitution of this Political Community with supranational sovereign powers. On March 10, 1953, Dr. von Brentano's committee submitted the new Constitution. It was approved unanimously by the Ad Hoc Assembly and referred to the Council of Ministers of the six Continental European nations for submission to their respective parliaments. By 1953, two of the six parliaments had approved, and there was no question of approval in two others.

Popular support was equally notable. Writing from Bonn on January 13, 1952, following the ratification of the Schuman Plan by the West German Parliament, Anne O'Hare McCormick noted "the student demonstrations following the vote in the Bundestag," and added that they could be interpreted only as "celebrating the promise that the merger will put an end to wars between France and Germany." [14] Speaking for France, Robert Schuman wrote a year later:

Nationalism is going out of fashion. It no longer attracts the crowd. Nor does it satisfy the young who are pursuing a new, more humane and generous ideal. During an election campaign, when I made numerous speeches in France, only once did I encounter demonstrators who were inspired by the old nationalist doctrine.[15]

In the summer of 1952, the French Institute of Public Opinion conducted a poll which, as reported by Anne O'Hare McCormick in *The New York Times*, showed then that the majority of Frenchmen were "definitely in favor of a European Army as the best means for the defense of Western Europe" and that "61 per cent believed the danger was less if German troops were incorporated into [such] an international army." [16] The response of the German people in the federal election in September 1953 was practically equivalent. This election was fought by Dr. Adenauer and his coalition over the question of whether the West German people would forgo an immediate attempt to unify their country and to achieve a wholly German controlled army or would instead place themselves, their economy and their soldiers under supranational Continental European leadership and control. Notwithstanding the chauvinistic appeals to German militarism and nationalism made in the election by the Nazi Right, the Communist Left and the large Liberal Socialist party in Left Center, 58 per cent of the West German people voted for this rapprochement between France and Germany.[17] In the Italian election of 1948, Premier de Gasperi's coalition of Christian Democrats, Liberals, Republicans and Right Socialists, which stands for EDC and Continental European Union generally, won 61.9 per cent of the votes.[18] Their receipt in the 1953 election of but 49.7 per cent of the vote (a recount which they waived actually gave them over 50 per cent) is probably due more to diplomatic ineptitude upon the part of the United States and Great Britain following the promise of Trieste to Italy in the earlier election, than to a change of heart with respect to Continental European Union upon the part of the majority of the Italian people. Popular support of Continental European Union is even greater in Luxembourg, Belgium and the Netherlands.

Such is Continental European Union as it showed itself in fact in Western Europe in the summer of 1952 and in West Germany in September of 1953. The French initiated this rapprochement between themselves and the Germans; Belgian, Netherlands, German, Luxembourg and Italian statesmen collaborated with them to bring it, step by step, into economic being and toward military and political implementation; and the German people repudiated their chauvinists to welcome it in a decisive vote. Regardless, therefore, of signs of a French change of mind which appeared in the fall of 1952 and grew in intensity in 1953, and whatever the future brings forth, this is a remarkable phenomenon.

Considered merely as an experiment in bringing traditionally competing, embittered and warring nations under the rule of supranational law it is unique. In its hesitations and its obstacles as well as its triumphs, even though incomplete, it must certainly have something important to teach us.

For the people of the United States Continental European Union is especially important. There is an essential connection between it and United States foreign policy.

Chapter 2

The Relation of Continental European Union to U.S. Foreign Policy

The foreign policy of the United States since 1949, of both the Truman and the Eisenhower administration, has rested on the rearming of the Germans inside the European Defense Community. This establishes an essential tie between Continental European Union and United States foreign policy. The following sequence of events establishes the treaties by which this tie is bound.

On April 4, 1949, the North Atlantic Defense Pact was signed in Washington, D.C., by the official representatives of the following twelve nations: Belgium, Canada, Denmark, France, Iceland, Italy, Luxembourg, the Netherlands, Norway, Portugal, Great Britain and the United States. On July 21, 1949, it was ratified by the Senate of the United States, and on August 24, 1949, its North Atlantic Treaty Organization (NATO) went into effect, with Greece and Turkey joining actively in February 1952. The 1949 Pact asserted in Article 5 that

an armed attack against one or more of them in Europe or North America shall be considered an attack against them all and consequently they agree that, if such an armed attack occurs, each of them, in exercise of the right of individual or collective self-defence recognized by Article 51 of the Charter of the United Nations, will assist the party or parties so attacked by taking forthwith, individually and in concert with the other parties, such action as it deems necessary, including the use of armed force, to restore and maintain the security of the North Atlantic area.[1]

To this end it authorized "a Council, on which each of them shall be represented . . . [to] establish immediately a defence committee." [2]

The Council of NATO is composed of a Permanent Representative from each of the fourteen member nations. The headquarters are in Paris, temporarily at the Palais de Chaillot. Its Military Committee is composed of the Chiefs of Staff of the fourteen nations, or their representatives. This Committee has a permanent Standing Group which functions continuously, is located in Washington, D.C., and is composed of three members—one each from France, Great Britain and the United States.

In December of 1950, the Council of NATO authorized the establishment of an integrated force for the defense of Western Europe under a Supreme Headquarters Allied Powers, Europe (SHAPE).[3] General Eisenhower was its first Supreme Allied Commander and opened SHAPE's Headquarters in Paris on April 2, 1951. General Ridgway was his successor. He was succeeded in 1953 by General Gruenther, also an American.

Clearly, NATO is focused heavily around the United States. The treaty which launched it was signed in Washington. Secretary of State Acheson was the first Chairman of its Council, and even its European military implementation has been continuously under American leadership with its Standing Group located in the United States. It is equally evident that for its success it depends upon unity among the free nations of the Western world, and especially, because of its permanent Standing Group, upon collaboration on foreign policy between France, Great Britain and the United States.

But while NATO and SHAPE were being established other things were also happening. The European movement toward a European supranational community of the fourteen European nations, initiated at London on May 5, 1949, was going forward with the creation of, and the debates in, the Council of Europe at Strasbourg. Even in 1949, however, the gulf between the British desire to keep it a merely consultative assembly and the Continental European desire to achieve a supranational community with sovereign powers began to show itself. Reporting on developments in the French Parliament in

1949, the *Annual Register* of London quotes M. Pleven as saying that Britain had not "made her choice between imperial self-sufficiency and European economic co-operation." [4] Clearly, the way to Continental European Union was being prepared in the days immediately after the signing of the NATO pact.

Also, the United States was making additional commitments with respect to its foreign policy. On April 8, 1949, but four days after the NATO Treaty was signed, France, Great Britain and the United States agreed to merge their military zones in Germany and to establish the West German Republic. About the same time, in Paris, M. Pleven proposed the European Defense Community with West Germany as a member and the Germans rearmed within it. On July 2, 1949, John J. McCloy arrived in Germany as the first United States civilian High Commissioner there. Soon he gave public expression to the opinion that Western Europe cannot be defended without the inclusion of German troops. General Eisenhower expressed the same judgment later when he made his first survey of the European military situation, following upon President Truman's request that he become the first Supreme Military Commander of NATO.[5]

On May 23, 1949, the Federal Republic of Germany was announced at Bonn after a liberal democratic constitution had been drawn up by a constituent assembly representing eleven states (Länder) in southern and western Germany. These eleven states were Bavaria, Württemberg-Baden, Hesse and Bremen in the United States zone; Rhineland-Palatinate, South Baden, and Württemberg-Hohenzollern in the French zone; and Schleswig-Holstein, Hamburg, Lower Saxony and North Rhine Westphalia in the British zone. On September 12, 1949, Theodor Heuss of the Free Democratic party was chosen President, and three days later Dr. Konrad Adenauer of the Christian Democratic party was made Chancellor. On September 21, 1949, the Allied High Commission announced the Occupation Statute which, subject to specified restrictions, placed the civil affairs of West Germany under German control.[6]

On October 7, 1949, the German Democratic Republic in East

Germany was set up in the Russian sector, between West Germany and the Oder-Neisse, with Wilhelm Pieck of the Socialist Unity (Communist) party as its President.[7]

The Federal Constitution of the West German Republic said nothing about the right to have an army. Also, while the arrangement of September 21, 1949, gave the West German people control over their civilian affairs, military affairs were still in the hands of the three Western High Commissioners and their occupation forces. German consulates abroad were authorized in 1950, and on July 2, 1951, the United States officially resumed diplomatic relations with Germany (West Germany). Also, on May 2, 1951, the Bonn Republic became a full member of the Council of Europe, after having been an associate member.

Meanwhile it became clear to the Continental European nations in the Council of Europe that a supranational European community with sovereign powers must be restricted to themselves. Hence, on May 9, 1950, the French government proposed the economic unification of the coal and steel industries of the six nations in the European Coal and Steel Community. On August 10th of the same year, the French Foreign Minister, Robert Schuman, explained its nature to the Council of Europe, describing its High Authority as "independent both of private interests and State power." [8] As noted in the previous chapter, the Treaty authorizing it was signed on April 18, 1951, by the Foreign Ministers of Belgium, France, Italy, Luxembourg, the Netherlands and West Germany in Paris. Forthwith, under the Presidency of M. Monnet, Germans, Frenchmen and the other Continental Europeans found they could work together constructively and harmoniously in its headquarters at Luxembourg.

This success of Franco-German economic collaboration inside the Continental European Community undoubtedly encouraged the French, British and Americans to move toward rearming the Germans inside the Community also, as suggested by M. Pleven in 1949. The decision occurred at Bonn on May 26, 1952, when the foreign ministers of France, Great Britain, the United States and West Germany signed the Convention on Relations Between the Three Powers and the Federal Republic of Germany.

Among other things the Convention says that

the Three Powers and the Federal Republic recognize that both the new relationship to be established between them by the present Convention and its related Conventions and the Treaties for the creation of an integrated European community, in particular the Treaty on the Establishment of the European Community for Coal and Steel and the Treaty on the Establishment of the European Defence Community, are essential steps to the achievement of their common aim for a unified Germany integrated within the European Community.[9]

This is the first official tie of United States foreign policy to Continental European Union. Article 4 of the treaty adds, "The Federal Republic will participate in the European Defence Community in order to contribute to the common defence of the free world," insuring that West Germany place herself under a Continental supranational military, as well as economic, authority and ally herself with the free world.

The next day, May 27, 1952, in Paris two other treaties were signed—the first by the six foreign ministers of the Continental European nations, the second by the foreign ministers of the fourteen NATO nations. The first treaty authorized the creation of the European Defense Community. The second, a Protocol to the NATO Treaty, related the European Defense Community to NATO.

The Treaty Constituting the European Defense Community specifies that "a permanent contact shall be established between the staffs of the European Defense Community Commissariat and of the civilian agencies of the North Atlantic Treaty Organization." It adds, "As soon as the European Defense Forces shall have been placed under the command of a Commander responsible to the North Atlantic Treaty Organization, members of the European Defense Forces shall become members of such Commander's Headquarters and of appropriate subordinate Headquarters." [10] This is why the military General Staffs of NATO and the EDC are together in the Palais de Chaillot in Paris.

The NATO Protocol asserts, "An armed attack . . . on the territory of any of the members of the European Defense Community . . . shall be considered an attack against all the Parties to the North Atlantic Treaty." [11] This commits NATO and the United States, as the leading member of NATO, to come to the defense of the Continental European Community if it is attacked. Article II adds:

The present Protocol shall enter into force as soon as each of the Parties has notified the Government of the United States of America of its acceptance and the Council of the European Defence Community has notified the North Atlantic Council of the entry into force of the Treaty setting up the European Defence Community.[12]

The two treaties signed at Paris on May 27, 1952, constitute, therefore, a second official binding tie between United States foreign policy and Continental European Union.

The Bonn Convention and the two Paris treaties, together with the Treaty Constituting the European Coal and Steel Community, were submitted by President Truman to the Senate of the United States on June 2, 1952, for its approval or information. Those signed by the Secretary of State of the United States were later ratified by the Senate and the entire arrangement was approved.

One item bearing on the relation of West Germany to NATO is to be noted. Whereas France, Belgium, Luxembourg, the Netherlands and Italy are members of NATO quite independently of their membership in the European Defense Community, West Germany is related to NATO only indirectly through her membership in the European Defense Community. The Socialist party in West Germany used this fact in its appeal to German national pride and chauvinism in the election of September 1953 as an argument against the Contractual Agreements and Continental European Union, claiming that it dishonored the German people and the German soldier by not relating West Germany to NATO on the same basis as the French and other Continental European nations. The Socialist argument brings out the point that to be in EDC without being in NATO eliminates one's right to use one's military forces unilaterally, whereas to be in NATO without being in EDC leaves a nation free militarily, aside from its obligations to NATO, to act unilaterally. Again we see how Continental European Union entails a real transfer of national sovereignty to the Continental European Community.

The most dramatic evidence of the essential connection between Continental European Union and United States foreign policy appeared in France in the fall of 1952 during the election campaign in the United States when it appeared that U.S. foreign policy might be shifted from the Kennan-Truman-Acheson policy of the containment of Communism to the Eisenhower-Dulles policy of the rollback crusade against Communism in both Asia and Eastern Europe. The significance of these events will not be appreciated until one misconception about the instability of French governments since World War II is removed and certain facts about the European Movement, noted in the previous chapter, are recalled.

It is frequently asserted that the continuous succession of defeated French governments since World War II demonstrates the incapacity of the French to agree upon anything. Whereas this judgment expresses some truth so far as French domestic policy is concerned, it is completely false with respect to French foreign policy from the end of World War II to January of 1953. During this lengthy period Robert Schuman was either the Premier or the Foreign Minister and every government supported his foreign policy. M. Schuman's foreign policy rested on two principles: (1) Franco-German collaboration economically, militarily and politically inside Continental European Union and (2) Franco-American collaboration inside NATO and inside the United Nations to police the peace of the world against Communist aggression in Europe and Asia.

Moreover, Premier or Foreign Minister Schuman, during this period, implemented the two principles with the backing of the French Parliament. French troops were beside those of the United

States in the United Nations police action in Korea. French troops were also battling, without other Western allies, in Indo-China. The French government and the Belgian were the first two governments to come out officially for the Council of Europe. One postwar French Premier proposed the European Defense Community, and M. Schuman, as the Foreign Minister of a governmental majority committed to it, signed the treaty authorizing it and the European Political Community. Furthermore, by a decisive majority the French National Assembly ratified the Treaty Constituting the European Coal and Steel Community, thereby permitting it to come into being. These are hardly signs of a government or a people that cannot make up its mind or implement it afterward. This implemented French mind up to late 1952 and January 1953 comprised two essentially connected factors: Franco-German collaboration and Franco-American collaboration vis-à-vis Communist military and political aggression in Europe and Asia.

Recall also the different Frenchmen and parties who had collaborated to build this French mind about foreign policy: Premiers Herriot and Pleven of the Radical Socialist party; former Premiers Blum and Ramadier and Guy Mollet of the Socialist party which voted unanimously for the Coal and Steel Community; and Premiers Schuman and Bidault and Minister Teitgen of the Christian Democratic party. Even Premier Pinay's Independent-Peasant-led coalition government of 1952 was unequivocally committed to Franco-German and Franco-American collaboration by the presence of Robert Schuman as its Foreign Minister.

Imagine, therefore, the shock which ran through France, the remainder of Europe and the Department of State in Washington in October of 1952 when M. Herriot, the oldest and most revered French statesman, who had pioneered in the movement for a United States of Europe in Geneva before World War II and in Paris and London afterwards, made a dramatic public address attacking both the European Defense Community and the foreign policy of the United States. M. Herriot's speech was all the more shocking because, at the time, his own Radical Socialists were members of

Premier Pinay's government which was committed to both of these things.

The Christian Democratic party saved the situation momentarily by an ultimatum to Premier Pinay's government and M. Herriot's Radical Socialists, informing them that if Premier Pinay and M. Herriot wanted Christian Democratic support for their domestic policy they must keep the Christian Democratic Foreign Minister, Robert Schuman, in the Quai d'Orsay and pursue his foreign policy.

By late December 1952, however, the popular and parliamentary criticism of the United States became so strong that Premier Pinay's government fell and M. Schuman departed from the Foreign Office. With his departure there came into being the first French government since World War II whose majority lacked the agreement on foreign policy necessary to place France in the European Defense Community and to support Franco-American collaboration to police Communist aggression in Europe and in Asia. After December 1952, France found it impossible to form a government without including Gaullists who oppose both Franco-German and Franco-American collaboration in foreign policy. This state of affairs continued through the Four Power conference at Berlin in February of 1954, even though both Premier Laniel himself and his Foreign Minister Bidault were personally for the European Defense Community.

In fact, Foreign Minister Bidault's firmness at Berlin in February 1954 was somewhat deceptive. As Harold Callender wrote to *The New York Times* from Paris on February 20, 1954:

When M. Bidault resisted the blandishments of the Russian Foreign Minister at the Berlin conference and took a strong stand with the Western powers for a European army, he probably represented a majority of his countrymen. But about one-third of the Cabinet for which he nominally spoke are opposed to the European army, as is probably a still larger proportion of Parliament. . . . What M. Bidault said and did at Berlin was misleading in so far as it suggested that France, as distinguished from M. Bidault, had a foreign policy.[13]

The fact which justifies his observation is that the government of Premier Laniel, for which M. Bidault spoke in Berlin, like every

French government since January of 1953, contained Gaullist cabinet members, and the Gaullists, like the Communists in France, oppose both Franco-German and Franco-American collaboration vis-à-vis Communism and stand instead for a unilaterally acting, nationalistic and chauvinistic France returning to its traditional power-politics alliance with Poland, Czechoslovakia and Russia vis-à-vis Germany.

The reason for this shift of the French from the constant mind with respect to foreign policy, which they had up to December 1952, to the indecision and division, present in every party, that characterized them afterward must wait until Chapter 9, when we have examined the positive legal proposals of Continental European Union and the living law factors upon which it depends for its effectiveness and for French acceptance. For our present purposes, the important consideration is the dramatic demonstration which M. Herriot's October 1952 speech gave of the essential connection between Continental European Union and the foreign policy of the United States. It showed that the two stand and fall together. If EDC in Continental European Union fails to come into being, the foreign policy of the United States, of both the Truman and Eisenhower administrations, with respect to Communist expansion in Europe fails also.

But European policy is essentially connected with Asian policy. Besides collaborating with the United States by signing the Contractual Agreements, the EDC Treaty and NATO Protocol to re-arm the Germans, vis-à-vis Communism, in a European Defense Community that is related to the U.S.-directed NATO, France has cooperated with the United States by contributing troops to the U.N. police action in Korea and by standing as the sole *Western* military force in Indo-China that is between Mao's Chinese and the Communist take-over of Southeast Asia. On March 28, 1953, President Eisenhower noted the "interdependence" of Korea and Indo-China.[14] In February 1954 at Berlin, Secretary of State Dulles found it necessary to include not merely Indo-China but also Mao's China in order to get Minister Molotov's support for reopening peace negotiations on Korea at the Geneva conference of April 26, 1954. On February 22, 1954, Secretary Dulles explained to a group of Congressional leaders the agreements he made at Berlin with respect to the Geneva conference. *The New York Times* of the next day reported some members of Congress who attended this meeting as understanding that "if the Secretary had not agreed to put Indo-China into the Geneva discussion, the last hope for favorable French action on the European army project would have vanished." [15]

One reason for this inescapable connection between Continental European Union and United States foreign policy with respect to Asia is the French belief, due to the remarkable economic resurgence and potential military strength of West Germany, that Germany will have too much military power and influence relative to France in the supranational European community if France must have military forces in Indo-China also. In order, therefore, to make the French contribution to the European Defense Community more nearly equal to that of the Germans, France wants peace in Indo-China. Hence, Foreign Minister Bidault demanded of Mr. Dulles in Berlin that the United States meet the Russian condition for negotiating peace in Indo-China at Geneva: the inclusion of Communist China in the Geneva conference.

The Soviet Foreign Minister undoubtedly had, however, one other motive for this condition: to woo France back to the old Russian alliance, and away from collaboration with Germany in Europe and with the United States in Asia, by encouraging the French to postpone decision on EDC still further, until at least after the Geneva conference. A report from Paris to *The New York Times* of February 23, 1954, suggested that Mr. Molotov had succeeded. It bore the title, "Move for Delay Gains: French Find Support in Stand of U.S. Senators," and concluded as follows:

Officials who had been present at the Berlin conference of foreign ministers quoted the Soviet Foreign Minister, Vyacheslav M. Molotov, as having said that Moscow calculated that if the European army treaty were not ratified this year it never would be. [16]

The desire of the French to obtain peace in Indo-China is understandable. With the movement against imperialism sweeping the world, many Frenchmen believe that they are not fighting in Indo-China for the French Empire but are fighting instead merely to withdraw from Asia as gracefully as possible. After President Eisenhower has negotiated a cessation of fighting with the Communist Asians which gets American boys home from Korea "with honor," the French see no reason why they should be the sole Western people losing their boys in Asia in order to prevent the fall of the remainder of Asia to the Communists, especially when it leaves them weak relative to Germany in the European Defense Community which the United States insists they join. This means not merely that Indo-China and Korea are tied to Continental European Union, but that the fate of the foreign policy of the United States for preventing the Communists from taking over the whole of Southeast and South Asia is tied to it also.

Moreover, it is tied to it in a way that probably neither the French nor the Americans appreciated before the Geneva conference of April 1954. Obviously the price of Russian support of France in achieving peace in Indo-China would be French repudiation of collaboration with Germany in Europe and with the United States vis-à-vis Communism in Asia, and return to the old Franco-Russian power politics alliance vis-à-vis Germany. This means not only that EDC is essentially connected to Indo-China and Korea, as the participation of Communist China in the Geneva conference of April 1954 clearly demonstrates, but also that if EDC fails the foreign policy of the United States for securing the necessary allies in the United Nations to prevent the Communist military conquest of Asia may fail also.

Looked at from the French standpoint, Mr. Molotov's proposal to France does not appear at first glance to be entirely implausible. Several American students of modern European politics, such as James P. Warburg [17] and, to a certain extent, Walter Lippmann,[18] have regarded the rearming of Germany in the European Defense Community as unwise. Aneurin Bevan, the leader of the Left wing of the British Labor party, holds the same opinion. On February 23, 1954, his wing came within nine votes of defeating the Attlee majority motion to "accept the inclusion of Western Germany in the collective organization of Western Defense within which German forces could serve without danger to their neighbors." [19] Protestant leader Pastor Martin Niemöller in West Germany agrees with the Bevan group. These men and their followers believe the wiser policy, and the only hope for a settlement between the free nations of the West and the Soviet East, is to keep Germany unarmed, or very weakly armed, as a kind of buffer no man's land between the Soviet East and a stronger rearmed free West. They tend to believe also that France and Western Europe's long-range danger is the German problem rather than the Russian problem. The history of Europe since Bismarck and 1870 gives weight to this opinion. Traditionally, a rearmed Germany has been a war-producing Germany. Why not, therefore, turn away from allied collaboration between the free nations on the continent of Europe and through the United Nations in the world generally with respect to the Communist danger, and return to bilaterally arranged power politics balancing which dictates always that one enters an alliance not with the nearest neighboring national power, but with the power on the other side of one's strongest neighbor? This clearly points toward a French alliance with the Soviet Union to prevent the unification and remilitarization of Germany.

What is more likely though is continuous temporizing on EDC and neutralism. This also would be a Russian victory, since it would mean that the Communist policy of dividing the free world and isolating the United States from her allies had succeeded. Should France not accept EDC, what would the "agonizing appraisal" by the United States have to be? Either (a) she would give up the basic conviction of the Truman administration, General Eisenhower the Supreme Commander of NATO, President Eisenhower, Senators McCarthy and Knowland and Secretary of State Dulles that Western free Europe is in danger from the largest land army in the world on its eastern border and cannot be protected from this danger without the contribution of a rearmed Germany, or (b) she would keep her troops in Germany and oppose both the French and the Communists by rearming the Germans under unilateral German control, thereby driving the French even further into Soviet Russia's arms. Both alternatives call for a complete about-face in the foreign policy of the United States, and neither is likely to stop Communism or preserve the peace of Europe. Certainly the latter of the two—the rearming of the Germans outside the European Defense Community —meets one problem, the Communist threat, by adding another, the threat of a purely German controlled rearmed Germany. This would seem to be about the quickest road to war in Europe that the mind of man can devise.

Let no one suppose, however, that we shall not be traveling down this road very soon and very fast if EDC and Continental European Union generally fail. Immediately following the Four Power conference at Berlin in February of 1954, *The New York Times* correspondent in Germany, M. S. Handler, wrote from Berlin as follows:

The time is rapidly approaching when Chancellor Adenauer must "deliver" on his foreign policy—the effective establishment of the European Defense Community . . . and the securing of a peace treaty returning a measure of sovereignty to the West German people. . . . Defeat for the treaty in Paris or another long delay could have the result of sweeping away the entire foundation of Chancellor Adenauer's foreign policy and leaving him empty-handed before the German people. [Should this happen] old nationalist tendencies could be expected to reassert themselves, with the irresponsibles arguing that the West Germans had tried to be good Europeans but had been rebuffed, and that it was therefore time to seek alternatives. The alternatives might narrow themselves down to one: a return to adventurous nationalism—the time-worn, bankrupt program of a long line of German demagogues.[20]

But let us, for the purposes of argument, suppose two things that are exceedingly improbable: First, that if EDC breaks down, thereby placing the Germans on their own, the Germans in return for a united Germany west of the Oder-Neisse will be content to remain in an inferior or unarmed military position, as a neutral no-man's land between France and the Soviet East. Second, that, confronted with the prospect of a France and Western Europe that rejects Continental European collaboration under supranational law for bilaterally arranged power politics, the Soviet Union will be willing to give up its foothold in East Berlin and the Russian-occupied center to withdraw behind the Oder-Neisse. Where would France and the free world be then? It has just been noted that the Soviet Union has the largest land army on the face of the earth. Mao's Chinese army is the second largest. This means that Russia can place her land army on the eastern banks of the Oder-Neisse. Remember now that we are assuming Europe to be operating without allied collaboration in a power-politics world. Can one suppose for a moment that in such a world the Soviet Union would leave that German power-politics vacuum unoccupied, or that France could do anything about it if the Russians moved in, under a trumped-up or real threat of German rearmament, to take over the whole of Germany after the manner in Rumania, Hungary and Czechoslovakia?

There is another danger if EDC fails. This danger centers in the Saar. France is now its trustee. It has been noted that if Continental European Union fails, Chancellor Adenauer's Christian Democratic coalition government will likewise fail. Its likely successor will be a Socialist government. The West German Socialist party has been led by Kurt Schumacher and his successor, Erich Ollenhauer, since World War II. Both have attempted to out-Nazi the Nazis in their appeal to German nationalism and militarism. As a consequence, the German liberal Socialists have opposed the Contractual Agreements and Continental European Union and have insisted upon the recovery of the Saar as the primary order of business. Moreover, if such a German Socialist government fails to deliver on these promises when in power, it will fall, and a party which will act to unify Germany and attach the Saar will take over. This is the real danger of the return of a Nazi Germany. In short, if Continental European Union fails, not only will the Communist chances of dividing and taking over free Europe be markedly increased, but also it is not unlikely that France will be the Czechoslovakia and the Saar will be the Sudetenland of World War III.

The tragedy of this trend of events in early 1954 is that its end product need not occur. Realistic French, German and other Continental European statesmen—men like Messrs. Schuman, Monnet, Adenauer, Spaak and de Gasperi—have faced the difficulty of the Saar question and the Franco-German problem generally and have found a practicable and constructive solution.

The difficulty, as described by an informed Belgian leader, is that the Saar is most needed by the French economy and fits most naturally into this while its linguistic and family ties make it culturally German, so that there is no practicable solution of the problem in a chauvinistic power-politics Europe: any government in either France or Germany which allowed the other nation to have the Saar would fall—obviously it cannot belong to both France and Germany.

Yet the Saar can belong to both if there is Continental European Union. Then Germany, France, Italy, the Saar, Luxembourg, the Netherlands and Belgium, all are integrated parts of a single economic, military, legal and political system. The Saar then can belong to France in one respect and to Germany in other respects because it belongs to both together.

In short, the choice for France, Europe and the United States, so far as the German problem is concerned, is not, as Messrs. Molotov, Warburg, Bevan, de Gaulle, the Nazis and Pastor Niemöller suggest, that between an unarmed Germany and a rearmed Germany. The choice instead is between a rearmed Germany controlled solely by the old-fashioned Junker-Nazi Germans and a rearmed Germany collaborating in and directed by a supranational Continental European Community. Upon a rearmed Germany collaborating in and directed by this larger community depend the peace of Europe, the future of freedom in Asia, and the success of the foreign policy of the United States in both Asia and Europe. As *The Economist* of London stated on November 28, 1953, "the European Defence Community project . . . remains the only satisfactory formula for the common defence of Europe." [21]

Even so, can Continental European Union be effective even if it is voted by all the six member parliaments? May not the historical forces and habits of nationalism be too strong for it? May it not be entirely too artificial and utopian? Can one make supranational law and supranational institutions out of whole cloth in this manner?

As we turn to the answering of these questions, one additional consequence of the essential connection between Continental European Union and United States foreign policy is to be kept in mind. This connection works both ways. As the fate of the foreign policy of the United States since World War II depends on the fate of Continental European Union, so conversely the fate of Continental European Union depends on the Europeans' confidence in the direction which the United States foreign policy will take. Because of the commitment of Continental European Union to NATO, established by the EDC treaty and the Protocol to the NATO Treaty, and because of the central role which the United States plays in NATO and in SHAPE, the French, Italian and other continental Europeans will not accept EDC, even though from a purely Continental European standpoint they deem it practical and wise, unless they have confidence also in the present and future foreign policy decisions of the United States. This means that, after answering the foregoing questions concerning the practicality and likely effectiveness of Continental European Union, we shall also have to examine the foreign policy of the United States particularly since the summer of 1952, when the foreign policy of the Eisenhower administration became evident.

Chapter 3

European Union: An Experiment in Sociological Jurisprudence

The European Movement toward European Union, which was launched at the Hague on May 10, 1948, produced two international groupings of nations: the Council of Europe, sometimes referred to as Greater Europe; and the Continental European Community, which is at times called Little Europe. The latter is a member and offshoot of the former. Both are important. In fact, the experience of the Council of Europe throws almost as much light on the question of the practicality and wisdom of Continental European Union as does the study of the latter Community itself.

The aim of European Union is to bring the relations between the member nations under the rule of law implemented with power, and away from bilaterally arranged power politics and war. The aforementioned treaties, instituting its Council of Europe and the economic, military and political institutions of the Continental European Community, introduce a new supranational positive law.

Sociological jurisprudence informs us that the introduction of new positive law is unlikely to be effective unless the norms which it expresses are supported by common norms in the underlying living law of the peoples to whom it is applied. The sociologist of law, Ehrlich, defined the living law as "the inner order of society," i.e., the binding normative ties in which the people participate apart from the constitutions, statutes and legal institutions of the positive law.[1] Hence European Union is an experiment in sociological jurisprudence.

That European Union is significant, the previous chapters have shown. From any significant experiment something important is to be learned. Therefore, whatever the future brings forth, the study of the Council of Europe and Continental European Union, with respect to the positive law that is proposed and the living law of the European peoples to which it is now applied, has important lessons for every student of international law and international relations and for any statesman or private citizen who is concerned about foreign policy and the peace of the world.

This European experiment raises two crucial questions: (1) Are there common norms in the living law of the European peoples which correspond to the supranational norms of the new positive law that is proposed for them? (2) If so, are they strong enough to overcome the traditional nationalistic living-law norms and rivalries? In short, are there communal living-law European norms which correspond to the proposed supranational European positive law and are they strong enough to make this positive law effective?

The principle to be used in answering the questions is specified by sociological jurisprudence. This science tells us that positive legal norms such as are proposed in the Continental European Coal and Steel Community, Defense Community and Political Community will not be effective unless there are common norms in the living law corresponding to and supporting the norms of the newly proposed Continental European positive law. Our task, therefore, becomes twofold. First, the specific transfers of sovereignty from the national to the supranational level required in the treaties constituting the Council of Europe and the new economic, military and political Continental European positive law must be noted. Second, the living law of each people to whom this positive law is to be applied must be examined to determine (a) whether it has norms in common with the living law of the others, and (b) whether they are strong enough relative to the nationalistic habits, norms and values of the traditional living law to overcome these, thereby making the newly proposed supranational positive law effective.

The determination of the norms of the supranational European positive law is relatively easy and will concern us first. It consists in examining the positive legal rules that have been laid down in the two treaties and in the statute constituting the larger Council of Europe and the three Continental European Communities.

The second portion of our task, however—determining the living law—confronts us with a difficulty. The founders of sociological jurisprudence, such as Ehrlich, failed to specify the method by which the living law of any society is to be determined. Ehrlich touched on the problem at the end of his *Fundamental Principles of the Sociology of Law*, suggesting that the method of sociological jurisprudence should be like the scientific method of the neo-classical Austrian school of economic science. Actually, however, he never indicated how the scientific method of the Austrian economists or any other scientific method could be applied to a specific society to determine its living law. Underhill Moore attempted to overcome this weakness.[2] The method which he introduced is of great theoretical significance and effective for the simple social situations to which he applied it; but it is inapplicable to the 157,000,000 people involved in Continental European Union and to the countless millions more involved in the wider European union of the Council of Europe. This is true because it requires the observation and description in spatio-temporal terms of the bodily movements of the people whose living law is being determined. Moore's method gave no clue either to the criterion for a reform of the living law.[3] In a sense it is precisely such a reform in traditional nationalistic living-law habits that European Union is attempting to achieve.

How then is their living law to be determined? If the method specified by Moore is impractical, what method is practical? Or, to put the matter positively, how must Moore's method be modified so that a practical way of determining the living law of the contemporary European peoples is at hand?

Ehrlich gives the first clue. He tells us that the living law of any society is not to be found in any particular fact or class of facts in that society, such as the observable behavior of its inhabitants, their climate, economic needs or physical power. Instead, the living law is not any fact, or even all the facts, but the *inner order* of all the facts.

Contemporary anthropologists, such as Professor A. L. Kroeber, concur with Ehrlich and add a further clue when they tell us that every culture has a pattern, and that the communal norms and values of a people are *essentially* connected with this pattern of their culture.[4] For scientists the adjective "essential" expresses that which is given in the scientific definition of anything. Thus, to say that values are essentially connected to the pattern of a culture is to say that values define the pattern or the inner order of a society, which is its living law. The normative character of law suggests this conclusion also.

Values, however, do not exist in the sky. They exist only as specific individuals freely believe in them and embody them in their behavior. It follows, therefore, that a society can have an inner order only as a majority of its people have common, living, embodied normative beliefs and values. The method, therefore, of determining the living law of the European peoples is to examine the quantitative statistics which specify how these peoples group themselves with respect to their personal, religious, political and economic beliefs. With respect to personal, living-law religious beliefs, the task is easy because the European people fall into a small number of normative religious groups. The economic and political groupings, though larger in number, are equally objective and relatively easy to determine. They show in the major political parties with their respective ideologies and policies and the number of adherents, as given in recent elections.

In determining the living law of the European peoples, one error, very prevalent in the United States, must at all costs be avoided. It consists in judging the living-law norms of Europe as if they were those of the majority of people in the United States. Such procedure violates the fundamental principle of sociological jurisprudence, which is that the positive law of a given people must be determined by their own living-law norms and not by the positive or living norms of some other people.

The majority of people in the United States are Protestant in their religious living-law beliefs. With time and the influences of modern secular philosophy, economics, politics and technology, even the living-law beliefs of many Protestants have become secularized. Furthermore, the political and economic beliefs of the majority of the American people derive from British empirical modern philosophy and from economists such as Smith, Jevons, Marshall and Keynes who based their science on the assumption of this philosophy. Similarly the doctrines and procedures of the legal institutions of the United States are an extension of British common law.

These Protestant religious and British empirical secular living-law norms exist also in the Scandinavian countries and Great Britain. The sovereign powers of the House of Commons and the Scandinavian parliaments are their positive legal expression. But beside them in these European countries there exist also other living-law institutions and customs, not present in the United States, such as a national church in certain instances and such as royal families and a hierarchically ordered type of society with different classes of people in their respective stations. The living law of Western Continental Europe is even more unique. Its religious living-law beliefs are overwhelmingly Roman Catholic. Its primary secular, modern, economic and political thinking derives (1) from Rousseau, the Encyclopaedists, Comte and the French Socialists like Proudhon and (2) from Continental rationalistic, rather than from British empirical, modern philosophy.

Sociological jurisprudence prescribes, therefore, that we be prepared to expect different living-law norms and hence different effective positive-law practices among the European peoples than in the United States. Failure to relate our judgments, concerning Continental European Union and the foreign policy of the United States vis-à-vis the Defense Community, to these differences in living

law between Europeans and the people of the United States will lead
to nothing but error, and perhaps even tragedy. It is imperative,
therefore, that we be objective with respect not merely to the positive legal institutions now proposed in European Union, but also to
the living law of the hundreds of millions of Europeans upon whom
the supranational positive law must draw if it is to be effective.

To these two objective tasks we must now turn. As we do so,
the limited character of our conclusions must be noted. We restrict
ourselves to determining whether there are common norms in the
living law of the European peoples upon which a wise statesmanship
guided by the principles of sociological jurisprudence can draw and
thus make effective the supranational positive law proposed in European Union. Even if such living-law norms exist, European Union
may not come into being, or be effective. First, statesmanship is not
always wise. Common living-law beliefs present in a people may not
be brought to expression by its politicians. In short, latent living-law
resources may be left dormant, unused, just as natural resources are
left unused by a people in an underdeveloped area. Also, even if the
statesmen of a European nation should desire to implement common
living-law norms among their people which are sufficient to make a
supranational community effective, the foreign policies of other
nations may make such action impossible.

The inquiry of the next four chapters restricts itself, therefore, to
two questions: (1) What is the new positive law of the Council of
Europe and Continental European Union? (2) Granted a favorable
external environment, are common living-law norms embodied in
the living beliefs and values of the European peoples which, if drawn
upon by a realistic and jurisprudentially wise European political
statesmanship, will make the proposed supranational positive legal
norms of European Union effective?

In answering, one usage is to be noted. The positive law of European Union will be regarded as including the newly proposed
economic and military communities as well as the purely political
community. Several considerations justify this usage. First, the High
Authority for Coal and Steel is as much a positive political and legal

institution as it is an economic one. It has its own court. It has also its own political assembly within the Council of Europe at Strasbourg. Moreover, the Treaty of Paris of April 18, 1951, which instituted it, specifies the positive legal rules that define its sovereign powers, aims and procedures. The same is true of the treaty constituting the European Defense Community. Second, observation of the introduction of Western economic, mechanical and military ways into non-Western cultures shows that these proposed positive processes and institutions obey Ehrlich's rule that effective positive proposals must correspond to the underlying living law, as much as do purely legal constitutions and statutes.[5]

Chapter 4

The Positive Law of the Council of Europe

The Council of Europe, it will be recalled, was set in motion by a statute signed in London on May 5, 1949, by the following ten European governments: Belgium, Denmark, France, Ireland, Italy, the Grand Duchy of Luxembourg, the Netherlands, Norway, Sweden and the United Kingdom. Later Greece, Turkey, Iceland, the Federal Republic of Germany and the Saar joined.

The Preamble of the Statute of the Council of Europe is as follows:

> Convinced that the pursuit of peace based upon justice and international cooperation is vital for the preservation of human society and civilization;

The signatory governments,

> Reaffirming their devotion to the spiritual and moral values which are the common heritage of their peoples and the true source of individual freedom, political liberty and the rule of law, principles which form the basis of all genuine democracy;
>
> Believing that, for the maintenance and further realization of these ideals and in the interests of economic and social progress, there is need of a closer unity between all likeminded countries of Europe;
>
> Considering that, to respond to this need and to the expressed aspirations of their peoples in this regard, it is necessary forthwith to create an organisation which will bring European states into closer association;

Have in consequence decided to set up a Council of Europe.[1]

The reference to "the spiritual and moral values which are the common heritage of their peoples and the true source of . . . the rule of law" suggests the conviction of the signatories that the vital, common, living-law norms necessary for a single European supranational positive law are present. Chapter VIII ("Europe's Cultural Heritage") of the handbook of the European Movement tells us what the authors of the Statute of the Council of Europe believed its living-law norms to be:

Western Europe, after a centrifugal period that began with Luther, is again becoming aware of a deep unity in culture, in tradition, and in outlook. No doubt it has become aware of this unity owing to the threat of external danger, but as the external danger takes an ideological form the reply to it must also have its ideology.[2]

Even so, paragraph (d) of Article I of the Statute adds, "Matters relating to National Defence do not fall within the scope of the Council of Europe." [3] Therefore, the Council of Europe has no military organ corresponding to the European Defense Community in Continental European Union. Similarly with respect to political matters, the Statute says, "The Committee of Ministers is the organ which acts on behalf of the Council of Europe," [4] and Article 23 specifies that the Consultative Assembly (the legislative branch of the Council of Europe)

shall discuss, and may make recommendations upon, any matter . . . which (i) is referred to it by the Committee of Ministers with a request for its opinion, or (ii) has been approved by the Committee for inclusion in the Agenda of the Assembly on the proposal of the latter.[5]

Article 41 similarly makes all amendments to the Statute of the Council of Europe subject to the recommendations of the Committee of Ministers. The Committee of Ministers is appointed by the respective governments, so that not merely all legislative and executive functions but also all future possible amendments of the positive law of the Council of Europe are under the sovereign unilateral control of the member nations. This becomes all the more evident when one notes that the Committee of Ministers "alone can conclude Conventions or Agreements" [6] and decide "with binding effect all matters relating to the international organisation and arrangements of the Council of Europe." [7]

The personnel of the legislative branch of the Council of Europe is similarly under the control of the national governments. Its very name, the Consultative Assembly, suggests this. As constituted in 1951, it contained representatives from fourteen countries, the number in each case being determined by the population of the nations concerned. Article 25 says, "The Consultative Assembly shall consist of representatives from each Member [nation] appointed in such a manner as the Government of that Member shall decide."

The *Concise Handbook of the Council of Europe* summarizes the situation accurately, therefore, when it concludes: "The Assembly proposes; the Committee disposes, being free to reject, amend or adopt the Recommendations of the Assembly. In theory, even if the Committee of Ministers accepts a Recommendation and transmits it to Member Governments, those Governments are not compelled to put its provisions into effect." [8] No real transfer of sovereignty from the national to the supranational level has occurred, therefore, in the positive law of the executive or legislative branches of the Council of Europe.

Precisely this fact at one time threatened the destruction of the Council of Europe and led to Continental European Union. Six member nations within the Council of Europe desired a real transfer of legislative, judicial and executive sovereignty to the supranational European level. The result was the positive law of the Continental European Community.

In the judicial branch of the Council of Europe, its positive law did specify one transfer of sovereignty from the fourteen member nations to its European Community. This occurred in its Convention for the Protection of Human Rights and Fundamental Freedoms.

At the meeting of the European Movement at the Hague in May 1948, two resolutions, among many others, were passed unanimously:

The European Union or Federation should be open to all democratic European nations which undertake to respect fundamental human rights.

A European Court of Human Rights backed with adequate sanctions should be established to adjudicate in cases of alleged violation of these rights.[9]

In February of 1949, the International Council of the European Movement set up an International Judicial Section under the chairmanship of Pierre-Henri Teitgen, former French Minister of Justice and present leader of the Christian Democratic party (MRP) of France. On July 12, 1949, after the member governments had set up the Council of Europe, M. Teitgen's committee submitted to its Committee of Ministers the draft of the European Convention on Human Rights. After debate, criticisms and suggestions, the Consultative Assembly drafted and passed the final "Convention for the Protection of Human Rights and Fundamental Freedoms." In Rome and Paris on November 4 and 28, 1950, the foreign ministers of the fourteen governments making up the Council of Europe signed this Convention.

It begins with two reasons why it is introduced. One is the attempt of the United Nations to achieve such a convention for all the nations of the world. The other is that "the Governments of European countries . . . are likeminded and have a common heritage of political traditions, ideals, freedom and the rule of law." [10] The latter amounts to a reassertion that there are common living-law norms throughout the fourteen member nations which will make this supranational European positive legal norm effective.

This solitary supranational positive legal norm of the Council of Europe is distinguished from the supranational positive legal norms of Continental European Union by the fact that the latter prescribe common norms for the economic, military and political inner order of the peoples affected, while the former refers only to the protection of the rights of individual persons qua individual persons. No norms for ordering their social relations are specified. Thus Article 2 of Section I opens as follows: "Everyone's right to life shall be protected by law. No one shall be deprived of his life intentionally save in the execution of a sentence of a court following his conviction of a crime for which this penalty is provided by law." Article 3 reads: "No one shall be subjected to torture or to inhuman or degrading treatment or punishment." Paragraph 1 of Article 4 adds, "No one shall be held in slavery or servitude." Article 5 continues: "Everyone has the right to liberty and security of person. . . . No one shall be deprived of his liberty save . . . in accordance with a procedure prescribed by law." Furthermore, it specifies the only five cases in which a person can be arrested. Paragraph 2 of this Article adds: "Everyone who is arrested shall be informed promptly, in a language which he understands, of the reasons for his arrest and of any charge against him." Paragraph 2 of Article 6 affirms, "Everyone charged with a criminal offence shall be presumed innocent until proved guilty according to law."

Forthwith are listed five specific "minimum rights" which any such person possesses. Articles 9, 10 and 11 guarantee the right to "freedom of thought, conscience and religion . . . expression . . . [and] peaceful assembly," subject only to such limitations "as are prescribed by law and are necessary in a democratic society . . . for the protection of the rights and freedoms of others." Article 14 adds: "The enjoyment of the rights and freedoms set forth in this Convention shall be secured without discrimination on any ground such as sex, race, colour, language, religion, political or other opinion, national or social origin, association with a national minority, property, birth or other status." This, let it be noted, is the ethics of the law of contract according to which moral and political man is universal man, rather than family or tribal man, that arose first with the ancient Greek philosophers and Stoic Romans.

To implement these protective legal rules, Section II authorizes the establishment of (1) a European Commission of Human Rights and (2) a European Court of Human Rights. Section III specifies the constitution and duties of the Commission; Section IV, those of the Court. Each of the contracting states has one member on the Commission. They are elected by the Committee of Ministers of the member states "by an absolute majority of votes, from a list of names drawn up by the Bureau of the Consultative Assembly" of the Council of Europe.[11] They remain in office for six years, except for seven members of the first group, whose terms expire at the end of three years in order to insure continuity.[12] Article 23 specifies that they "shall sit on the Commission in their individual capacity." Article 24 reads: "Any High Contracting Party may refer to the Commission, through the Secretary-General of the Council of Europe, any alleged breach of the provisions of the Convention by another High Contracting Party."

Qualifications, however, soon began to appear. Article 25 recognizes the competence of the Commission to receive petitions of violations of the Convention from any person, "organization or group of individuals claiming to be the victim of a violation by one of the High Contracting Parties," provided that the High Contracting Party in question "has declared that it recognises the competence of the Commission to receive such petitions." No anonymous petitions are to be considered.[13] Article 26 adds that the Commission "may only deal with the matter [sic] after all domestic remedies have been exhausted, according to the generally recognised rules of international law." Article 28 specifies that upon receipt of the petition the Commission will work in conjunction with the member state and the party making the appeal to determine the facts and "shall place itself at the disposal of the parties concerned with a view to securing a friendly settlement . . . on the basis of . . . this Convention." Certainly, Articles 25 and 26 come very close to taking back with the left hand any sovereign powers given with the right hand in Article 24 and elsewhere by a member state to the Community of the Council of Europe. It is evident that, in this solitary attempt at a transfer of sovereignty to the Council of Europe, the achievement is difficult.

Nevertheless, Article 31 does add that if no solution is reached the Commission "shall draw up a Report on the facts and state its opinion as to whether the facts found disclose a breach by the State concerned" of the Convention. The Commission may also "make such proposals as it thinks fit." [14] Its report must be transmitted to the Committee of Ministers and to the states concerned, "who shall not be at liberty to publish it." [15]

If the question is not referred to the Court, Article 32 specifies that the "Committee of Ministers shall decide by a majority of two-thirds of the members . . . whether there has been a violation." If the decision is in the affirmative, the Committee must prescribe a period within which the member state concerned must implement the decision of the Committee.[16] If the decision is not implemented, the Committee of Ministers shall decide by majority vote "what effect shall be given to its original decision and shall publish the Report." [17]

The Court is composed of one judge from each state.[18] Judges shall be elected by a majority of the Consultative Assembly of the Council of Europe from a list nominated by the members, each member state proposing three candidates, of whom two at least shall be its own citizens.[19] Each judge, after proper staggering is established, will serve for nine years and can be reelected.[20] The Court elects its own President and Vice President, who may be re-elected.[21] Each case shall be heard by a Chamber of seven judges. A judge who is a national of, or who is chosen by, the member state judged in any case concerning a violation shall sit as an ex officio member of the Chamber. The other judges of the Chamber "shall be chosen by lot by the President." [22]

When one turns to the Court's jurisdiction, the same phenomenon appears as occurred above with respect to the Commission. Sovereignty transferred to the Court in one article tends to be withdrawn in another article. Article 44 reads: "Only the High Contracting Parties and the Commission shall have the right to bring a case before the Court." Article 48 qualifies this with the provision "that the High Contracting Party . . . or . . . Parties concerned . . . are subject to the compulsory jurisdiction of the Court . . . or, failing that, with the consent of the High Contracting Party . . . or . . . Parties concerned."

Which of these two possibilities applies, depends upon whether any signatory to the Convention takes advantage of its Article 46 to declare that it recognizes the jurisdiction of the European Court "as compulsory *ipso facto*." [23] In 1952, when the Council of Europe published its Convention on Human Rights, only Sweden had so declared. Clearly transfer of sovereignty to the larger European community, which is the Council of Europe, is not easy.

A Protocol amending the Convention, signed at Paris on the 20th of March, 1952, by the foreign ministers of the fourteen member states, had as its purpose "the collective enforcement of certain rights and freedoms other than those already included in Section I of the Convention" of 1950.[24] Article 2 is interesting:

No person shall be denied the right to education. In the exercise of any functions which it assumes in relation to education and to teaching, the State shall respect the right of parents to ensure such education and teaching in conformity with their own religious and philosophical convictions.

This brings the positive-law rules of the Convention into relation with the living-law beliefs of the people. The next Article also encourages the bringing of the living-law choices and beliefs of the people to bear upon the legislative and executive decisions of their respective states:

The High Contracting Parties undertake to hold free elections at reasonable intervals by secret ballot, under conditions which will ensure the free expression of the opinion of the people in the choice of the legislature.

It appears, therefore, that only in the domain of personal human rights does the positive law of the Council of Europe achieve any transfer of sovereignty from the individual state to the European Community and even in this case (except for Sweden to date) this transfer is made in one Article only to be curbed, if not withdrawn, in another.

Chapter 5

The Positive Law of Continental European Union

As previously noted, the positive law of Continental European Union prescribes the establishment of three interrelated communities: (1) the Coal and Steel Community, (2) the European Defense Community and (3) the European Political Community.

Article 1 of the Treaty of April 18, 1951, which defines the positive law of the Coal and Steel Community, asserts that it is "based on a common market, common objectives, and common institutions." [1] This suggests that, notwithstanding its novel supranational positive law, it none the less has roots in Continental European living law.

Viewed from the standpoint of positive law, this Coal and Steel Community has five parts: (1) the High Authority, (2) the Common Assembly, (3) the Council of Ministers, (4) the Consultative Committee and (5) the Court of Justice. The High Authority is its executive arm; the Common Assembly is its legislative branch; and the Court of Justice is the judicial component. The function of the Council of Ministers is to relate the sovereignty of the High Authority to the sovereignties of the six member governments. The Consultative Committee relates the High Authority to the living-law producer, labor and consumer groups in the Community.

The High Authority is composed of (1) nine members chosen by common agreement by the six participating nations and (2) a technical staff of approximately three hundred people. The function of the nine administrative members of the High Authority is to carry out the provisions of the Treaty of April 18, 1951. In other words, their task is to exercise the explicit supranational sovereignty it confers upon them.

Speaking before the Consultative Assembly of the Council of Europe at Strasbourg on August 10, 1950, when this new legally constituted European Community was first proposed, Robert Schuman, Foreign Minister of France, described the sovereign rights conferred upon the High Authority by the Treaty-making powers as involving "two essential characteristics: an independent Authority, and a single market." [2] The High Authority, he added, "will not be a Committee of Ministers or of Delegates of Ministers." [3] Instead, it

will be an institution that is autonomous and, in consequence, one that has its own responsibilities. The signatories of the Treaty will, with certain guarantees, submit to the authority that they will have set up. In spite of its contractual origin, the Authority will exercise its powers according to an unfettered estimation of the needs and possibilities, but always within the limits of its Charter. It will itself be subordinated only to the objectives specified and the rulings arising therefrom. The Authority thus set up will be the first example of an independent supranational institution.[4]

Becoming even more explicit, M. Schuman added that the "participating States will be abandoning some degree of sovereignty in favour of the common Authority" and "will in advance accept the notion of submission to the Authority that they will have set up and within such limits as they themselves will have defined." [5]

The Common Assembly is the legislative branch of the Coal and Steel Community, as initially constituted. Its powers as defined in the Treaty of April 18, 1951, are merely consultative, like those of the Consultative Assembly of the Council of Europe. It can propose, but not dispose. In fact, its membership is that of the Belgian, the Netherlands, West German, Luxembourg, French and Italian portion of the Consultative Assembly of the Council of Europe. Thus it relates the Coal and Steel Community to the Council of Europe. This is insured by a Protocol to the 1951 Treaty. Article 1 of the Protocol reads:

The governments of the member States are invited to recommend to their respective Parliaments that the members of the Assembly, which these Parliaments are called upon to designate, should preferably be chosen from among the representatives of the Consultative Assembly of the Council of Europe.[6]

This means that the personnel of the legislative branch of the Coal and Steel Assembly, as initially authorized, are chosen by the member governments.

As the sequel will show, however, the signatories of the Treaty of April 18, 1951, envisaged this merely Consultative Assembly as something temporary, to be replaced by a Political Assembly with sovereign legislative powers of its own and by a lower house elected directly and democratically by the 157,000,000 people of the Community voting as Europeans rather than as Germans, Frenchmen, *et al.* The Defense Community Treaty, signed by the six foreign ministers in May of 1952, makes this explicit.

The Council of Ministers of the Coal and Steel Community, like its present Assembly, is identical in personnel with the Belgian, French, West German, Italian, Luxembourg and Netherlands portion of the Council of Ministers of the Council of Europe. However, the foreign ministers of these six nations have much less power when they sit in the official capacity of members of the Council of Ministers of the Coal and Steel Community than the positive law gives them as members of the Council of Ministers of the Council of Europe. In the latter body, as we noted above, they possess all executive powers and determine even what the legislative branch of the Community may consider. In the Coal and Steel Community, they possess no executive powers whatever, these being given to the High Authority. Nor does the Council of Ministers have any control over legislation so far as a control of the executive branch of the Coal and Steel Community is concerned.

The executive branch gets its legislative authority from the powers assigned to it in the Treaty of April 18, 1951, and the approval of the Treaty, already voted, by the legislative branches of the contracting governments. So long, therefore, as the High Authority of the Coal and Steel Community acts within the positive legislative prescriptions assigned to it by the Treaty of April 18, 1951, the Council of Ministers and their respective governments have no control over it: its decisions are mandatory upon them and their respective governments. Hence, the High Authority not merely proposes; it also disposes.

Even if the High Authority at Luxembourg assumed sovereign powers which the Council of Ministers (i.e., the foreign ministers of the member governments) thought were not assigned to it by that treaty, neither the Council of Ministers of the Coal and Steel Community nor the member governments could interfere directly. Instead, they would have to appeal to the Court of Justice of the Coal and Steel Community. Using the Treaty of April 18, 1951, as its positive norm, this Court's decision in the matter would be binding and final. As Article 14 says, decisions of the High Authority "shall be binding in all their details." Furthermore, Article 38 adds: "On the petition of a member State or of the High Authority, the Court may annul the acts of the Assembly or of the Council." This means that, should the Council of Ministers and the Assembly vote that statutes of the Treaty of April 18, 1951, bearing on the sovereign powers of the High Authority should be changed by new legislation, such action would be unconstitutional—the reason being that both the Assembly and the Council of Ministers owe their legal existence to the implementation of the sovereign powers of the High Authority as specified in the aforementioned Treaty. Clearly, so far as its positive law is concerned, the supranational High Authority of the Coal and Steel Community has real sovereign powers. The member nations face a Court and law which is, in certain specified matters, above their own courts and their own national sovereign powers.

This Court is composed of seven judges appointed by common agreement of the governments of the member states. Appeals to it may be made by any of the other institutions of the Coal and Steel Community, by governments, firms or individuals.

But if the Council of Ministers of the European Coal and Steel Community has neither executive power nor control over legislative changes within the sovereign powers given to the High Authority in the treaty, what then is its function? It is a liaison between the High Authority and the member governments. It communicates the sovereign decisions of the High Authority and of the member governments, within their respective sovereign spheres, each to the other. It harmonizes, and avoids conflicts between the respective but different sovereign powers and acts of the six member nations and the European High Authority. In the official publication by the Council of Europe on the Schuman Plan, the sovereignty of the member governments, as related by the Council of Ministers to that of the High Authority, is described as "States' Rights." [7] It follows conversely that the High Authority has sovereign federal powers which are related by the Council of Ministers to the sovereign States' Rights of the member governments.

The fifth institution of the European Coal and Steel Community is the Consultative Committee. Just as the Common Assembly serves as the legislative liaison between the Coal and Steel Community and the Council of Europe, and just as the Council of Ministers is the executive liaison between the member national governments and the High Authority, so the Consultative Committee relates the High Authority to the living-law member groups of the Continental European Community. In other words, it relates the High Authority to producer, labor and consumer groups. Its task is to advise the High Authority on economic matters affecting these groups. It is made up of not fewer than thirty, and not more than fifty-one, members chosen by the Council of Ministers of the Coal and Steel Community from the three economic groups.

Viewed, therefore, from the standpoint of the positive law, the European Community for Coal and Steel involves a truly remarkable transfer of sovereign powers from six Continental European nations to a supranational European community. It has executive, legislative and judicial branches, each with autonomous, specified powers of its own. The specification of these powers is contained in the Treaty of the Coal and Steel Community, which was signed by the six foreign ministers and passed later by their respective parliaments.[8]

Events have proved this new supranational Continental European positive law to be something more than verbal. On August 10, 1952, it and the institutions which implement it went into effect. Jean Monnet of France became the first President of its executive branch. Chancellor and Foreign Minister Adenauer of West Germany became the first President of its Council of Ministers. Paul-Henri Spaak of Belgium became the first President of its Common Assembly and Massimo Pilotti of Italy became the first President of its Court of Justice.[9]

The High Authority and the Secretariats of the other four institutions of the Community are located in Luxembourg. The Assembly meets in buildings of the Council of Europe at Strasbourg. In all five institutions of this Continental European Coal and Steel Community representatives of its six peoples are working together. To realize in fact what this means, one must have been in Luxembourg or talked to those who have been there.

With M. Monnet, the President of the High Authority, and those around him, it has become almost a passion to regard oneself as a European rather than a Frenchman, a German, a Belgian, an Italian, a Netherlander or a Luxembourger. An American whose official business it has been to observe the administration, at Luxembourg, of this institution through every phase of its development, and who has known its President personally over many years, informed the writer that M. Monnet regards himself as having undergone almost a change of citizenship and feelings, sloughing off purely French attachments for a wider European loyalty. For him personally European, as compared with merely French, citizenship is a living reality. His manner of action is direct, practical, as simple as possible and matter-of-fact. His inspiration in part is the non-doctrinaire, pragmatic way of doing things which he experienced when working with Americans in the United States during World War II. Moreover, he takes his sovereign powers seriously. Speaking as President of the High Authority of the European Coal and Steel Community, he has said:

> The sole justification of our authority lies in the fact that we cannot and should not take a national point of view. If we should forget this in the future, it would constitute a veritable diversion of our powers and would call for sanction by a decision of the high court.[10]

Anne O'Hare McCormick described him as "a self-effacing, behind-the-scenes operator whose greatest contribution to the 'peaceful revolution' he engineers is to persuade and inspire the men who have the position and power to translate his ideas into action."[11]

The mandate of his High Authority is to create a single market for the 157,000,000 people in the Continental European Community. Ultimately, the goal is to remove all tariffs, import controls, exchange inconvertibilities and immigration restrictions between the member states. The last-named goal, as the sequel will show, is what gives Continental European Union its special appeal to the Italians with their excessive overpopulation. These goals are to be reached not in one single step, but in several stages. The first stage went into effect on February 10, 1953, when the common market was established for coal, iron ore and scrap metal. Five years are allowed before all protection of national coal and steel industries is removed.

In *The New York Times* of June 23, 1953, Michael L. Hoffman reported some of the results as follows:

> The first effect . . . was almost indescribable confusion in the marketing of steel. . . . Consumers were taken completely by surprise. . . . Industries that had enjoyed a form of protection merely by virtue of being situated nearer than competitors to Thionville suddenly discovered that concerns on the other side of France could get steel cheaper than they. . . . In Italy, steel companies for the first time in history have had to establish firm prices and, what is even more revolutionary, publish them. . . . The common market in scrap and iron ore is a functioning reality. . . . Prices for most types of steel . . . moved toward the kind of balance that would prevail in a competitive market. . . . There is not much evidence, however, of any agreement between the different regions.

The High Authority is just now watching the cartel problem very closely. . . . The evidence of price changes suggests that . . . [the common market] is already beginning to demonstrate the kind of capacity for adjustment to the situation in the whole of the community that its organizers intended it to have.[12]

[Furthermore, the men in control of the coal and steel industries] are thinking entirely in terms of getting ready to meet common market competition when the protective barriers are lowered.[13]

In addition to these immediate, actual accomplishments, the High Authority has executive power of taxation. A British observer has described its operation as follows:

Every month, a reminder note goes out from the High Authority to the various coal and steel businesses in the six countries. Every business calculates its own tax, based on the value of its production, and pays it into a local bank. The High Authority believes that pride in their production figures will help most firms to confess their fair share of tax. The revenue expected is about £20,000,000 a year. Very little of it will be spent on maintaining the coal and steel institutions. Most of it will be used for modernising machinery and getting houses built for the workers. M. Monnet describes it as "the first European tax," meaning the first tax collected not for a national but for a supra-national government. It will add substantially to the power and independence of the Coal and Steel Community.[14]

Nevertheless, all these achievements will not insure success. In *The New York Times* of February 15, 1953, Harold Callender reported from Paris concerning the European Coal and Steel Community as follows:

Its destiny is linked with that of the hastily devised European army plan, which has provoked strong opposition. For if the Monnet technique is not successful for defense, its achievements in the sphere of coal and steel will be weakened by a return of nationalism. It now seems necessary, or at least desirable, to secure some kind of European defense unity in order to avoid a setback for the new step toward economic unity taken when the single market was inaugurated.[15]

In short, notwithstanding its achievements, the success of the European Coal and Steel Community depends on the acceptance of the

European Defense Community. If the latter fails to materialize, the former will fail also. A return to bilaterally arranged power politics on the continent of Europe would force each nation to have its own autonomous national coal and steel industry. This, incidentally, is clear proof that society is not determined by the economic factor alone, but that instead the economic is a function of the military which in turn depends upon the political as the sequel will show.

THE EUROPEAN DEFENSE COMMUNITY

On May 26, 1952, the Secretary of State of the United States and the foreign ministers of France, Great Britain and Germany signed at Bonn the "Convention on Relations with the Federal Republic of Germany and a Protocol to the North Atlantic Treaty." The next day at Paris the foreign ministers of the six nations in the European Coal and Steel Community signed a treaty and six protocols constituting the European Defense Community.

The May 26 Convention had the purpose of ending the war status and the military government of West Germany by the three Western occupying powers. It provided that the Federal Republic of Germany should be an equal partner in the European Community and in the free world generally. The four contracting parties affirmed that

the Three Powers and the Federal Republic recognize that both the new relationship to be established between them by the present Convention and its related Conventions and the Treaties for the creation of an integrated European community, in particular the Treaty on the Establishment of the European Community for Coal and Steel and the Treaty on the Establishment of the European Defence Community, are essential steps to the achievement of their common aim for a unified Germany integrated within the European Community.[16]

Section 2 of Article 11 is:

The present Convention shall enter into force immediately upon
(a) the deposits by all the Signatory States of instruments of ratification of the present Convention and of all the Conventions listed in Article 8; and

(b) the entry into force of the Treaty on the Establishment of the European Defence Community.

The foregoing statements make it clear that the Convention does not take effect, and hence West Germany does not return legally to a peacetime sovereign status, unless West Germany enters into, and accepts the provisions of the European Defense Community and this Community is similarly approved by the parliaments of its other members. In short, in order for West Germany to achieve the legal status of a free nation, rather than that of a defeated power occupied by Great Britain, France and the United States, it must enter into and accept the responsibilities and controls of both the European Coal and Steel Community and the European Defense Community.

The Treaty Constituting the European Defense Community attempts in the military field what the European Coal and Steel Community attempts and has in part achieved in the economic field. Article 1 of Chapter I reads:

By the present Treaty the High Contracting Parties institute among themselves a European Defence Community, supranational in character, consisting of common institutions, common armed Forces and a common budget.[17]

Article 7 adds, "The Community shall have juridical personality." Article 8 implements these purposes as follows:

The institutions of the Community shall be:
—a Council of Ministers, hereinafter called the Council;
—a Common Assembly, hereinafter called the Assembly;
—a Commissariat of the European Defense Community, hereinafter called the Commissariat;
—a Court of Justice, hereinafter called the Court.

The Treaty provides further that the Community is to have at its disposal Armed Forces which are to be called "European Defense Forces."[18] *This insures*, not merely supranational law, but *supranational law with its own police force*. The armed forces are to be made up of contingents "placed at the disposal of the Community by the member States with a view to their fusion." [19] Furthermore, "No member State shall recruit or maintain national armed forces aside from those provided for in Article 10" of the Treaty.[20] The latter article permits member states to "recruit and maintain national armed forces intended for use in the non-European territories with respect to which they assume defense responsibilities," and "as a bodyguard for the Chief of State." [21] Policemen and "forces of gendarmerie" are also to be left entirely under the sovereignty of each member state.[22] The Treaty also prescribes that the European Defense Forces "shall wear a common uniform" [23] and shall be under a joint European Supreme Commander.[24]

The Commissariat, which is the executive branch of the European Defense Community, is similar to the High Authority of the European Coal and Steel Community. It consists of nine members appointed for six years, no more than two being appointed from one state.[25] Section 2 of Article 20 prescribes:

In the discharge of their duties, the members of the Commissariat shall neither solicit nor accept instructions from any Government. They will abstain from all conduct incompatible with the supranational character of their functions.

Each member state agrees to respect this supranational character and to make no effort to influence the members of the Commissariat in the execution of their task. "The members of the Commissariat shall not exercise any other professional activity during their terms of office." [26] The Commissariat is appointed by the governments of the member states "by agreement among themselves." [27] The first appointees "shall hold office for a period of three years."[28] At the end of the first three-year period, "a general reappointment shall take place." [29] After that, "one-third of the members of the Commissariat shall be reappointed every two years." [30] Article 25 prescribes that the President of the Commissariat shall be appointed by the governments of the member states "by agreement among themselves." [31] His term shall be for four years except in the case of the first President, whose term will be three years in length.[32] He may be reappointed.[33]

One task of the Commissariat is to establish "general organizational regulations," [34] on "the basis of the principle of collegiate responsibility." [35] After the Commissariat as a whole has thus determined the organizational regulations, it is the duty of the President to coordinate the respective duties of the members of the Commissariat and to insure the execution of its decisions.[36]

Article 31 prescribes, "Ranks higher than Commander of a basic unit of homogeneous nationality shall be conferred by the Commissariat with the unanimous concurrence of the Council." [37] Article 29 requires the Commissariat to report to the Council at periodical intervals and to supply the Council with such information and to undertake such studies as it requires. Consultations and information exchange between these two groups are to be mutual.

Article 33 specifies that the Assembly of the European Defense Community shall be that of the European Coal and Steel Community except that the German Federal Republic, France and Italy shall have three additional delegates each.[38] It must hold an annual session, and may be convened "in an extraordinary session at the request of the Commissariat, the Council, the President of the Assembly or the majority of its members." [39]

The Council, like the Council of the European Coal and Steel Community, is composed of representatives of the member states.[40] Its task is to harmonize the sovereign power of the Commissariat with the different sovereign powers reserved to the member states.[41] It may also issue directives, provided they are within the framework of the Treaty, for action by the Commissariat, provided they are by unanimous vote.[42]

The Court is the Court of Justice of the European Coal and Steel Community. It adjudicates all disputes between different institutions and members of the European Defense Community by means of the Articles of the Treaty of May 27, 1952, just as it adjudicates all disputes within the European Coal and Steel Community by recourse to the Articles of the Treaty of April 18, 1951.[43] It appears, therefore, that the European Defense Community involves a specified transfer of national sovereignty to a supranational European body in the same manner and degree to which this occurs in the European Coal and Steel Community.

With respect to implementation, however, there is a difference. The transfer has actually occurred in the case of the latter Community. The transfer has been agreed to by the foreign ministers of the six nations in the case of the European Defense Community but, as late as April 1954, has been approved only by the Parliaments of the Netherlands, West Germany, Belgium and Luxembourg.

In West Germany there were constitutional difficulties which threatened in early 1953 to be insurmountable. When the present constitution for West Germany was framed in consultation with the occupying powers, their representatives had Nazi Germany in mind. Consequently, they framed a constitution with the greatest possible number of restrictions upon the executive and with no provision for a West German government with an army. The result is that the West German government has two supreme courts to restrain the executive rather than the usual one. One of these has as its function the passing of judgment upon any issue that raises a question concerning the interpretation of any statute in the constitution itself. The other has as its jurisdiction the constitutionality of any statute passed by the legislative branch of the government. Furthermore, any amendment which might alter this state of affairs or anything else in the constitution requires a two-thirds vote of both houses of the West German parliament.

The matter is further complicated in fact by the circumstance that in 1952 and 1953 the first of the two supreme courts had a majority of judges who came from the Christian Democratic party, whereas the second had a majority whose political background was that of the Socialist party. Furthermore, the German Socialist party under its first postwar leader, Kurt Schumacher, and his successor, Erich Ollenhauer, has been opposed both to the Contractual Agreements and to Continental European Union. In 1953 and 1954, the Socialists took advantage of the fact that the West German constitution contains no statute granting the German government the right to have an army, to declare any parliamentary approval of the Contractual Agreements and the European Defense Community to be unconstitutional, and appealed to the supreme courts for a decision. Thus, even though it was evident in 1952 that Chancellor Adenauer's Christian Democratic coalition government had the majority necessary, in all probability, to gain parliamentary approval of the Contractual Agreements and the placing of a German army under supranational leadership and control in EDC, he did not have the two-thirds vote necessary to add a statute to the constitution authorizing an army, should the supreme court declare the Contractual Agreements and the EDC Treaty to be unconstitutional.

Informed German observers of the West German legal and judicial mind told me in Germany in November 1952 that it was not at all unlikely that the courts would so declare. The reasons were twofold: The German judicial mind tends to think only in terms of the positive law and its verbal literal meaning, and because there was no law in the constitution specifying the right to have an army it was likely to support the Socialists' contention. Second, the supreme court whose majority was from the Socialist party would have an additional inclination to do this. Also, the desire to embarrass the foreign powers who were instrumental in framing the existing constitution might play a part.

This indicates the folly of basing constitutions on the meeting of a particular temporary, practical concern instead of on the living-law norms of the people to whom they are applied. This observation applies as much to the introduction of a Continental European Defense Community to stop Communism as it does to the introduction of a West German constitution to prevent the rise of Nazi militarism. The irony of the situation becomes the more evident when one notes that the Socialists' insistence on the unconstitutionality of any vote involving a German army arose not from their conviction that Germany should not have an army, but from their desire (1) to defeat the Adenauer coalition and (2) to out-Nazi and outchauvinize the Nazis by insisting upon a purely German-controlled army.

It became evident in the fall of 1953, however, that even if the two supreme courts, meeting conjointly as they had decided to do, should declare the Contractual Agreements and the EDC Treaty to be unconstitutional this obstacle could none the less be overcome. Two events in 1953 made this possible: The first was the unexpectedly large majority which Chancellor Adenauer's Christian Democratic party obtained in the 1953 West German elections. The second was the remarkable victory which his party won in the later municipal election in Hamburg. The federal election victory enabled Chancellor Adenauer to form a West German coalition government which was assured of two-thirds of the votes in the lower house or Bundestag. On February 26, 1954, this body of the West German Parliament approved the constitutional changes to permit rearmament by a vote of 334 to 144. The Hamburg municipal victory gave him the required additional three members which he needed in the upper house or Bundesrat in order to have a two-thirds majority there. This two-thirds approval by the Bundesrat has occurred. On March 30, 1954, President Heuss signed the parliamentary act ratifying both the Contractual Agreements and the EDC Treaty.

The decision, therefore, as to whether the European Defense Community will become a fact turned in April 1954 around the parliaments of Italy and France. The failure of Premier de Gasperi's Christian Democratic party to win an absolute majority in the 1953 Italian elections left Italy's decision in doubt. The matter was complicated by opportunistic British and American promises made in the previous election with respect to Trieste, which were not fulfilled. Again, as in Germany, one sees the folly of basing one's foreign policy with respect to another nation on transitory, vote-catching power-politics advantages of the moment. The exceedingly serious flare-up over Trieste in 1953 demonstrates that such apparently clever practices in one election turn out to be liabilities in a later election.

It is likely that Prime Minister Giuseppe Pella's quick movement of troops to Trieste in 1953, immediately upon taking office, was aimed to prevent the chauvinistic Fascist nationalists of the Right from making a monopoly of the Trieste issue. Had the liberal Christian Democratic, Republican and Socialist groups in the middle allowed this to happen, democratic government in Italy would have been crushed between a Communistic dictatorship from the Left and a chauvinistic Fascist dictatorship from the Right. When Prime Minister Pella prevented it and then restored a sober atmosphere he saved both liberal democracy in Italy and supranationalism on the continent of Europe from immediate destruction. The possibility of Italian acceptance of EDC was preserved.

The fate of the European Defense Community in the French National Assembly became equally precarious in January of 1953 after the Pinay government fell and Robert Schuman departed from the Foreign Office. As previously noted, notwithstanding the personal approval of the European Defense Community by Premier Laniel and Foreign Minister Bidault, their 1953-1954 government could not ratify the EDC Treaty because it included Gaullists and depended for its majority on the followers of M. de Gaulle, who is for a strong one-party, chauvinistic France and opposed to Franco-German collaboration generally.

Before reaching the conclusion, however, that the positive law of the European Defense Community was shown by the composition of the Laniel government in 1953 to be artificially utopian and impractical, we should note one other fact. On September 17, 1953, at Strasbourg, Guy Mollet, the head of the Socialist party of France, announced that his party would vote for the European Defense Community on two conditions: (a) that Britain associate herself with the Treaty in ways that Britain has already indicated she may be willing to consider, and (b) that the European Political Community with real supranational sovereignty be voted at the same time.[44] The first condition probably means that Britain relate herself to the European Defense Community as she has associated herself with the European Coal and Steel Community. In *The New York Times* of February 23, 1954, Drew Middleton reported from London: "The

British Government is prepared to make public at an appropriate time the draft of a treaty linking the United Kingdom politically and militarily to the European Defense Community, under which West Germany is to be armed." [45]

The significance of Guy Mollet's Strasbourg announcement is that the Socialists, 105 in number, were not members of Premier Laniel's majority government. This means that the Socialists might provide that government with the votes on foreign policy, replacing those of its Gaullist members, which are necessary for the majority required to approve the European Defense Community Treaty and the European Political Community Statute. In other words, even in the French Parliament of 1953 there may have been a majority in favor of the European Defense Community and Continental European Union on the condition of favorable foreign policies in Great Britain and the United States.

In any event, Guy Mollet's Strasbourg statement makes it evident that the positive law of the European Defense Community requires for success the positive law of a European Political Community. In fact, Article 38 of the Treaty Constituting the European Defense Community instructed its Assembly to study "the creation of an Assembly of the European Defense Community elected on a democratic basis" and to report the results of the study, within a period of six months after the date of its first convening, to the Council of the European Defense Community. [46] This means that even the foreign ministers who designed and signed the Treaty Constituting the European Defense Community intended to bring both the High Authority of the Coal and Steel Community and the European General Staff of the Defense Community under the control of a European Political Community elected directly by the 157,000,000 people voting as Europeans.

This observation of the six foreign ministers that the economic and the military communities must be made secondary to the political community has important implications. First, it brings two bureaucracies under direct European democratic control. Second, it makes any weakness of liberal democracy and any development of Fascist or Communist chauvinism in one member state less dangerous to the other member states and the community as a whole. This explains the following statement to me by one of the most informed observers of Continental European Union in Paris in late October of 1952: "Pick the strongest argument which you can find against French participation in the European Defense Community or in Continental European Union and, upon further analysis, you will always discover that it is an argument for participation." He illustrated his statement as follows: "Take, for example, the French fears of the Germans, born of three German invasions since 1870. Add to this the recent (1953) German foreign-trade statistics which show that West Germany possesses already the strongest economic power and hence military potential on the continent of Western Europe. Upon a first reflection these facts are terrifying to the French. Upon a second reflection, however, the realistic situation is seen to be, Is France going to leave this great West German economic and military power under the direction of German industrialists, militarists and politicians alone, or is she going to put it under the direction of a supranational Continental European Community in which six peoples, rather than the Germans alone, determine how it is to be used?"

The theoretical implications of the dependence of the parliamentary approval and success of the Coal and Steel Community and the Defense Community upon prior parliamentary approval and institution of the Political Community are equally important and far-reaching. This dependence demonstrates the priority of politics over either military power or economics in domestic and foreign policy. Were the European Coal and Steel Community able to succeed without the Political Community—which Europeans have found by experimentation not to be the case—there would be evidence for the thesis that economic factors are primary in social relations. Were the Defense Community able to stand on its own feet there would be evidence similarly for the prevalent thesis that power politics, and in particular military power, is what matters in domestic and in foreign policy. The failure, therefore, to get either an effective Coal and Steel Community or parliamentary approval for the

Defense Community, unless the Political Community is also approved and made basic, constitutes an empirical disproof of the thesis that power politics or economic considerations are the primary determinants of domestic social organization and foreign policy. Instead, the foregoing facts show that political organization must come first and be basic, and that economic or military organization, even if introduced first, is possible or effective only when it is made secondary to and brought under the control of political organization.

It is important for what will follow that we fully appreciate what the priority of the political means. The essence of the political is that it introduces norms. People never transfer to a larger communal body the sovereignty which they have as private individuals unless they are sure that the power transferred will express their norms and values.

Military power qua military power is neutral with respect to the goals at which it may be directed. Economics is also the science of efficiency of means, and is not qua economics a science of ends. Hence, like power politics, it is neutral with respect to values, norms and goals. This is why no people will give sovereign powers to an effective economic or military communal body unless the economists and the soldiers are under the control of a political body whose norms and social values and goals are their own.

THE EUROPEAN POLITICAL COMMUNITY

Article 38 of the Treaty Constituting the European Defense Community, signed at Paris on May 27, 1952, authorized the Assembly of the European Defense Community, which is also the Assembly of the European Coal and Steel Community, (1) to study the creation of an Assembly with specified sovereign powers, elected directly on a democratic basis by the 157,000,000 people making up the six member nations, and (2) to submit proposals within six months.[47] It referred to the original Assembly as a "transitional organization," [48] because, as noted in the previous chapter, the foreign ministers who founded the Coal and Steel and the Defense Communities wanted a Continental European legislative body with sovereign supranational powers to which the economic and defense community would be subject. Because the members of the original Assembly are appointed by the governments of the member states and its powers are merely consultative, it lacks the desired supranational sovereign legislative powers. Consequently the original Assembly must be merely transitional. Therefore it has now come to be officially called the Ad Hoc Assembly. In the EDC Treaty of May 27, 1952, the foreign ministers ordered it to make and execute plans to destroy itself, substituting an Assembly whose sovereignty would derive in part not from any national government but from the 157,000,000 European people themselves voting as Europeans.

The foreign ministers did not wait for the Ad Hoc Assembly, at Strasbourg, to proceed at its leisure. On September 10, 1952, in a meeting at Luxembourg, the six foreign ministers of the Coal and Steel Community instructed its Assembly to proceed immediately to construct the Ad Hoc Assembly called for in the Treaty of the European Defense Community. This meant that three members each would be added to the West German, French and Italian delegations in the Assembly of the Coal and Steel Community. It will be recalled that, for the other three member states in this Continental European Community, the number of representatives in the Assembly remained the same in the Defense Community as in the Coal and Steel Community.

On September 15, 1952, the Ad Hoc Assembly was constituted at Strasbourg. On March 10, 1953, its Constitutional Committee, under the chairmanship of Dr. Heinrich von Brentano of West Germany, brought in the Draft Treaty Embodying the Statute of the European Community.

Its Preamble is brief:

We, the peoples of the Federal Republic of Germany, the Kingdom of Belgium, the French Republic, the Italian Republic, the Grand Duchy of Luxembourg and the Kingdom of the Netherlands,

Considering that world peace may be safeguarded only by creative efforts equal to the dangers which menace it;

Convinced that the contribution which a living, united free Europe can bring to civilization and to the preservation of our common spiritual heritage is indispensable to the maintenance of peaceful relations;

Desirous of assisting through the expansion of our production in improving the standard of living and furthering the works of peace;

Determined to safeguard by our common action the dignity, freedom and fundamental equality of men of every condition, race and creed;

Resolved to substitute for our historic rivalries a fusion of our essential interests by creating institutions capable of giving guidance to our future common destiny;

Determined to invite other European peoples, inspired with the same ideal, to join with us in our endeavour,

Have decided to create a European Community.

Wherefore our respective Governments, through their Plenipotentiaries, meeting in the city of ...., with powers found in good and due form, have adopted the present Treaty.[49]

Its third clause referring to a "living, united free Europe" and to a "common spiritual heritage" expresses the conviction that the positive law which is proposed has real living-law roots common to all the peoples involved.

The fifth clause specifies one of the common norms which this European law embodies. It is that all men are to be treated the same before any of its statutes, regardless of differences in condition, race or creed, and that every statute shall safeguard the dignity and the freedom of any and all members of the Community. The next clause speaks of "our historic rivalries." These are facts. Moreover, the current hesitations and fears of the French with respect to the Germans indicate that they are facts in today's living law. The emphasis on "our essential interests" suggests, however, that the living laws of the six nations have a common factor strong enough, if it is drawn upon, to overcome the present rivalries. In judging whether this political community can be effective, we must, therefore, determine in the sequel what the "essential interests" in the living law are and whether they are held in common as living beliefs and practices by a sufficient majority of the European Community to make them effective as positive law.

Article 1 specifies that the proposed European Community is to be "supranational," founded "upon a union of peoples and States, upon respect for their personality and upon equal rights and duties for all," and adds: "It shall be indissoluble."

With respect to the words "States" and "personality," some searching questions will have to be asked in the sequel. An Italian Right-wing Monarchist, a French Gaullist or a Right-wing West German will conceive of the "State" or of the political person differently from a liberal Christian Democrat like Alcide de Gasperi or Chancellor Adenauer or a Socialist like Guy Mollet of France or Paul-Henri Spaak of Belgium. In judging, therefore, whether the positive law expressed in Article 1 is likely to be effective if instituted, we must examine the living law: Do a majority of people in the supranational community agree in their living social beliefs with respect to the personality of a political person and the nature of a political state? If they do not, sociological jurisprudence tells us that the Political Community is likely to fail notwithstanding all the military and economic advantages that would follow if it succeeded. This conclusion follows from the dictum of sociological jurisprudence that positive law is effective only when its norms correspond to those of the underlying living law.

Roughly the transfer of sovereignty from the participating states to the Continental European Community, which the constitution specifies as its positive law, has three components: (1) the positive legal principles and procedures respecting human rights which are specified in the European Convention on the subject of the Council of Europe; (2) the positive legal principles, institutions and procedures as specified in the Treaty establishing the European Coal and Steel Community; (3) the positive legal principles specified in the European Defense Community Treaty.

To this end five institutions are established: a Parliament, an Executive Council, a Council of National Ministers, a Court of Justice and an Economic and Social Council.[50]

The statute prescribing the composition of the Parliament indicates how the economic, military and political executives of this supranational European Community are brought under the control of the member states and under the direct will of its 157,000,000 people considered as European citizens. In short, the new positive supranational law subjects the three aforementioned sovereign powers over which it has jurisdiction to the control of a legislative body which is in part subject to state control and in part subject to direct popular democratic European control. To this end the Parliament consists of a Senate and a Peoples' Chamber. The members of the Senate, or upper house, are "composed of senators representing the people of each State." [51] Notwithstanding this reference to the people, the senators are elected by the national parliaments. France, Germany and Italy have 21 senators each, Belgium and the Netherlands 10 each, and Luxembourg 4, making a total of 87.[52]

The Peoples' Chamber, or lower house, is "composed of deputies representing the peoples of the Community." [53] In short, its members represent the people as Continental Europeans rather than as Frenchmen, Germans, Italians, Belgians, *et al.* France, Germany and Italy receive 63 deputies each, and France has 7 more representing her overseas territories; Belgium and the Netherlands have 30 each, and Luxembourg has 12, making a total of 268.[54] As Professors Bowie and Friedrich have pointed out, this would mean, if the national parliaments are representative of local popular opinion, that "the two houses will very closely resemble each other in party composition." [55]

Legislation, to be valid, must be passed by a simple majority of both houses of the Parliament. After specified periods for deliberation by the two houses and within a further specified number of days, the laws passed by the Chamber "shall be promulgated by the President" of the Executive Council.[56] He may, however, request the Parliament to hold a new debate.[57] Regulations to implement the laws may be issued by the Executive Council.[58]

The European Executive Council is the administrative instrument of the Community. Article 27 adds that it "shall have no powers other than those conferred upon it by the . . . Statute." All other sovereign powers are wholly reserved to the member states. Its

President is elected by the Senate in secret ballot by an absolute majority vote of the senators.[59] The President appoints the other members of the Executive Council.[60] As Professors Bowie and Friedrich have noted, this means that the Senate, and hence the member states, have a greater control over the Executive branch of the European Political Community than do the deputies in the Peoples' Chamber who are directly elected by the people as citizens of the entire community.[61] This represents the extent to which the new positive law keeps close to the nationalistic habits of the traditional living law.

Nevertheless, the existence of the Peoples' Chamber means that there is a real departure, so far as control of legislation is concerned, from the traditional nationalistic practices. The question which we shall have to answer with respect to the effectiveness of the departure from traditional practices in living and positive law is whether there are other factors in the living law of these peoples, not previously used by its traditional positive law, which will make the sovereign powers of the Peoples' Chamber effective in their influence upon the Executive.

Although the President appoints the members of his Executive Council, Section 3 of Article 28 prevents him from appointing more than two members of the same nationality. He must also restrict his choice to citizens of the member states.[62] No member of the Executive Council may be a member of the government of a participating state, nor may he be a judge or solicitor general in the Court or a member of the Economic and Social Council of the Political Community.[63] Section 2 of Article 30 says that no member of the Executive can "exercise any paid function" or be a member of "the Board of Directors of any enterprise conducted for profit."

The positive law of this Community bases the length of term of its Executive branch upon French and British rather than American practice. Thus the government in office must resign if "a vote of no confidence is passed against it" by either house of Parliament or if either house "refuses to grant its request for a vote of confidence." [64] Moreover, the Senate can pass a majority vote of no confidence merely by electing a new President.[65] A three-fifths majority vote by the Peoples' Chamber is required for its vote of no confidence in the Executive.[66] Again we see that the control of the Senate representing the member states over the Executive is stronger than that of the Peoples' Chamber. In fact, under certain circumstances, the European Executive Council has the right to order the dissolution of the Peoples' Chamber. The Executive may exercise this right if, after requesting a motion of no confidence from the Peoples' Chamber, the vote of no confidence is that of a majority less than three-fifths.[67]

The Council of National Ministers has the liaison function, as in the Coal and Steel Community and the European Defense Community, of harmonizing the sovereign powers of the European Executive Council with those of the member states. The Council of National Ministers and the European Executive Council are instructed to do this by consultation and exchange of information.[68] The Council of National Ministers is composed of six members, one from each state. The chairmanship rotates alphabetically.[69] Any member state or the European Executive Council may request the Chairman to convene the Council of National Ministers.[70]

The Court is made "identical with the Court of the European Coal and Steel Community and of the European Defense Community."[71] Its duty is to "ensure the rule of law in the interpretation and application of the . . . Statute" of the European Political Community.[72] This means that it applies not merely the positive prescriptions of the Statute of the European Political Community but also, except as the Statute modifies them, the positive laws of the treaties establishing the European Coal and Steel Community and the European Defense Community.

The number of judges shall not be more than fifteen.[73] They are selected "from a double list by the European Executive Council, with the approval of the Senate." [74] Each member state may submit three candidates. Their term is nine years, and they may be reelected.[75] Section 5 of Article 39 requires, "The judges shall be independent and subject only to the law." Article 44 gives the Court "exclusive

jurisdiction to decide on the validity of decisions or recommendations of the European Executive Council and of deliberations of the
Council of National Ministers, in cases where such validity is con-
tested in litigation before a national Court." It also has jurisdiction
over any dispute bearing upon any institution of the Community
with respect to the Convention for the Protection of Human Rights
and Fundamental Freedoms.[76] Article 47 empowers the Court to act
as an Arbitration Court.

The Economic and Social Council is an advisory body for the
Executive Council. It also has the duty, upon request, to deliver
opinions to either house of Parliament or to the Executive Council.
It may also transmit resolutions of its own to them.[77] The positive
legal rules governing its membership, competence and procedure
are left to the Parliament of the Community to determine.[78]

Part III of the Statute constituting the European Political Community defines its Powers and Competence. These fall into six sec-
tions: (1) General Right of initiative, (2) Integration of the European Coal and Steel Community and the Defense Community, (3)
International Relations, (4) Financial Provisions, (5) Economic
Powers and (6) Specialized Authorities.

The Political Community's initiative consists in the right to make
proposals to the member states which have as their object the attain-
ment of the general aims specified in Article 2 of the Statute. The
proposals are made by the Executive Council on its own initiative
or on a motion of either or both houses of Parliament. The executive
Council may also request member states for information on action
taken with respect to any proposals of the Community.[79] The integration of the previous Economic and Military Communities is to be
achieved in accordance with Article 5, which constitutes them as "a
single legal entity," within which the previous Executive organs
"may retain such administrative and financial autonomy" as is guar-
anteed to them by the two Treaties which constitute the European
Coal and Steel Community and the European Defense Community.
This means that any sovereign powers transferred from the member
state to the European Community in the two former treaties remain

transferred under the constitution of the European Political Community.

Articles 59 and 64, however, put a possible qualification upon this conclusion. They specify that "the budgetary and financial provisions of the treaty instituting the European Coal and Steel Community shall remain in force during a period . . . not exceeding two years" after the Peoples' Chamber of the European Political Community is established. After that period the financial provisions of the Statute of the European Political Community will apply.[80] Article 78, bearing on these financial provisions, reads:

The methods of determining the assessment, the rates of taxation and the manner in which the Community's taxes are levied shall be laid down by the European Executive Council in the form of bills, with the unanimous concurrence of the Council of National Ministers.[81]

Article 80 adds: "The basis for determining the contributions of Member States and the rate of contribution shall be unanimously decided by the Council of National Ministers, on the proposal of the European Executive Council." If the provisions of these two articles of the constitution of the proposed European Political Community are applied to the High Authority of the Coal and Steel Community, this will mean that sovereign powers to levy taxes, which they now exercise without appeal to the Council of Ministers, will be taken away from them. Thus as Professors Bowie and Friedrich have noted, "If the Draft Treaty cuts off this authority, it is to that extent a step backward." [82] The High Authority at Luxembourg will have less sovereign supranational power than it initially enjoyed and exercised.

Articles 67 through 74 do, however, give the European Community novel powers. Within "the limits of the powers and competence conferred upon it," it has the right to "conclude treaties" or international agreements.[83] Article 69 adds that it "shall ensure that the foreign policies of Member States are co-ordinated." Article 72 prescribes, "Member States may not conclude treaties or international agreements which run counter to commitments entered into

by the Community or adhere to such treaties or agreements."
Article 74 adds "the right to accredit and receive diplomatic representatives."

An additional clause in Article 69, however, requires "unanimous
decision of the Council of National Ministers" before the European
Executive Council may "act as the common representative of the
Member States." Because the Executive Council is chosen by the
member states, this keeps treaty-making powers and international
relations much under the control of the member states. Section 3 of
Article 70 does add that Parliament "may address proposals" through
the Executive Council "to the Council of National Ministers or to
the governments of Member States on all matters affecting the interests of the Community." [84] Parliament may also request the Executive Council to "invite the Council of National Ministers or the governments in question to make known what action has been taken on
. . . proposals." [85]

The economic powers of the European Political Community include the prescription that it "shall establish progressively a common market among the Member States, based on the free movement
of goods, capital and persons." [86] Article 84 gives the Community
one year before it exercises the latter power. The goal is to be
achieved step by step over a five-year period.[87] Article 87 is important. A common market and fair competition between all states
in the Community are impossible if a member state can manipulate its
currency, inflating or deflating it radically at will. This article begins:

> The Member States shall, particularly on monetary matters, consult the
> European Executive Council before taking decisions which might affect
> the interests of the said States, and before concluding among them-
> selves agreements likely to impede the free movement of labour and
> commodities.

It adds:

> Should the . . . Executive Council find that such decisions run counter
> to the aims of the present treaty . . . the European Executive Council
> may, with the consent of the Council of National Ministers, address ap-

propriate proposals to the Governments of the Member States concerned.

The Statute constituting the European Political Community is accompanied by two Protocols. The first defines the "Privileges and Immunities of the Community." Their character is illustrated by Articles 2 and 3, which specify in part that "the premises and buildings of the institutions of the Community, together with its archives, shall be inviolable . . . exempt from search, requisition, confiscation or expropriation." The second Protocol links the European Political Community to the Council of Europe. Its purpose is to keep the Council informed of the actions of the European Political Community and to insure the presence of the Executive Council of the European Political Community in any discussion of its actions in the Council of Europe.

So far as the positive law is concerned, it appears that the movement toward European Union has specified a genuine transfer of sovereignty from the traditional European nations to a supranational European Community to the following extent: For the fourteen member states of the Greater European Community which is the Council of Europe, there has been no transfer of sovereignty whatever except in the field of individual human rights and freedoms. On all political, economic or military matters—i.e., on all determinate, national communal matters—there is no transfer whatever of sovereignty in the larger Council of Europe. On social as opposed to personal rights, its powers are merely consultative.

With respect, however, to the smaller group of six nations within the larger Council of Europe group, there has been a genuine transfer, so far as positive law is concerned, from the six member nations to the supranational Continental European Community. The transfer with respect to individual human rights and freedoms, of course, occurs because the six members of the Continental European Community voted for it as members of the larger Council of Europe. What makes the positive law of the Continental European Community unique, not merely in Europe but also in the world as a whole, is that it prescribes a genuine transfer of communal national sovereign powers from the national to the supranational community and specifies the institutions necessary to implement the transfer.

The transferred sovereign powers are roughly three in number. One is economic and is in partial operation. Another is military, and the third is political. Of the three, the political is primary because both the economc and the military are brought under its control and will be neither approved by the national parliaments nor effective unless the Political Community is established first. Moreover, the political sovereignty of the Continental European Community involves more than the partial sovereignties previously assigned by the positive laws to the Coal and Steel Community and the European Defense Community considered independently. The Political Community also has treaty-making powers that permit it to function in its own right as a sovereign nation in the larger world community. Also half of its legislative powers are under the direct control of the citizens of the entire community, voting as individual Europeans, rather than merely as the traditional voters of a particular nation. This was not true of the legislative bodies of either the Coal and Steel Community or the Defense Community. The degree, therefore, to which the individual members will give priority to their European rather than their traditional national loyalties and norms will determine the extent to which the transfer of sovereignty specified by this new positive law becomes an effective living entity. The time has come, therefore, to turn from the positive to the living law.

Chapter 6

The Living Law of Greater Europe

It has been noted in Chapter 3 that the method used in determining the living law of any people must be both qualitative and quantitative. Qualitatively it must describe the diverse norms of the major normative groups of the peoples concerned. Quantitatively it must indicate the number of people in each nation belonging to each normative group.

A prevalent error to be avoided is the assumption that the qualitative and quantitative normative groupings in the European peoples are identical with those in one's own nation or community. This difference in norms that are used to guide community action shows in the names of the European political parties. In each of the six Continental European nations a major party is the Christian Democratic party, showing that not merely the religious, but even the political, normative groupings are determined by religious as well as secular living-law beliefs. Furthermore, even in the United States and in European nations like Great Britain the very absence of political parties distinguished by religious titles is the result of normative living-law religious beliefs. Such nations will be found to be overwhelmingly Protestant in the quantitative value of their living-law religious beliefs. Their lack of religious political parties expresses an essential part of the living-law religious norms of Protestants that, even for the best interests of religion, church and state should be separated and political groupings should be distinguished by secular normative principles which are neutral with respect to religious

75

beliefs. This is not true, however, in Continental Europe. Hence, an objective determination of the living law of Greater or of Little Europe must pay attention to its religious, as well as its secular, normative components.

THE RELIGIOUS LIVING LAW

The religious living laws of the European peoples represented in the Council of Europe fall into five qualitative normative groupings: (1) Protestant Christianity, (2) Gaelic Roman Catholic Christianity, (3) Latin Roman Catholic Christianity, (4) Greek Orthodox Christianity, and (5) Islam.

The Protestant Christian religious living law has a majority of adherents in Great Britain, Iceland, West Germany and the three Scandinavian countries in the Council of Europe. Gaelic Roman Catholic Christianity is the normative living religious belief of more than nine-tenths of the people of the Free Republic of Ireland. It is well known that a very large majority of the people in Belgium, Luxembourg, France and Italy adhere to Latin Roman Catholic Christian religious norms. The Greek people are overwhelmingly Greek Orthodox Christian, and the Turks are correspondingly Islamic. The foregoing qualitative religious living-law norms and quantitative statistics make one point clear with respect to the Council of Europe. In so far as the religious living law of the Community is concerned, there is not a common religious living law.

THE POLITICAL LIVING LAW

The different qualitative normative political groupings of the peoples in the Council of Europe are even greater in number. Great Britain, for example, has four qualitatively different political norms —those of the Conservative, Liberal, Labor and Communist parties —the last one named being quantitatively insignificant. The other three qualitatively different British political norms have one basic normative principle in common: the pluralistic principle of political sovereignty, which affirms that a good society must permit and encourage men to group themselves normatively under more than one set of religious, philosophical, economic, political or other beliefs.

Practically this means many religious denominations and a many-party political state. Any state which accepts the pluralistic theory of sovereignty will henceforth be referred to as a liberal democracy, regardless of differences between its normative religious and political groupings on other matters. Conversely, a liberal democratic party or government will be defined as one whose positive constitutional law affirms and implements that theory.

The Communist party, or any Communist state, illustrating as it does a monistic theory of political sovereignty, is opposed to liberal democracy. A Communist party in any democratic society if it is true to its basic normative convictions, must disrupt and destroy that society. The Nazi Right in Germany, the Gaullist Right in France and the neo-Fascist Right in Italy are additional examples of normative European groupings which affirm or are strongly inclined toward a monistic theory of sovereignty.

All four, moreover, are normatively opposed to Continental European Union. The opposition by the Communists arises from the fact that they must oppose any government whether national or supranational which is not built on Communist normative principles. The opposition by the Nazis, Gaullists and neo-Fascist Italians arises from their excessively nationalistic normative principles. None of the four would oppose Continental European Union were it obtained by a chauvinistic, militaristic imperialism of their own particular nation or normative persuasion.

Whether France can safely go into a political union with Germany in view of the threatened revival of German Nazism, or conversely West Germany can safely go into a political union with France in view of the threatened revival of Gaullist chauvinism, and whether the aforementioned supranational positive law of the Continental European Community will be effective, depend significantly on the numerical balance between adherents of the European parties affirming a monistic theory of political sovereignty and adherents of the European liberal democratic parties.

Ireland adds four more qualitatively different normative political groupings in the European nations. Represented in its Parliament in 1952 were Fianna Fáil, 70 members; Fine Gael, 42; Clann na Poblachta, 2; and the Clann na Talmhan, 6. Ireland has, to be sure, two other parties—Labor, 16, and the Independents, 11; but these may be assumed to have norms similar to the Liberal and Labor parties of Great Britain.[1] The 1953–1954 government of Prime Minister Eamon de Valera is a Fianna Fáil party government. The essentially Irish character of the norms of this government and of three other of the six Irish parties provides the living-law explanation of why, although the Irish are Roman Catholic Christian in their living-law religious beliefs, they do not join politically with the Latin Roman Catholic peoples in Continental European Union.

The leading Independent party of Iceland adds another unique normative political grouping. The Agrarian and Christian Popular parties of Norway add two more. The Land Tax party in Denmark is another. In Greece the Greek Rally, its largest party, adds another.

The fact that Greece has a Royal family and is a constitutional monarchy distinguishes it also normatively from Ireland, Iceland and three of the six nations in Continental European Union. When the British army took over Greece after the defeat of the Germans in World War II, Prime Minister Churchill found that the one dependable man available to command the living-law loyalty of the Greek people was the Greek Orthodox Patriarch.[2] This demonstrates the reality and vitality of Greek Orthodox Christian religious norms in even the political living law of the Greek people.

The two major present political parties of Turkey are liberally democratic. Notwithstanding the achievement of power by Ataturk and his Republican People's party through a military coup and an initial dictatorship, his party allowed itself to be voted out of office by democratic processes in a subsequent election. It was replaced by the Democratic party. Both parties, except for their Islamic religious living-law component, are similar normatively to two of the aforementioned parties of other nations.

At the moment in Turkey, however, there is an Islamic reaction and resurgence due to the fact that the masses in the villages distant from the Europeanized cities of Istanbul and Ankara do not understand the Western European secular norms and are guided instead by inner living beliefs, habits and practices which are Islamic not merely in their religious content but also in their secular legal and social prescriptions. Again one sees that positive law must sooner or later come to terms with the underlying living law of the overwhelming majority of people to whom it is applied. This large Islamic factor adds another unique living-law normative grouping to our list.

When we turn to the Continental European nations within the Council of Europe, the diversity of political norms becomes even more marked. France is a sufficient example.[3] Its political living law falls into roughly eight qualitative normative political groupings arranged on the basis of economic policy from Left to Right, with their 1951 representation in the National Assembly, as follows: Communists, 99; Socialists, 105; Mouvement Républicain Populaire, or Christian Democratic party, 83; the younger World War II Radical Socialists of M. Pleven, 14; the older party Radical Socialists of M. Herriot, 66; Independents, 43; Peasants, 34; others, 64; Rassemblement du Peuple Français, or Gaullists, 118.[4] The Gaullist group was divided in the days of the Pinay Independent-Peasant-led coalition government of late 1952 into two groupings: (a) the regular Gaullists who opposed both the domestic and the foreign policy of the Pinay government, 88, and (b) the dissident Gaullists who collaborated with the Pinay government on domestic economic policy but opposed its Continental European foreign policy, 30. The Socialists were not members of the 1952 Pinay coalition government because they did not accept its domestic policy. They did, however, guarantee it the necessary votes on Continental European Union, replacing those of the Gaullists and enabling it to retain Robert Schuman as Foreign Minister.

The Socialists of France, like the liberal Socialists in Belgium, the Netherlands, Luxembourg and Italy, have quite different philosophical, religious and other living-law roots from the Labor party (Socialist) of Great Britain, with its largely Protestant and British empirical living-law background. Hence the Continental European Socialist parties add another qualitatively unique normative grouping to our list. Because the Socialist party of West Germany, unlike the Socialist parties in the other five Continental European Union nations, opposes Continental European Union, it also is normatively unique.

There is also the Christian Democratic party, present in all six of the Continental European nations. Its normative economic and political principles must not be confused with those of the Roman Catholic hierarchy in the United States. It is further to the Left generally in its economic thinking than either the Republican or the Democratic party in the United States, or than any other party in Continental Europe except the Socialist and the Communist. In fact, the Left wing of the Christian Democratic party is frequently further Left than the Right wing of the Socialist party.

Between the Christian Democratic party in the Left Center and the three chauvinistic, nationalistic Continental European parties at the extreme Right stand several parties—such as the French Radical Socialists, the Italian Liberal and Republican parties, and the Belgian Liberal party—which are laissez-faire or New Deal liberal in their economic policy, Roman Catholic in their private religious living-law background, and anticlerical in their secular educational and political philosophy. They may be grouped together normatively under the title of Roman Catholic laissez-faire liberal. There is a corresponding Protestant laissez-faire liberal Continental European group, of which the Free Democratic party in Germany and the corresponding party in the Netherlands are examples. It, too, is anticlerical in its educational and political philosophy. In our final analysis we shall put these two laissez-faire Continental European liberal parties together under the name of the Liberal party.

This group is not to be completely identified in its normative doctrine with the British Liberal party, although they have much in common. Whereas both the economic and the political norms of the British Liberal party derive from British empirical philosophical thinkers, such as Hume, Bentham, Jevons, Austin and Marshall, those of the Radical Socialist liberal party of France, following Proudhon, rest only their theory of liberty upon British empirical thinkers and root their theory of equality and fraternity in Kant's theory of justice, which derives from modern Continental rationalistic philosophy. The latter half of their doctrine, therefore, is nearer to that of the British Labor party philosophy of the late Lord Lindsay than to that of the British Liberal party.[5]

Because modern Continental rationalistic philosophy is the creation of both Frenchmen and Germans, the living-law roots of the French liberals' political and religious norms are as German as they are French. In fact, the essence of Kant's concept of ethical and political man is that he cannot be identified with German, French or Italian man, but must be identified instead with the universal man of the categorical imperative of a universal law before which all men, regardless of color, nation and creed, are equal.

Within this normative grouping of the liberal Continental European parties are to be found the Independents and the Peasants of M. Pinay's 1952 coalition government, who are further to the Right economically and politically than the Radical Socialist liberals. This is undoubtedly due to their laissez-faire, inborn attachment either to their small businesses in the towns or to their local plots of ground. Such people do not easily transfer their personal sovereign rights even to a federal government, to say nothing about a supranational government. At this point, however, their Roman Catholic Latin religious personal living law may fill in what their laissez-faire attachment to the soil omits. This evidently happened when M. Pinay's Independents and Peasants voted for Robert Schuman as their Foreign Minister, thereby supporting the transfer of national sovereignty to the supranational Continental European Community, and when Premier Laniel of these same parties supported it personally in 1954.

The norm of the Roman Catholic religion, especially of a Latin Continental European, as compared with the Gaelic lovers of Eire, is not a nationalistically focused religious living law; instead it is European in range and emphasis. Therefore in throwing the middle parties—between the Christian Democrats in Left Center and the chauvinists at the extreme Right—into one normative liberal grouping it is important in judging the living-law support they will provide for Continental European Union to distinguish the parties with Roman Catholic from those with Protestant religious living-law norms.

The normatively different political groups, described above, in the fourteen European nations of the Council of Europe, total twenty-three. Nineteen affirm a pluralistic theory of sovereignty, and hence are liberally democratic. The other four affirm a monistic theory of sovereignty and hence stand for or tend toward an undemocratic, one-party political dictatorship.

With respect to the nineteen different normative groupings which have liberally democratic theories of sovereignty, one caution on nomenclature must be observed: liberal democracy is not restricted to the parties among them which use the word "liberal" in their names. The British Conservative party, the Christian Democratic party and the Socialist party, for example, are as liberally democratic as the British Liberal party or the Continental European Liberal parties because the normative principles of all prescribe a pluralistic theory of the state, i.e., a many-party system. This is precisely what distinguishes them from the Communists, some Left-wing Italian Socialists and the Nazi, Gaullist or neo-Fascist Right.

It appears, therefore, that there are at least five different normative religious groupings and twenty-three different normative political groupings within the living law of the Council of Europe. This explains why there was no transfer of normative communal sovereign powers from the fourteen member nations to the supranational Council of Europe Community, even in its positive law. These nations simply do not have common religious and political living beliefs for ordering their economic, military and political lives together.

Their religious living law falls into five normatively different, and often conflicting, groupings. The religious beliefs of the follower of Islam require him to live according to the rules of the traditional *shariat*, or Islamic law. Its norms for ordering men politically and socially are not shared with any other significant religious or political grouping in Europe. The religious and political norms for government of the conservative party with the largest number of representatives in the French parliament (the Gaullists), similarly, are not shared with the British Conservatives nor any other European party. None of the three parties in Great Britain has an exact normative equivalent on the Continent, as our comparison of (1) the French Liberal parties and the British Liberal party, (2) British Conservatism and M. de Gaulle's conservatism and (3) the British Labor party and the Continental Socialist parties has shown. But without norms, the same in the member nations, there cannot be a communal "supranation," because there is no shared communal law.

Why, then, were the member nations able to achieve some slight transfer of sovereignty to the supranational community with respect to the Convention for the Protection of Human Rights and Freedoms? Consideration of the reason for the Bill of Rights in the Constitution of the United States gives the answer. The purpose of the Bill of Rights, as called for originally by Jefferson, was to protect minority normative beliefs from being outlawed by the living-law beliefs of the majority. In short, the purpose of a Bill of Rights is to protect the diversity of religious and political norms within the living law. Certainly the living law of the people of the Council of Europe contains plenty of normative diversity. Thus it sustained a bill of personal rights but did not sustain a transfer of sovereignty with respect to the specific norms to be used for ordering the political, economic and military communal relations of men in the Council of Europe.

Even so, the Convention on Human Rights would probably never have been signed by the foreign ministers of the fourteen nations in the Council of Europe without the presence of one other fact in the living law of these fourteen nations: that the majority in each nation, notwithstanding diversity of their religious and political norms, shared a belief in a pluralistic theory of political sovereignty and hence in a many-party system operated by liberal democratic processes. This encourages normative diversity and its protection through a Bill of Rights. Had one of the fourteen governments been Communist, Nazi or even Gaullist, guided by a monistic principle of sovereignty, unanimous parliamentary support of a Council of Europe Bill of Rights either would not have been forthcoming, or it would not have been implemented by that particular nation.

Chapter 7

The Living Law of Each
Continental European Nation

When one turns from the living laws of the fourteen nations in the Council of Europe to those of the six nations in Continental European Union, a radically different situation becomes evident. Instead of five different normative religious groups, there are but two; and both are Western Christian rather than Eastern Orthodox Christian or Islamic. Moreover, of the two normative living-law religious groups, the Roman Catholic represents almost the entire population in four nations (Belgium, Luxembourg, France and Italy) out of the six and is surpassed only slightly by the Protestant group in the latest official statistics in the other two (the Netherlands and West Germany).

This explains the outstanding role which Christian Democratic leaders have played in creating the positive law of Continental European Union. They include former Premiers Schuman and Bidault, and Ministers de Menthon and Teitgen in France; Ministers van Zeeland and Eyskens of Belgium; Chancellor Adenauer and Dr. Heinrich von Brentano of Germany; Deputy Prime Minister Beel of the Netherlands; President Dupong and Minister of Foreign Affairs Joseph Bech of Luxembourg; and Premiers de Gasperi, Pella and Scelba of Italy. It is imperative, therefore, in judging the practicality of Continental European Union to pay especial and initial attention to the religious component of the living law of the 157,000,-000 people who make up this Community.

It is well known that the members of this community in Belgium, Luxembourg, France and Italy are overwhelmingly Latin and Roman Catholic in their living-law religious beliefs and institutions. The latest approximate statistics are as follows: Belgium, 99.3 per cent; Italy, 99.6 per cent; France, 97.5 per cent; and Luxembourg, 98 per cent.[1]

The Royal Family and almost 3,000,000 citizens of the Netherlands, according to the census of 1947, belonged to the Dutch Reformed Church, which, of course, is Protestant. The denomination, however, with the largest number of adherents in 1947 was the Roman Catholic church with slightly more than 3,700,000 members. The membership of all Protestant churches other than the Dutch Reformed church totaled 1,259,000.[2] This means that the people of the Netherlands were, in 1947, approximately 38.5 per cent Roman Catholic and 44.3 per cent Protestant in their religious living law. Informed religious and political leaders of the six Continental European nations told the writer, however, in the fall of 1952 that in the Netherlands the Roman Catholic living law had just gone beyond the Protestant living law in the number of its followers. If this be true, then the majority religious living-law norms of the people of the Netherlands are qualitatively identical with those of the majority of the peoples in Belgium, Luxembourg, France and Italy.

Even before 1952, however, the living-law norms of the Roman Catholic and other groups had expressed themselves in eight political party groupings in the lower house of the Netherlands parliament, here listed with their representation: Catholic People's party, 32; Netherlands Labor party (Socialist), 27; Anti-Revolutionary party (Protestant), 13; Christian Historical party, 9; Party for Freedom and Democracy, 8; Communist party, 8; Political Reform party (Protestant), 2; and Catholic National party, 1.[3] Since the lower house has 100 members, the numbers also express percentages.

The statistics just given make several facts clear. First, the party with the largest number of members, previous to 1952, was the Catholic People's (Christian Democratic). Second, party distinctions in the Netherlands are determined by normative differences which are religious in character. Only three of the eight parties—namely, the Socialist, the Liberal and the Communist—are devoid of normative religious connotations; and the sequel will show that this is not wholly true for the Socialists.

Third, when the Protestant living law comes to expression it tends to divide itself politically, whereas the Roman Catholic religious living law tends to keep united politically. This is demonstrated by the fact that notwithstanding the greater number of Protestants in the 1947 population the Catholic People's party was much the largest political party in the Netherlands. The influence of Roman Catholic religious living law upon the political forces in the Netherlands becomes even more evident when one notes that the Socialist party, which is the next largest, contains a considerable Catholic minority.

The norms of the Netherlands Labor party (Socialist) with respect to Dutch religious as well as secular living law are especially interesting. One of its basic normative principles is "spiritual federalism," [4] which has two aspects. First, socialism in the Netherlands has freed itself from the anti-religious secularism of much previous Continental European socialism and of communism. Second, the Netherlands Labor party is substituting for purely secular socialism one grounded in religious pluralism. To this end, it has established three "working groups"—Catholic members, Protestant members, and "the so-called humanitarian group" [5]—so that socialism in the Netherlands is at least two-thirds Christian. Members of the laboring class in the Netherlands tend to be more Roman Catholic than Protestant; therefore, it is safe to assume that at least one-third of the party's membership is in the Roman Catholic "working group" and that at least 9 of its 27 representatives in the lower house of parliament represent that group. This means that in the lower house 32 (Catholic People's party) plus 1 (Catholic National party), plus 9 Catholic working group (Labor party), or, in other words, 42 per cent of the total membership, are normatively Roman Catholic in both their living religious faith and their political voting habits, and indicates the existence of additional living-law norms common to the people of the Netherlands and the largely Roman Catholic peoples of Belgium, Luxembourg, France and Italy.

By the time of the 1952 elections, two additional changes had occurred. First, there had been an increase in the ratio of Roman Catholics to Protestants in the Netherlands, so that the former probably passed the latter in the number of believers. Second, the Labor party had formulated its normative doctrines more explicitly, implementing them through the Catholic, Protestant and humanitarian working groups and had brought its normative program more and more to the attention of the electorate. Its "Programme of Principles" contains the following important items:

[1] The Party's aim is . . . an economic structure without class-contrasts . . . in which . . . the principal means of production in the sectors of industry, banking and transport will be socialized, . . . [and] a social structure . . . founded on a legal order of labour . . . [2] The Party rejects State-socialism [and] . . . every form of state absolutism, dictatorship or one-party system. . . . In order to prevent bureaucratic abuse of power, it wants the trade organizations, which have to be founded by law, to be self-governing organs.

Note the bringing of labor under the rule of law. Here the Stoic Roman, Continental type of legal mentality, so typical of the living law of Latin Continental Europe, shows itself.

[3] The State shall be a constitutional one; its task the establishment and vigorous maintenance of the law, to which the State itself must also submit.

Here again the Stoic Roman legal mentality, reinforced by the Continental Rationalistic, modern philosophic outlook, comes to positive legal expression. Supranational sovereignty then becomes natural. Hence,

[4] The Party aims at an international community of nations. . . . In this future world order every state has to be willing to transfer part of its sovereignty to higher organs.[6]

In the 1952 election, the Netherlands Labor party tied the Catholic People's party in the number of representatives in the lower house of parliament (30) and surpassed it by 16,000 in popular votes received.[7] In the later elections of April 21, 1954, the Catholic People's party recaptured its position as the largest single party, with the Socialists making gains in the eleven provincial councils.[8]

Both the Catholic People's party and the Netherlands Labor party stand normatively for a transfer of national sovereignty to the supranational European Community, so that, in 1953, 60 per cent at the very least of the Netherlands lower house supported Continental European Union. Moreover, these objective results, a logical implication of their normative beliefs, represent something much more fundamental and lasting than the threat of a foreign power or power-politics political expediency of the moment. The Stoic Roman, Continental type of legal mentality and the Continental Rationalistic philosophical mentality are not artificial or transitory. They are living-law beliefs built into the minds and emotions of Continental Europeans by centuries of reflection and education. Moreover, initiated by Descartes and Malebranche in France, advanced by Spinoza in the Netherlands and completed by Leibniz and Kant in Germany, they are living-law norms holding as much for Belgians, Luxembourgers, Frenchmen, Italians, and even West Germans as they do for the people of the Netherlands. Similarly, the domestic norms peculiar to the socialist parties of the six nations are the same in all six and are, therefore, also supranational, rather than chauvinistically national in their qualitative content.

The importance of the Catholic working group in the Netherlands Labor party should not be overlooked. This group provides common living-law support for the 1952–1954 Socialist-Christian Democratic coalition government of the Socialists and Christian Democrats. The Protestant working group provides a common living-law basis for a similar coalition between the Socialist party and the Netherlands Protestant parties.

It would be a mistake to leave the impression that only the Catholic Christian Democratic party and the Socialist party in the Netherlands stand for Continental European Union. These Catholic and Socialist normative factors have been emphasized because, if Continental European Union is to have living-law support, a majority of the people must hold common religious and secular living-law norms similar to those of a majority of the peoples in the five other Continental European nations. The living-law norms of the Roman Catholics and the Socialists provide this all-embracing common living-law factor. But there are also Protestant supporters of Continental European Union. It has been noted that the Royal Family belongs to the Dutch Reformed Church, which is Protestant, as do 30 per cent of the Dutch people. Queen Juliana said in her visit to the United States in 1952:

Europe is the only part of the globe where nations are at all seriously negotiating about giving up part of their sovereignty. We [in Holland] feel we can be a reliable pillar of European unity, a unity which is growing by means of the Schuman Plan and other economic and defensive and—perhaps eventually—political integration. Constitutional amendments have been voted lately by the Netherlands Parliament in order to remove some remaining obstacles to our partnership in future supranational organizations.[9]

With collaboration between the Socialist, Protestant and Catholic party groups and the Royal Family the living-law support for Continental European Union in the Netherlands is decisive.

The religious and secular living-law statistics of West Germany are similar to those of the Netherlands. We are accustomed to thinking of the Germans as an overwhelmingly Protestant people. This was true of the prewar Germany and was the reason why it was under Prussian political leadership. Many people, such as James Warburg,[10] suggest that a West Germany in Continental European Union is an artificial positive-law marriage between present Germany and the other Continental European nations, with no underlying common norms in the living law to support it. It would be nearer the truth to say that the old Germany was the artificial political unit. Since Bismarck, Germany has been without common religious or secular living-law norms. Western and southern Germany, embracing the Rhineland and Bavaria, was Roman Catholic in its religious and secular living-law beliefs. Northern and central Germany, the present Russian sector and East Prussia, all focused at Berlin, were Protestant. This gave the Protestants a decisive majority before both World War I and World War II, and meant in fact that western and southern Germany, the Rhineland, the Saar and Alsace-Lorraine, over which Germany and France fought in three major wars after 1870, were forced to live under a positive law that was foreign to their own living-law religious and political beliefs. Certainly, if the adjective "artificial" is to be used, it must be predicated of the old Germany. Moreover, precisely this failure of the positive legal unity of the old German state to correspond to the underlying plurality of the living-law realities forced Bismarck to find an enemy abroad in order to cover up living-law divisions at home.

Present West Germany is far different. To assume that West Germany under Chancellor Adenauer or anyone later who represents a majority of the people will behave like the old Germany that embraced all the Prussian and East Prussian Junkers to the east of the Oder-Neisse is to ignore two facts—(1) the area of former Germany now under Communist control, which the Communists are unlikely to give up, and (2) the living law of the present 48,000,000 West Germans—which add up to one conclusion: For the near future, at least, Germany will be determined by the living law of the present West Germans. The Four Power conference in Berlin in February of 1954 made this clear to all. Realism dictates, therefore, that we base our judgment concerning the relation of Germany to Continental European Union on the content of the living law of the present West Germans.

The 1946 religious statistics of the Western and Russian sectors, which embrace all of Germany west of the Oder-Neisse, were as follows: Protestant, 59.7 per cent; Roman Catholic, 35 per cent.[11] The failure, however, of the four occupying powers to come to an agreement on a peace treaty for the entire area and the resultant establishment of the West German Republic results in a religious living law in the present West German Republic as follows (1951 statistics): Protestant, 51 per cent and Roman Catholic 45.2 per cent.[12] In short, the religious living law of West Germany is practically the same as that of the Netherlands in 1947.

Again, as in the Netherlands, the Protestants divide politically—some voting with Chancellor Adenauer's Christian Democratic party, which is a Protestant as well as a Roman Catholic party, many voting Socialist and many voting with the Free Democratic party, the Refugee party and with the Right-wing parties. This has the result of giving the Protestant and Roman Catholic Christian Democratic party the largest number of followers in West Germany. As in the Netherlands, the Roman Catholics divide, the majority supporting the Christian Democratic party and a very considerable group voting with the Socialists. The latter German group, which is largely in Bavaria and the Rhineland, corresponds to the Roman Catholic working group in the Labor (Socialist) party of the Netherlands. In the 1949 elections to the lower house of the German Parliament, the Christian Democratic party received 31 per cent of the votes and the Socialist party 29.2[13]—percentages practically identical with those received by the corresponding parties in the Netherlands.

However, the qualitative norms and the religious living-law beliefs of Socialist party members in Germany differ from those of Socialists in the Netherlands or in any other Continental European nation, for three reasons: First, German Socialism at the federal level is for the most part secularly minded and neutral if not, in part at least, antithetical to religion, somewhat after the manner of Marxist Socialism and much French and Italian Socialism. Second, except in Bavaria and the Rhineland, it draws its support mainly from the northern and eastern commercial and industrial cities, where most of the people are Protestant in their religious living-law beliefs. Thus in West Germany at the federal level collaboration between Socialists and Christian Democrats is not fostered to the same extent as in the Netherlands by a shared religious living law.

In this connection, the state government in Bavaria is most interesting. In the elections to the Bavarian state legislature on November 26, 1950, the Christian Democratic party (Christian Social Union) received 27.4 per cent of the votes, the Socialist party, 28 per cent; in the March 30, 1952, local elections, the results were 26.4 per cent and 26.1 per cent respectively.[14] The living-law religious norms of the majority of Bavarians were overwhelmingly Roman Catholic. This means that the leaders and members of the Bavarian Christian Democratic and Bavarian Socialist parties, unlike the corresponding majority groups at the federal level, have majority living-law religious norms in common, permitting the active Christian Democratic and Socialist coalition government that exists in Bavaria. The August 14, 1949, Bavarian vote in the Federal elections is also interesting. There the Christian Democrats polled 29.2 per cent, and the Socialists 22.8 per cent,[15] showing that many Bavarians who vote against the Christian Democrats in Bavaria on domestic policy vote for it on federal policy where the main issues are the European Defense Community and Continental European Union.

The third, and the crucial, factor preventing a coalition between Chancellor Adenauer's Christian Democratic coalition and Erich Ollenhauer's Socialist party in the Federal government is the Socialist party's diagnosis of the reason why liberal democracy failed in the days of the Weimar Republic—made after World War II by the former Socialist leader, Kurt Schumacher, and shared by his successor. The diagnosis is that liberal democracy failed because it allowed the Prussian chauvinistic Junkers and their colleagues, Hitler's Nazis, to gain a monopoly on chauvinistic nationalism and militarism. The Socialists conclude that, if liberal democracy is to survive in Germany, it is imperative that one liberal party at least stand for German militarism and nationalism. This explains the Socialists' attempt, in the municipal elections of 1952, to out-Nazi the Nazi Right in their appeal to German militarism, nationalism and chauvinism, and the primary importance assigned by the two leaders to a strong nationalistic German army, the immediate recovery of the Saar and the unification of Germany, combined with opposition both to the Contractual Agreements and to the prior entry into Continental

European Union. The Socialist opposition to the Contractual Agreements is not, therefore, opposition to militarism in Germany; quite the reverse. The stand, instead, is that the Contractual Agreements and Continental European Union dishonor the German people and the German state because the German army is placed in a Continental European army on an unequal footing with the French army, which is in NATO.

Two points are to be noted with respect to this diagnosis. The first is that its aim, if implemented, would defeat and destroy the Socialist party and liberal democracy in Germany, instead of saving them. To meet the Nazis on their own chauvinistic, nationalistic battleground is obviously to court defeat. If the Germans are asked to decide whether the Nazis or the Socialists are the more chauvinistically militant and nationalistic, the answer is obvious. The ideology of Socialism, by its very origin and nature, is international and not chauvinistically German.

Moreover, the Socialist diagnosis of the cause of the fall of the Weimar Republic is as erroneous as it is unwise. One has but to read the recent autobiography of Franz von Papen to note the real cause. After all his attempts to justify his own behavior with respect to Hitler are discounted the facts which he presents make one thing clear: that liberal democratic government failed because the liberal parties refused to collaborate and chose instead to cut one another's throats, leaving Germany without any liberal government that could act. This result is precisely what the refusal of German Socialists and Christian Democrats to collaborate may bring about again.

Fortunately, however, in the election of 1953 the German people gave the Christian Democratic party alone 45 per cent, and its coalition with Free Democrats and the German party 58 per cent of the vote—a decisive majority.[16] Consequently, in the new West German lower house, liberal democracy does not need the support of the Socialist party, with its 29 per cent of the votes, for effective government.

But the favorable circumstance of a spontaneous uprising in East

Berlin is not one on which liberal democracy can count before every election. Democratic processes may fail in the future in Germany if the Socialists continue to regard a spurious appeal to chauvinistic nationalism as more important than the principles of liberal democracy which they share with the Christian Democrats and other liberal democratic German parties.

In the latter half of 1952, the liberal Socialist leaders of the five other Continental European nations urged two matters upon Herr Ollenhauer: first, that he reconsider his insistence on a purely German-controlled remilitarized and united Germany as primary; second, that he collaborate with the Christian Democratic coalition in approving the Contractual Agreements and rearming his countrymen within the Continental European Community, thereby bringing the German army under European, rather than under nationalistic German, control. He rejected the advice on the ground that he still felt that negotiation with the Russians to recover the Eastern sector might succeed if West Germany stayed out of Continental European Union. Before accepting the Contractual Agreements and committing West Germany to Continental European Union he wanted at least one more four-power meeting with the Russians to attempt recovery of the Russian sector.

The subsequent elections of 1953 indicated that the majority of Germans were convinced that additional negotiation was useless: two-thirds of them voted for the Contractual Agreements and for entering Continental European Union. Even the usually socialistic Hamburg voted later in the same way. A dispatch from Germany to *The New York Times* in November of 1953 reported that the election results had caused the convening of a Socialist party meeting to re-examine the traditional policy. The meeting confirmed their old policy.

In February of 1954, the four powers granted Herr Ollenhauer's plea for "one more attempt" to unify the Russian and Western sectors. The results should prepare at least some of Germany's liberal Socialists to reconsider the advice of their ideological colleagues to the west and see that a consistent application of Socialist doctrine is incompatible with a chauvinistic nationalism and militarism which would out-Nazi the Nazis, and calls instead for a European community. This would mean practically that the German Socialists could collaborate with the Christian Democrats on foreign policy and even, at certain times, upon domestic policy.

Table I [17]

Parties	% of Total Vote		Bundestag Seats		
	1953	1949	1953	1949	
Christian Democrats	45	31	244	141	
Free Democrats	10	12	48	53	
German party	3	4	15	17	
C.D. Coalition totals	58	47	307	211	
Socialists	29	29	150	136	
(Chr. Dem. + Soc.)	(74)	(60)	(394)	(277)	
Refugees	6	–	27	–	
Communists	2	6	–	15	
Neo-Nazis	1	–	–	–	
Others	4	18	3	40	
Totals	100	100	487	402	

The first practical step toward such a coalition of Socialists and Christian Democrats at the federal level might be for the Bavarian Socialists in the Federal Parliament to support collaboration at Bonn similar to that in Bavaria. This having been accomplished, the Rhineland Westphalia Socialists in the Federal Bundestag, who were in a similar coalition in their own state government from 1947 to 1950, might follow. It would then not be a difficult step for the majority of the Socialists at Bonn to do likewise. This would make liberal democracy in Germany *doubly* secure, as the 1953 and 1949 election results presented in Table I show. Also, it would insure two liberal coalitions with majority support, at different times, thereby giving Germany effective liberal changes of governments in fact as well as theory. One coalition would not have to win continuously to insure a liberal government and German collaboration in the Continental European Community.

It is to be noted that in 1949 the coalition of Christian Democrats,

Free Democrats and German party obtained only 47 per cent of the votes and but 211 of the 402 Bundestag (lower house) seats. Were but one-third of the 29 per cent of the votes and of the 136 seats obtained in 1949 by the Socialists added to the Christian Democratic coalition, liberal democracy in West Germany would have had a decisive popular majority. In fact, it would need the support of neither the German party nor the Refugee party.

In a federal coalition of Christian Democrats and Socialists (CDU–SPD), no other party support would be necessary. Then, even with the lower 1949 Christian Democratic figures, liberal democracy would have 60 per cent of the popular vote and over 68 per cent of the seats in Parliament. With the higher 1953 Christian Democratic Union figures, the result would be 74 per cent and 80 per cent respectively.

Nor is such a coalition normatively difficult. We have already noted that the party next to the Socialists, toward the Left, in its economic and social policy is the Christian Democratic party and that its Left wing is farther Left than the Socialist Right wing. The Christian Democratic Karl Arnold, former President of the Bundesrat (upper house) of the Federal government and President of the State of Rhineland Westphalia, is generally considered to be the leader of the Left wing of the federal Christian Democratic party. In his youth he attended a labor college in Munich, sponsored by Catholics, which was "dedicated to social reform on a Christian basis." [18] Before 1933 he was a trade union organizer; and he has been one since World War II. He is undoubtedly further Left than the Socialist Mayor of Hamburg, Max Brauer, who was an adviser to Chiang Kai-shek's National Government in the 1930's and was a typical citizen of the United States in the 1940's.[19] To be sure, the Christian Democratic party as a whole in Germany is rather conservative; but so is the German Socialist party. No party in Germany is much Left of Left Center except the Communist. Hence, there is no normative reason why a coalition of Christian Democrats and Socialists cannot be effective—perhaps not so effective at Bonn as in Bavaria, but even so able to pursue a positive common policy.

Under such a coalition or under one of Christian Democrats and Free Democrats, such as exists at present, liberal democracy would be secure in Germany. In fact, future German domestic politics might oscillate between the two coalitions. In either event, Franco-German collaboration within a supranational European Community would be sustained.

These conclusions gain support from an examination of the specific normative principles of the German Christian Democratic party and its supporters. *The Economist* of London has summarized the normative aims of Chancellor Adenauer as follows: He has used his political position "in a determined effort to change the whole trend of Germany's development from a nationalist, predatory, eastward-looking power, dominated by Prussia, and without a real friend in the world, into a firm base for a free, federated Western Europe." [20] Noting that the very small German Party (Deutsche Partei) and certain Right-wing elements in the Free Democratic party and the Christian Democratic party may have some neo-Nazi associations, *The Economist* adds: "The moral leadership rests with the Christian-Democrats under the strong religious influence of Dr. Adenauer." [21]

"The Bonn correspondent of *The New York Times* reported in August 1953:

While the aggregate [of neo-Nazis] may be impressive, the fact remains that numerous splinter groups and individuals have been pinned down to the ground and cannot move because of Chancellor Adenauer's determination that they shall not move. . . . The Chancellor's determined opposition to Nazis and neo-Nazis is founded on political as well as on ideological grounds.[22]

Any success of the Nazi Right will be at the expense of "the Center which is occupied by his own Christian Democratic Union party." Thus political self-interest as well as a living-law moral and religious conviction puts Chancellor Adenauer and his party against what France and the European Community have most to fear in Germany.

Interviews in the fall of 1952 with representative Continental

European religious and political leaders revealed another normative factor in Dr. Adenauer and his party. An outstanding leader of the Christian Democratic party in Belgium told me that when the leaders of this party in the six nations had their first meeting after the war Dr. Adenauer set one absolute condition for his participation in their joint deliberations. It was that the Continental European Christian Democratic party be a Protestant as well as a Roman Catholic party, standing unequivocally for a pluralism of religious and party faiths.

Moreover, Chancellor Adenauer's liberal religious and political convictions are implemented. Three major German Protestant leaders are Bishop Otto Dibelius of West Berlin, Propst D. Asmussen of Kiel and Pastor Martin Niemöller of Wiesbaden. Only the last of the three is opposed to the Christian Democratic party program, to the Contractual Agreements and to the entrance of Germany into Continental European Union. He no longer speaks for German Protestants as a whole. He represents at best little more than the Protestants of his home state of Hesse. Propst Asmussen, the head of the Lutheran Church of Schleswig-Holstein was asked to lead the Christian Democratic party in this state; and he is an unequivocal supporter of the party and its Continental European Union program. Bishop Dibelius of West Berlin has been Chairman of the German Protestant church since 1949 and a member of the Christian Democratic party since 1945.[23] Such facts insure that any coalition government headed by, or containing, Christian Democrats must respect the pluralistic principle of religious and political sovereignty.

Furthermore, the contribution of the Protestant leaders to Dr. Adenauer's Christian Democratic party has been significant. On September 17, 1953, following the Christian Democratic coalition's election victory, a British observer reported:

One of the reasons for the success of the Christian Democrats has been the energetic campaign conducted by Protestant leaders in the north—a reminder that the party draws its support not only from Catholic but also from Protestant votes. . . . In Italy it was the Communists, the Monarchists, and the neo-Fascists who gained votes; in western Germany neither the Communists nor the neo-Nazis have won a single seat in the new Bundestag, while the right-wing parties of the Government Coalition—the Free Democratic Party and the German Party, both of which made a bid for ex-Nazi and Nationalist support—have lost votes to the Christian Democrats. Even the new Refugee Party, with its powerful appeal to a refugee population amounting to nearly a quarter of the electorate, has secured less than six per cent of the votes.[24]

Even more remarkable than these fruits of Protestant and Catholic collaboration in Germany's Christian Democratic party is the collaboration itself. These are the people who produced Luther and the bitterness of the Reformation. This is the land in which one has had but to scratch the surface to find the passions and hatreds of the religious wars still smoldering. If the achievement of Continental European Union in fostering harmonious collaboration between Frenchmen and Germans is, as it truly is, a remarkable phenomenon, its accomplishment in bringing Catholics and Protestants together in Germany is even more notable.

The converse is also true. An essential contribution is made to Continental European Union by the Protestant-Catholic collaboration in Germany's Christian Democratic party. Its Catholic majority and leaders tie West Germany to Latin, Western and Southern Europe, rather than to chauvinistic East Prussia, thereby insuring the common living-law norms in Germany and the other five nations which are necessary to make Franco-German collaboration in the supranational Continental European Community effective. This point cannot receive too much attention. It is the key to the success or failure of Franco-German collaboration, EDC and Continental European Union generally.

In any event, it appears that the religious and secular living law of West Germany is practically identical qualitatively and quantitatively with that of the Netherlands. Also the norms of its two major parties—the Christian Democratic and the Socialist—are international in origin and content and are similar to those of the two major liberal parties in the other five Continental European nations.

What of Italy? The 1953 election and the Trieste affair, follow-ing upon it, suggest that there may not be support in the Italian parliament for the positive law of the Continental European Com-munity. As we have noted, however, it is likely that this situation is caused more by avoidable errors in the foreign policy of the United States and Great Britain with respect to Trieste and by diplomatic or undiplomatic participation in the 1953 Italian elections than by any inherent failure of the living law of the Italian people to sup-port the positive law of Continental European Union. The entrance of a foreign diplomatic representative into the domestic politics of any nation is always an error. It inevitably places the party leader supported by the foreign agent in the position of being the pawn of a foreign government. This may very well account for the Christian Democratic coalition's failure, by 0.4 per cent, to achieve a majority in the federal elections of 1953, after obtaining 61.9 per cent in 1948.

What really matters, however, with respect to the Continental European Community in Italy, is the living law of the Italian people. Its religious component is almost entirely Roman Catholic and thus even more like that of France, Belgium and Luxembourg than the living law of the Netherlands and Germany. The geographical posi-tion of the Vatican City in Italy and its status of virtual inde-pendence, surrounded by a much larger state, makes the Roman Catholic living law of Italy somewhat different, however, from that of other countries.

Because of its small geographical territory and the fact that it is a spiritual community without an army, the Vatican must depend upon negotiation with each Italian government to preserve its posi-tion in Rome. The type of government which Italy has is, therefore, a life and death matter for the Vatican. However much it tries to remain neutral on domestic Italian political issues, this inevitably puts the Vatican into politics. The effect upon the Italian people of this necessary concern of the Vatican with domestic Italian politics is the opposite of what many outsiders suppose. It makes the majority of Italians anticlerical and anti-Vatican politically, even though they are Roman Catholic—and in this sense pro-Vatican—in their personal religious faith. Several times in conversation informed Italians of many diverse interests and ages in 1952 expressed the following opinion to me: "There are two things you can count on always in Italy regardless of changes of government. The one is that the Italians are Roman Catholics in their personal religious faith. The other is that they are anticlerical politically."

One other factor reinforces this political anticlericalism in the living law of the Italian people. All graduates of the Italian secondary schools and universities know of Machiavelli and have been educated in Roman Stoicism and the modern Continental Rationalistic philosophy. All three influences are secular in their economic, political and legal norms and hence anticlerical politically. In this respect the Italians are like all the other Continental Europeans.

Awareness of this peculiar union of religious clericalism and political anticlericalism in the living-law beliefs and behavior of the Italian people is important. Otherwise the paradoxical problem confronting EDC, United States foreign policy and Dr. de Gasperi's Christian Democratic coalition in the 1953 federal election will not be appreciated. The paradox consisted, as it always consists, in needing the support of the clerics to obtain a majority, yet finding such support to be, at the same time, a political liability.

Failure to realize this probably explains why the public participation of the Eisenhower administration's top diplomat to Italy in the 1953 Italian election campaign did not have the beneficent influence which she may have supposed her recent conversion to Roman Catholicism, her association with clerics and her publicized visit to the Vatican would produce. It was common knowledge that the opponents of liberal democracy were associating EDC, United States foreign policy and the Christian Democratic coalition with the Vatican, and that the Communists were trying their best to pin the tag of clericalism on Dr. de Gasperi and his Christian Democratic, Right-wing Socialist, Republican and Liberal associates. As C. L. Sulzberger reported in *The New York Times* of March 16, 1954, " 'clericalism' has been a fighting word in Italy for more than a century" and the

Communists "have made the most of Christian Democracy's alleged 'clerical' ties. They have gained great strength in the Region of Emilia on this basis." On March 20, 1954, *The Economist* of London noted, "Anti-clericalism is part of the democratic tradition in both France and Italy." [25] In any event, the outcome was that those favoring EDC and Italian collaboration with the United States on foreign policy failed to obtain a majority in the officially accepted popular vote, and the Christian Democrats, Right-wing Socialists, Republicans and Liberals received 17.4, 36.2, 34.8 and 21.2 per cent fewer votes respectively in 1953 than in 1948.

These events illustrate the objective basis that sociological jurisprudence, with its attention upon the living law as well as upon positive procedures and particular deeds, provides for judging concrete matters, such as the wisdom of President Eisenhower's ambassadorial appointment to Italy in 1953. It is to be remembered that the diplomat's function is to represent and convey the wishes and aims of his own country with such sensitivity to the values, sentiments and mentality of the country to which he is assigned that its people will be inclined to respond favorably. Toward the personal religious living law of the Italian people, therefore, President Eisenhower's appointment showed both objectivity and sensitivity. Moreover, as our study of Christian Democracy in Germany has shown, anything which contributes to sympathetic understanding and collaboration between Protestants and Roman Catholics is of great importance not merely for Christianity but also for Continental European Union and United States foreign policy. It is only the insensitivity to the anticlericalism in the political living law of Italy that made the appointment questionable and its effect upon the 1953 Italian elections what it was.

What makes these events the more regrettable is that Dr. de Gasperi is respected throughout Europe for his personal Roman Catholic religious faith and his equally deep convictions concerning the secular character of the state and the pluralistic principle of political and religious sovereignty. Hence, in fact, he and the other leaders of the Italian Christian Democratic party combine the same

Roman Catholic personal religious norms and secular political norms as do the Italian people generally and the majority of the Christian Democrats in the other five Continental European nations. This means that the Italian Christian Democratic party possesses norms which are Continental European rather than provincially Italian in their content and appeal.

The norms of the liberal Right wing of the Italian Socialists under Giuseppe Saragat are similarly European, and so are those of the Liberals and Republicans of whom the philosopher Croce and Count Sforza were the leaders. Unfortunately, the majority of the Italian Socialists vote with the Communists, who stand for a one-party rather than a many-party state and hence, in effect, are opposed to liberal democracy and to Continental European Union. This leaves liberal Socialism very weak in Italy. Its percentage of the popular vote was 7.1 in 1948 and but 4.5 in 1953. The combined vote of the Republican and Liberal parties is equally weak, being but 6.3 per cent of the popular vote in 1948 and 5.1 in 1953.[26]

Because of the weakness of liberal Socialism and the Liberal and Republican parties there is but one possible grouping of Italian parties that will give a liberal democratic government; namely, the coalition of Christian Democrats, Right-wing Socialists, Republicans and Liberals. This coalition must win continuously if liberal democracy is to survive in Italy. Such a situation would not be healthy, even if it always won; and it failed to do so by 0.4 per cent in the officially accepted popular vote of 1953. What Italian politics clearly needs is a shift of the Socialists from their heavy 1953 vote for the Communist ticket to the liberal Right-wing Socialist party ticket. Then there could be two liberal Italian majority coalitions at different times—one with the liberal Socialists in the majority, the other with the Christian Democrats in the majority. This would make the quantitative political living law of Italy more like that of the other Continental European Union peoples. Qualitatively, let it be recalled, it is the same.

Such a development is less unlikely than the Italian election statistics of 1953 suggest. First, some at least of the leaders of the

Italian Christian Democratic party wish a stronger liberal Socialist party would arise. Second, the Communist vote of 31.3 per cent in 1948 and 35.3 per cent in 1953 is subject to some qualification.[27] Many Italians told me in 1952 that a large part of the Communist vote was a protest designed to make the Christian Democratic coalition government energetic in its agricultural and other social reforms. In proof it was noted that many peasants had surrendered their Communist party cards and become loyal supporters of the Christian Democratic coalition after farms were provided which they bought on mortgage from the government and could own outright after annual payments over twenty or thirty years, and that many Italians who voted the Communist ticket were Roman Catholic in their personal religious living-law beliefs—beliefs unequivocally opposed to Communist doctrine.

Two things are clear, therefore, concerning Italian living law. First, if interference by foreigners in Italian elections is avoided, and if those who voted the Communist ticket but in fact want a Christian Democratic or liberal Socialist majority are added to the 61.9 per cent of 1948 and the 49.7 per cent of 1953 who voted for liberal democracy and a coalition of Christian Democrats, Liberals and Socialists favoring Continental European Union, then both liberal democracy and the positive law of the Continental European Community are decisively supported. Second, if to the political component is added the religious component, which is 99.6 per cent Roman Catholic, the living-law support becomes even greater. In this connection the outspoken support of the Continental European Community by His Holiness Pope Pius XII is important.

Another factor is not to be overlooked. Italy's basic problem is its overpopulation relative to scanty raw materials and resources. The positive law of Continental European Union, if made effective by its common living law, will have the practical consequence of removing not merely tariff but immigration barriers between member states. This will provide France with a much needed increase in population and at the same time contribute greatly to the solution of Italy's serious population problem. When such a practical expansion of jobs in the whole of Europe becomes an immediate actuality for Italian workers, many of them, now moved by domestic reasons to vote the Communist ticket and incidentally to vote against joining Continental European Union, will undoubtedly change their votes.

Also, many interviews in October of 1952 with the younger and older leaders of the Italian government made it evident not merely that they believe in Continental European Union, but also that the common Continental spiritual and cultural living-law norms necessary to make it effective are present. Minister of Finance Pella emphasized that these spiritual and cultural living-law values common to the majority of the six peoples in the Continental European Community, rather than the economic and military advantages, however important, convince its creators that the Community is realistically practicable and genuine rather than transitory and artificial.

The reason for the primacy of the spiritual and the normative, it may be noted again, is that no government transfers even a part of the sovereign control of its people to a supranational body unless that body is guided by the people's own norms and values. Without the common, indigenous values, therefore, Continental European Union would fail, regardless of military and economic advantages to be derived from it. Younger members of the Italian government emphasized that what makes this radical venture in supranational postive law so realistic and practical is that its leaders, such as MM. Schuman, Spaak, Adenauer and de Gasperi, not only have living-law ancient religious and modern secular liberal norms and convictions in common but also know what they are.

Signor Pella pointed out also that the Continental European Community was fortunate because the leaders in 1952 of foreign policy in the three major nations—Drs. de Gasperi of Italy, Schuman of France and Adenauer of West Germany—were born on or near the borderlands of the nations and hence embody the cultures of two peoples and nations. Informed North Europeans pointed out to me later that this is true also of Paul-Henri Spaak, the Socialist leader of Belgium and major proponent of Continental European Union. All come from what many Europeans today call Middle

Rome—that persisting portion of the former Roman Empire which extends from Italy northward over the Brenner Pass, embracing not only Austria, Bavaria and the West German Rhineland and West-phalia but also the entire Rhine valley and its western tributaries in middle France, Alsace-Lorraine, the Saar, Luxembourg, Belgium and the lowlands of western Holland. Every Italian, like every Austrian and every Frenchman, dreams daily of his culture as the epitome of a civilization that is universally European in the religious and secular values for which it stands. This was the source of Mus-solini's living-law appeal, as it was of Napoleon's. Continental Euro-pean Union enables the Italians and the French, as well as the Romanized West Germans, the Netherlanders and the Belgians, to fulfill such dreams of a universal Europe together in the name of peace with one another and with the rest of the world without the death throes in each generation of the irrational outbursts of a provincially local and chauvinistically national imperialism.

Nor is this vision of a common, enlarged and united Middle Rome the sheer fantasy of some imaginative historian. The realistic states-men of the six nations in Continental European Union embody its living realities. They belong at one and the same time to more than one nation and to this over-all common Middle Roman modern world. Dr. de Gasperi's first language was German, and the culture of his youth was Austrian. His home city was in Austria before World War I. He studied the Stoic Roman type of law so typical of the Continent and received his Doctorate in Law from the University of Vienna. Since World War I, his language and his life both politi-cally and religiously have been Italian. Robert Schuman comes from Metz in Lorraine. He fought in the German army in World War I, Lorraine then being a part of Germany. Since World War I, after the manner of Lorraine, he has been truly French—a member of the French underground fighting Hitler's Germany in World War II. Like Chancellor Adenauer, he is a devout Roman Catholic respected by Frenchmen, Germans and other Europeans alike for the depth and sincerity of his political and moral convictions. He has two de-grees—one from the University of Bonn, the second a Doctorate in

Law from the University of Munich. This means that his legal mentality is identical with that of Dr. de Gasperi. Chancellor Adenauer holds similar degrees from the universities of Bonn and Munich. Dr. Heinrich von Brentano, floor leader of the Christian Democratic party in the West German Parliament, Chairman of the Committee which wrote the Statute of the European Political Community, and former Vice President of the Consultative Assembly of the Council of Europe, though of a family prominent in the cultural and political life of Germany for two centuries, is, as his name indicates, the patrilineal descendant of the Brentano family of Tremezzo, Italy.[28] Clearly this is the living-law stuff, transcending national boundaries, of which a vital European leadership can be made.

Furthermore, under such a leadership, the Saar can unite France and Germany, instead of dividing them. Because of its geographical location in the heart of old Middle Rome nearer French industry, it can be French in its natural economic relations under the European High Authority at Luxembourg, while remaining German linguistically and in most of its family ties.

This brings us to the living law of France itself. Its Socialist party leader, Guy Mollet, agrees with Italy's Christian Democratic Prime Minister Pella that Continental European Union, if it is to pass the parliaments and be effective, must have a common basis in norms and values within, not in dangers and pressures from without. In late October of 1952 at the Socialist party headquarters in Paris, M. Mollet spoke to me in substance as follows: "Military and economic advantages may be the occasion for, and the by-products of, Continental European Union; but they cannot be its basis. Its basis must be in the common norms of the European peoples involved."

As noted above, the living-law norms of the majority of the French people are qualitatively the same as those of the five other Continental European peoples. The religious living law of France is in major part Roman Catholic, tinged with a Cartesian and Voltairian skepticism born of the primacy of the *cogito* of the individual self in the Frenchman's judgment of the church's dicta and the source of any earthly authority. This skeptical element makes French Roman

Catholic religious living law almost Protestant in its temper with respect to the Vatican hierarchy.[29] Hence the religious living law of France is much nearer than might at first be supposed to that of the Netherlands and West Germany, where there are major Protestant components.

We have already noted the qualitative similarity of the diverse French political norms to those of the other five continental nations, in describing the major French political parties. In fact, the parties of the six countries are practically identical. When they differ, it is for the most part in name. The two major liberal parties in all six nations are the same—the Christian Democratic and the Socialist. Moreover, the third largest liberal party is the same in all six nations, even though it bears different names in different countries, such as Radical Socialist in France, Liberal in Belgium and Italy, Protestant Liberal in the Netherlands, Free Democratic in Germany and both Republican and Liberal in Italy.

Moreover, even quantitatively the political living laws are similar. Only the non-liberal Right-wing and Left-wing parties are stronger quantitatively in France than in the other nations. Even so, the French liberal parties muster roughly two-thirds of the votes in the French parliament. Since World War II the Christian Democrats (85) and the Socialists (104) have vied with each other for the lead among the liberal parties, the Socialists going ahead in the 1951 election (the situation is similar in the Netherlands). The French Radical Socialists (80) of Herriot and of Pleven come next in popular support, and are followed by the more conservative Independent-Peasant liberals (77).

The foregoing figures show that domestic political difficulties in France are the opposite of those in Germany and Italy where the problem is to get more than one liberal democratic coalition. France suffers from an oversupply of such coalitions. Hence the frequent change of French governments. Nevertheless, through all these changes between World War II and January 1953, each liberal democratic coalition favored Continental European Union. The reason for the agreement is now clear. The norms of the major

French liberal parties are those of the liberal parties of the other five nations in the Continental European Community. Where there are common living-law norms, there can be an effective positive-law community. This is why the realistic statesmen of Continental Europe, between World War II and January of 1953, believed a supranational Continental European Community to be possible and practicable.

The reason for the difference between the positive law of the Council of Europe and that of the Continental European Community now becomes clear. The former achieved no real transfer of sovereignty from the fourteen member states to the larger community because the member states lacked a common religious or political living law. The six Continental European nations achieved such a transfer because they approximated a common living law.

The experiment in sociological jurisprudence which is European Union establishes the following conclusions of considerable import for legal science, international law and foreign policy generally.

First, the international sphere independently confirms the fundamental thesis of sociological jurisprudence that law is more than positive law, and that positive law is effective only where there are corresponding common norms in the living law.

Second, the method of sociological jurisprudence for determining the living law of any nation, which Ehrlich, Professor Pound and Underhill Moore left in an indeterminate or impractical form, is shown to be to specify qualitatively and quantitatively the major normative groupings of the people in question.

Third, the positive law of any supranational community of nations may be suggested by a foreign danger, the economic advantages or the desire for peace; but these cannot be its basis. The basis instead must be in a living law with a normative content common to all the nations and peoples involved.

Fourth, there is more than one way of bringing the many nations of the world under the rule of law. As *The Taming of the Nations* pointed out in 1952 in addition to the way of the United Nations which would include as many nations as possible, there is also the way of culturalism, which consists in bringing those nations with common religious beliefs and political parties into a single "supranation." The comparison of the positive law of the Council of Europe with that of the Continental European Community shows that a much greater transfer of sovereignty from the national to the supranational community is possible where nations have common religious and political groups and beliefs.

Fifth, the experiment in sociological jurisprudence which is European Union shows also that culturalism is much more effective, as a basis for international collaboration, than the regionalism suggested by Prime Minister Churchill in World War II. The reason is clear. The geographical proximity of regionalism is no guarantee of a common living law. Culturalism—that is, a common culture—provides the common living law. Because the Continental European nations have a common culture with explicit normative content, they are able to achieve an economic supranational positive law in the Coal and Steel Community and for the military and political communities which expresses a real transfer of sovereignty from its member nations. Conversely, because there are not common religious or political norms in the fourteen regionally associated nations of the Council of Europe, it is unable, in its positive legal constitution, to achieve any significant transfer of communal national sovereignty.

Sixth, a theory of foreign policy which would base itself on power factors or economic aid alone is unrealistic. These may be by-products; they are not foundation stones. Moreover, such a foreign policy neglects the living-law norms, from the standpoint of which nations or groups of nations will (a) use their power, (b) order their social relations economically, and (c) make their decisions with respect to both domestic and foreign policy. Whether the Continental nations, for example, will muster the power necessary to defend themselves from external attack by Russia or from internal attack by a revived Nazi Germany depends upon whether they have common living-law norms that enable them to trust one another to place their fragments of potential power in one large single, efficient Continental European pool under the control of leaders sincerely committed to, and directed by, these common norms.

Part of the answer to this question is already known, as specified by the qualitative and quantitative content of the living law of each of the six Continental European nations considered independently. It remains to combine the living-law findings. Then we shall have the living law of the Continental European Community seen collectively in its unity. With this information, the probable party make-up of the Lower House of the Continental European Community should be made evident. Also, if the foreign policy of outside nations be favorable, an objective answer should be at hand to the question: Is Continental European Union practicable?

Chapter 8

Is the Continental European Community Practicable?

The treaties establishing the positive law of the Continental European Community prescribe unity in two different ways. First, they combine into one community what appear initially as three different communities. Second, they transfer to one sovereign "supranation" certain sovereign powers, traditionally exercised by six different nations. Both cases are present when the Coal and Steel Community and the European Defense Community become instruments of the European Political Community, while maintaining the distinctive sovereign powers and functions specified in the treaties that initiated them. This means that the Continental European Community introduces a common supranational positive law for ordering the economic, military and political relations of its 157,000,000 members.

Sociological jurisprudence tells us, however, that a common positive law is never effective unless it is supported by a common living law. Is this the case with respect to Continental European Union?

Upon first thought, the answer seems to be clearly negative. The six traditional living laws of the six Continental European nations have been mutually antagonistic economically, militarily and politically. Witness the three major European wars between France and Germany in the last eighty years. Is not France the epitome of nationalism in the world? Is this not what the French Revolution and modern France mean? Have not the traditional living-law habits of

113

these six peoples been chauvinistic and antagonistic toward one another rather than cooperative? How then can Continental European Union possibly work?

Before acquiescing in the conclusion which these questions suggest, let us note certain facts. First, the European Coal and Steel Community and the proposed European Defense and Political communities are not empty dreams of speculative armchair thinkers. Instead, they result from the practical, official decisions of realistic politicians, who from January 29, 1946, to January 8, 1953, were supported in everything that they did by the governments in power and by the peoples behind the governments. Clearly political developments and deeds like these cannot be wholly unrealistic and fanciful. Second, geographically *the present Germany is not the old Germany*; and the Four Power conference of February 1954 in Berlin made it abundantly clear that tomorrow's Germany is not likely to be the old Germany in the foreseeable future. This suggests that a Franco-German collaboration in Continental European Union may be supported by the living law of the present Germany although the living law of the old Germany made it impossible. Third, there may be common living-law resources in the six nations which were left undeveloped in the past and never brought to positive legal expression politically; just as there are natural resources in the underdeveloped nations of Asia and Africa which have never been developed and brought to social expression through new positive legal forms and institutions.

The foregoing considerations make it clear, therefore, that the question of the practicality of Continental European Union is not to be answered in the facile manner that a first impression, and its critics, might suggest. Instead, we must let the qualitative and quantitative character of the *de facto* living law of the community itself provide the answer.

To this end, the comparative study in the previous chapters of (1) the living law of the fourteen nations in the Council of Europe, and (2) the living law of the six nations in the Continental European Community has already made several things evident.

In the fourteen nations there is no common religion: the religious living law of Turkey is overwhelmingly Islamic; that of Greece, similarly Greek Orthodox; that of the six Continental European nations, in major part Latin Roman Catholic; that of Ireland, similarly Latin Roman Catholic but with a Gaelic isolationistic and nationalistic focus; whereas the other nations in the Council of Europe are overwhelmingly Protestant Christian.

The same is true of political parties in the fourteen nations. There is no significant Socialist party in contemporary Turkey. Conversely there is no Islamic living-law mass movement in any other nation in the Council of Europe comparable to the present Islamic reaction of the masses of Turks in the villages. Furthermore, for the orthodox followers of Islam the *shariat*, or positive law, is as important as the Koran; and the principles it sets up for ordering social relations are incompatible with those of any other Western European state. The British Labor party has been lukewarm and often opposed even to the Council of Europe, and has shown little interest in collaboration with the Right-wing Socialist parties on the continent. In fact, as was noted in Chapter 6, none of the three political parties of Great Britain is matched in any of the six Continental European nations. The major political parties of Ireland are similarly provincial. Hence there is no common inner order in the living laws of the fourteen nations of the Council of Europe by which the economic, military or political life of all fourteen can be regulated. This is why the Council of Europe, even in the realm of positive law, achieved no genuine transfer of sovereignty from its member nations to its international community. A Consultative Assembly alone was possible.

The Council of Europe can become more effective than it has been. However, for the greatest effectiveness, it, like the United Nations, must ground its internationalism in the objective fact of living-law religious and political pluralism. I have indicated elsewhere how such a stronger international law is to be achieved for nations with diverse and conflicting living laws.[1]

The living laws of the six nations in the Continental European

Community are, however, quite different from those of the eight additional nations in the Council of Europe. The major political parties in all six are practically the same. The religious living laws in the six nations also are similar, with the Latin Roman Catholic group comprising the majority in five of them and exercising the major political influence in the sixth.

The similarity of the six major political parties in each of the six nations merits more detailed consideration. It is such that the competing normative principles for ordering economic, political, military and social relations in any given nation are approximately identical with those in the other member nations. Practically this insures that the six Continental European nations do not have to create new political parties, or even a single new political party in committing themselves to Continental European Union. The leaders of the Christian Democratic parties of the six nations have been meeting together since World War II and will probably continue to meet together whether Continental European Union goes into effect or not. The same is true of the Communist parties, the Socialist parties and, to a lesser extent, the Liberal parties of the six nations. Similarly, military leaders of the six nations have been planning a common military command at the Palais de Chaillot with Germans present in a civilian status, since May 27, 1952, when the European Defense Treaty was signed in Paris. These living-law facts are already present. They permit the creation of a supranational community with common living-law norms, without the departure of any citizen from his traditional religious, political, economic or other beliefs for ordering the relations between men in society.

To be even more specific, let us recall, from the previous chapter, the specific normative political principles of the six major parties common to the six Continental European nations. Far to the Left in economic theory, the Communist party has its monistic conception of political sovereignty and its Marxist ideology for ordering the social relations of men generally. Next, towards the Left, the liberal, or Right-wing, Socialist party has a pluralistic theory of political and religious sovereignty and emphasizes a strong nationally controlled, legally and federally regulated economy. Next is the Christian Democratic party with its pluralistic theory of political and religious sovereignty, its emphasis upon Christian responsibility, and at times even Christian Socialism, in economic relations and its outstanding leadership. Beside the Christian Democrats in the Center is a secularly minded or Protestant Liberal party with its pluralistic theory of political and religious sovereignty and with its Protestant or secular skeptical insistence on the separation of church and state. There is also a Liberal party whose adherents are Roman Catholic in personal religious living law, yet anticlerical in political theory. Finally at the extreme Right, in each of the six nations there is an imperialistic, chauvinistic, nationalistic party that tends to a monistic theory of political and religious sovereignty and is opposed to any international collaboration.

Qualitatively speaking, therefore, the religious and political living-law norms of different groups in any one nation are absolutely identical in most cases with those of corresponding groups in the other nations of the Continental European Community, and approximately identical in the cases of the Radical Socialists, Liberal, Free Democratic and Republican parties. This gives the supranational European Community the same common living-law content for ordering the economic, military and political life in the supranational European Community that the separate nations have been using unilaterally.

Although qualitative similarity of the living laws of the six nations is necessary, it is not sufficient. Quantitative similarity is also required. Otherwise, the people of a given nation might find their economic and political lives ordered in the supranational community by the norms of only a small minority in their own nation. Thereby their own living beliefs and convictions, and their majority will, would be violated. Also, if in one of the six nations the chauvinistic normative group at the Right or the Communist group at the Left possessed unquestionable majority support, the Community would break down for lack of a common living law, because a living-law group affirming a monistic theory of political and religious sovereignty is incompatible with a living-law group denying this principle. The failure of all attempts to have coalition governments of liberal democrats and Communists is conclusive proof of this point.

The question must, therefore, be faced: Is the quantitative support for the two living-law religious groups and the six living-law political parties common to the six nations sufficiently similar in the six nations to make Continental European Union practicable? A preliminary answer to the question was published under the title, "United States Foreign Policy and Continental European Union," in the *Harvard Studies in International Affairs* of February 1954. The three tables which follow provide more recent and complete data. Table II gives in percentages the quantitative support which each of the six qualitatively different political parties enjoys in the six nations. Table III expresses, in percentages at the bottom, the quantitative living-law support which the six parties enjoy in the Continental European Community as a whole. Table IV gives in percentages the quantitative support which the two qualitatively different religious living-law groups possess in the six nations and in the Continental European Community as a whole.

The columns numbered 1 to 6 in Table II order the six parties from left to right in agreement with their economic beliefs. The four parties represented by Columns 2, 3, 4 and 5 stand for the pluralistic theory of religious and political sovereignty, and hence are liberal democratic parties. In any coalition of these parties liberal democratic institutions and values will be preserved. Therefore Column 7, which sums Columns 2, 3, 4 and 5, gives the present quantitative strength of liberal democracy in each of the six nations. Furthermore, any and every member state which fears that some particular member state of the Community will turn chauvinistically nationalistic, thereby destroying it and threatening the first state's existence, need not have serious fear so long as the quantitative living-law support for the parties represented by Columns 2, 3, 4 and 5 is a comfortable or decisive majority.

The following criteria govern the assignment of the political parties of each nation to the six columns. Only liberal Socialists are

Table II

COMPARATIVE QUANTITATIVE POLITICAL LIVING LAW OF THE CONTINENTAL EUROPEAN COMMUNITY IN PERCENTAGE OF POPULAR VOTE AND OF SEATS IN THE LOWER HOUSE OF PARLIAMENT

Country	(1) Communists		(2) Socialists		(3) Christian Democrats		(4) Roman Catholic Liberals		(5) Protestant Liberals		(6) Rightists		(7) (2)–(5) = Liberal Democracy		(8) (1) & (6) = Antiliberal Democracy	
	Vote	Seats	Vote	Seats	Vote	Seats	Vote	Seats	Vote	Seats	Vote	Seats	Vote	Seats	Vote	Seats
Belgium	4.7	3.3	36.4	35.8	47.5	50.9	11.2	9.9	–	–	–	–	95.1	96.6	4.7	3.3
France, 1951	26.7	16.4	14.6	16.5	11.9	13.6	24.9	34.4	–	–	21.6	18.8	51.4	64.5	48.3	35.2
France, 1946	29.5	29.3	18.4	16.0	27.1	28.0	24.8	26.5	–	–	–	–	70.3	70.5	29.5	29.3
Italy, 1953	35.3	36.9	4.5	3.2	40.1	44.2	5.1	3.8	–	–	12.7	11.6	49.7	51.2	48.0	48.5
Italy, 1948	31.3	32.0	7.1	5.7	48.5	53.4	6.3	4.9	–	–	4.8	3.5	61.9	64.0	36.1	35.5
Luxembourg	16.8	9.8	41.4	27.4	33.2	43.1	8.4	19.6			–	–	83.0	90.1	16.8	9.8
Netherlands, '52	6.1	6.0	28.9	30.0	28.6	30.0	–	–	31.4	32.0	2.7	2.0	88.9	92.0	8.8	8.0
Netherlands, '48	7.7	8.0	25.6	27.0	31.0	32.0	–	–	32.7	32.0	1.2	1.0	89.3	91.0	8.9	9.0
W. Germany, '53	2.2	–	28.8	30.8	45.1	50.1	2.4	.6	15.0	15.8	4.2	2.6	91.3	97.3	6.4	2.6
W. Germany, '49	6.4	–	32.6	33.8	34.5	35.0	8.1	9.9	17.7	17.4	–	–	93.0	96.1	6.4	–

The percentages have been computed from figures given in *The New York Times*, *Keesing's Contemporary Archives* and the Netherlands Information Service.

119

assigned to Column 2. The term "liberal" (uncapitalized) refers to any party affirming the pluralistic principle of religious and political sovereignty, i.e., parties 2, 3, 4 and 5. A party named Liberal (Columns 4, 5) is therefore but one among other liberal parties. By Roman Catholic Liberals (Column 4) are meant voters holding the Liberal party's secular norms, whose religious living law is Roman Catholic. Voters with Liberal secular norms whose religious living law is Protestant go in Column 5. However, a political party may be assigned to Column 4 or Column 5 without having the term "Liberal" in its name: the criterion is not the tag, but the content of the norms of the Liberal party as defined in the previous chapter. For example, the French Liberals in Column 4 include four groups none of which uses the word "Liberal" in its party name: the Herriot and Pleven branches of the Radical Socialist party, the Independent party and the Peasant party. A problem arose in assigning the Refugee party in West Germany. Its ideology is not specified, its unity being the product of its members' refugee status. Being from the Eastern sector, which is much more Protestant than Roman Catholic, they classify probably in Column 5 if they are liberals. Many observers believe, however, their Prussian and East Prussian background gives them Rightist inclinations.[2] Hence, for want of more objective information Table II assigns them arbitrarily half to Column 5 and half to Column 6.

To determine whether the frequently mentioned French fear of rearming the Germans inside the Continental European Community is justified, the percentages for Germany in Table II are crucial. Examination of the percentages for France reveals a possible fear which has not been noted before—the fear that liberal Germans may have of a Rightist France in the Bonaparte tradition. In short, perhaps there is a French problem for Germany and European peace generally as well as a German problem for the French and other Continental Europeans.

In the case of Germany, Column 7 of Table II shows that in the 1949 elections the nominally liberal German political parties won 93 per cent of the votes and 96.1 per cent of the parliamentary seats.

In the 1953 election they won 91.3 per cent and 97.3 per cent respectively. It is to be noted that notwithstanding the remarkable victory for Dr. Adenauer's Christian Democratic coalition in 1953 the total popular vote received by all the nominally liberal democratic parties decreased from 93 per cent in 1949 to 91.3 per cent. This expresses the fact that the defeated Nazi Right dared to appear openly in the 1953 election, with percentage results given in Column 6.

Informed students of Germany know, however, that even the popular vote of 91.3 per cent in 1953 for the nominally democratic parties of Columns 2, 3, 4 and 5 cannot be taken as the real strength of liberal democracy in West Germany. Each one of these nominally liberal West German parties contains a Nazi Right. Moreover the Nazi Right is probably weakest in the Socialist party (Column 2) and strongest in the Protestant Liberals (Column 5). It is to be noted that the latter group is the third largest political group in contemporary Germany, having about 17.5 per cent of the popular votes and seats in 1949 and 15.5 per cent in 1953. If we eliminate the Refugee party from West Germany's liberals in Columns 4 and 5, retaining within liberal democracy only the Socialists (Column 2), the Christian Democrats (Column 3) and those among the Roman Catholic liberals and the Protestant liberals who voted with the Christian Democratic coalition, we approximate more closely the strength of liberal democracy in West Germany. As shown in the Table in Chapter 7, it was 76 per cent of the popular vote in the 1949 elections and 87 per cent in 1953. With allowance for the effect of the East Berlin riots in the 1953 election, an average of these two figures, or 81 per cent, would probably be on the optimistic side. Even so the leeway between this figure and 49.9 per cent, the defeat of liberal democracy in West Germany, is great.

We cannot take 81 per cent as a measure of West German support for Continental European Union, because it includes the Socialists and they opposed union as late as 1954. However, many Socialist leaders in other Continental European countries believe that the German Socialists might modify their opposition if they came to power: while opposed to participation in Continental Europe under Christian Democratic German leadership, they might be for it under a Socialist German government. Certainly, their ideology, which is essentially European rather than provincially German both in origin and in content, points this way. In any event, the Christian Democratic coalition, which is both liberally democratic and favorable to Continental European Union, won 47 per cent of the popular vote and 52.5 per cent of the seats in the lower house of parliament in the 1949 elections and 58 per cent of the popular vote and 63 per cent of the seats in 1953.

Suppose, however, that instead of the coalition of Christian Democrats, Free Democrats and German party of the 1949 and 1953 elections, the Christian Democratic and Socialist coalition, suggested as a possibility in Chapter 6, should arise. It is to be recalled that in the late summer of 1952 the Socialist leaders of the other five Continental European nations urged Herr Ollenhauer, the leader of West Germany's Socialist party, to stand for a European rather than a chauvinistic German liberal Socialist foreign policy by collaborating with the Christian Democrats to pass EDC. Up to April of 1954 he had refused to do this. One of the outstanding liberal Socialists in Germany is Herr Kaisen of Bremen. In the federal election of 1953, the Socialists did better in Bremen than in any other state (*Land*) in Germany. In December of 1953 Mayor Kaisen had become a major German leader of the "Socialist Movement for a United States of Europe," working beside M. Spaak of Belgium and M. Monnet of France.[3] This is the first step toward a Socialist and Christian Democratic coalition at Bonn. Columns 2 and 3 of Table II show that such a coalition represented 67.2 per cent of the popular vote and 68.8 per cent of the parliamentary seats in 1949, and 73.9 per cent and 80.9 per cent respectively in 1953.

Undoubtedly the high percentage of the coalition of Christian Democrats, Free Democrats and German party in the 1953 election was due in part to the East Berlin riots just before the election and in part to the fact that had the West German people not supported Dr. Adenauer's European policy they would have returned legally, although not actually, to the status of a people without a peace treaty subject to foreign military government. Even so the foregoing percentages, and especially those in Column 7, show that liberal democracy and support for Franco-German collaboration in the Continental European Community can lose many votes, from the Right wing of each present West German liberal party, to the Prussian Junker and Nazi Right in future elections without a serious threat to liberal democratic institutions or German loyalty to the Continental European Community. In other words, if this Community is established in 1954 and the foreign policies of the United States and Great Britain are favorable (what this means will concern us later), there is a good chance that Dr. Adenauer and other Continental European statesmen will have the time to create European-minded, westward-looking habits in the German people and a similarly collaborative and loyal European-minded Continental Western Europe generally.

In judging the strength of liberal democracy and of loyalty to the Continental European Community it is necessary to pay attention, in Table II, not merely to the relative quantitative percentage strength of the Right as given in Column 6, but also to that of the Communist Left as given in Column 1, because, although the Communist Left and the chauvinistic Right are absolutely opposed in their economic norms for ordering social relations, they agree on the monistic theory of political and religious sovereignty and hence have a common interest in destroying liberal democracy. In order to determine the initial opposition which liberal democracy and Continental European Union must face in any nation, it is necessary to combine the quantitative percentages of Columns 1 and 6, as in Column 8. It shows Italy and France to be the only nations where there is a serious threat to liberal democracy or to Continental European Union from a combined Right and Left.

In the 1953 Italian election liberal democracy failed to obtain a majority of the officially accepted popular vote and surpassed the combined Right and Left by but 49.7 per cent to 48 per cent, and by but 51.2 per cent to 48.5 per cent in parliamentary seats. The marked difference from the ratios of the previous election in 1948 is, however, notable. Then liberal democracy surpassed the combined Right and Left by 61.9 to 36.1 per cent in popular vote and 64 to 35.5 per cent in parliamentary seats. This great discrepancy points to the significance of extraneous factors, such as unwise diplomacy from abroad in the 1953 results.

In the 1951 French election liberal democracy surpassed the combined Right and Left by but 51.4 per cent to 48.3 per cent—not a comfortable popular majority. In parliamentary seats, however, the ratio was 64.5 per cent to 35.2 per cent. Because the larger ratio in parliamentary seats is the result of positive legal rules, and popular vote may be assumed to be nearer the living law, the situation in France, so far as liberal democracy is concerned, is not too healthy. The French figures in Columns 7 and 8 undoubtedly explain why France became the main threat to Continental European Union in April of 1954 when General Juin dropped NATO for the Gaullist Right's policy and General de Gaulle threatened civil war in case the French parliament approved EDC, daring even to affirm the monistic principle of political sovereignty by blatantly asserting, "I myself was the state and the government in France." [4] Some contemporary politicians have given rise to the suspicion that they are dominated by a Napoleonic complex but General de Gaulle is the first one with the somewhat dubious distinction of having insisted that he has such a psychiatrical trait.

Notwithstanding the fact, however, that the French figures in Columns 7 and 8 show the living law to be less favorable to liberal democracy and to Continental European Union than the ratio of parliamentary seats would indicate, other living-law statistics, such as the French public opinion poll of June 1952, show opinion to be more favorable to Continental European Union than the 1951 election statistics suggest. The special bulletin from Paris to the magazine *World*, in the midmonthly issue of April 15, 1954, was probably correct, therefore, when it reported that the French statesmen who favored EDC might have obtained a slight majority for it had they forced a parliamentary vote in mid-April, but that this would have been at the risk of "*wrecking the Western Alliance* and threatening France with civil war." [5] The percentages for France in Columns 6, 7 and 8 show that, while the Gaullists are far from having the majority to achieve their normative aims by parliamentary means, they are sufficiently near a majority when supported by the Communist Left to make their threat to destroy liberal democracy by an army-led revolt a possibility with which other liberal French statesmen—and, it must be added, liberal German statesmen—must reckon.

Table II reveals one other important fact. The Socialist party and the Christian Democratic party are the major liberal parties in all six nations. This suggests that they will be the major liberal parties in the Continental European Community. In Belgium, the Netherlands, Luxembourg, West Germany and Italy, the Christian Democratic party is the largest liberal party, whereas in France it is tied for second place with the combined Herriot-Pleven Radical Socialists. In Belgium, the Netherlands, Luxembourg, West Germany and Italy the liberal Socialist party is the second largest liberal party, whereas in France it holds first place. In the Belgian elections of April 1954, which occurred after Table II was completed, the Socialist party increased in strength from 77 against the Christian Democratic (Social Christian) 108 to 86 against 95, thus making a coalition government of Christian Democrats and Socialists likely there.[6] Thus what Italy lacks in liberal Socialist strength, France makes up; and whereas Christian Democratic strength is tied with that of the Radical Socialists and the Pinay or Laniel Independents and Peasants for second place in France, it ranks first in quantitative support in the other five nations.

That the party differences in the Continental European Community will be practically identical qualitatively and quantitatively with those in each member nation becomes clearer when we combine the percentages of Table II to arrive at the qualitative and quantitative political living law of the Continental European Community seen in its unity. This occurs in Table III.

Table III

THE POLITICAL LIVING LAW OF THE CONTINENTAL
EUROPEAN COMMUNITY IN ITS UNITY

Population in Millions Supporting Each Party in Each Nation

	(1)	(2)	(3)	(4)	(5)	(6)	
Country	Commu- nist	Social- ist	Chris- tian Democrat	Roman Cath. Lib.	Protes- tant Liberal	Right	Total Pop. in Millions
Belgium, 1950	.41	3.17	4.14	.97	—	—	8.72
France, 1951	11.32	6.19	5.04	10.55	—	9.15	42.40
1946	*11.95*	*7.45*	*10.98*	*10.04*	*—*	*—*	*40.51*
Italy, 1953	16.55	2.11	18.80	2.39	—	5.95	46.88
1948	*14.28*	*3.24*	*22.13*	*2.87*	*—*	*2.19*	*45.64*
Luxembourg, 1948	.04	.12	.09	.02	—	—	.29
Netherlands, 1952	.63	3.01	2.98	—	3.27	.28	10.42
1948	*.74*	*2.46*	*2.98*	*—*	*3.14*	*.11*	*9.63*
W. Germany, 1953	1.06	13.96	21.86	1.16	7.27	2.03	48.47
1949	*3.07*	*15.66*	*16.62*	*3.89*	*8.50*	*—*	*48.03*
Continental Europe	30.01*	28.56	52.91	15.09	10.54	17.41	157.18
Percentages†	19.09%	18.17%	33.66%	9.60%	6.70%	11.07%	

16.30%

68.13%

* Ignoring italic numbers.
† Of population for each Continental European political group.

These figures have been computed from population statistics given in *The World Almanac*, for the nearest appropriate year, and Table II.

The figures in Table III represent populations in millions. The total population for each country is given in the column at the extreme right. The figures in the remainder of the table are determined by multiplying the total population of each nation by the percentages in that nation who voted for each of the six major political parties. This permits us to add the number of party adherents in a small country, like Luxembourg, with a total population of but 300,000, to the number in larger countries, like France and Italy, thereby obtaining the totals for the European Community as a whole which appear at the bottom of the six columns. Dividing the totals —30.01, etc.—at the bottom of Table III by 157.18, (that is, 157,180,000, the total population of the Continental European Community) gives an approximate appraisal of the percentage of popular support for each normative political group in the Continental European Community as a whole. These percentage figures, which appear directly under the population totals, are, of course, rough approximations. For example, they assume that the total population will distribute itself politically as the voting portion does. It will be noted also that the percentages expressing the quantitative support of the six major groups do not total 100 per cent. This expresses the fact that in each country there are individuals and parties who do not fall into any of the six major groupings listed. They total roughly 2 per cent.

The three major percentages at the bottom of Table III are significant. They indicate that for the Continental European Community as a whole the Communist party is supported by approximately 19 per cent of the population, the chauvinistic Nazi, Gaullist or Fascist Right by roughly 11 per cent and liberal democracy by 68 per cent of the total population. The controls, therefore, which a popularly elected supranational European parliament would place upon a chauvinistic dictatorship and imperialism of either the Communist Left or the Nazi-Fascist Right seem to be sufficiently strong quantitatively to be effective.

The percentages at the bottom of Table III indicate also that the normative political group with the largest number of supporters is the Christian Democratic party, representing 33.66 per cent of the people. The second largest party is the Communist with 19.09 per cent. Almost abreast of them, and the second largest liberal normative group, is the liberal Socialist party with 18.17 per cent. If we combine the Roman Catholic and Protestant Liberal parties, which are similar in their political and economic normative beliefs and differ primarily in their religious affiliation, this combined Liberal party represents 16.3 per cent of the people and is the fourth largest normative political group and the third largest liberal party. The parties then line up in the following order of quantitative strength: (1) Protestant-Catholic Christian Democrats 33.66 per cent, (2) Communist 19.09 per cent, (3) liberal Socialists 18.17 per cent, (4) Protestant-Catholic Liberals 16.3 per cent and (5) the chauvinistic Right 11.07 per cent.

The percentages show many important things: First, the top quantitative strength of the liberal Christian Democratic party in the Community as a whole, almost twice that of its nearest rival, explains the exceptional role which Christian Democratic statesmen like MM. Schuman, Bidault, van Zeeland, Bech, Adenauer, von Brentano and de Gasperi have played in the creation of Continental European Union. Their influence is not the accident it appeared to be to persons who looked at it merely from the traditional historical and positive-law standpoint. Second, the quantitative strength of the Communists in second place by nine-tenths of one per cent is significant. Add to their 19.09 per cent the 11.07 per cent of the Gaullists to obtain 30.16 per cent and one appreciates the opposition from within that Continental European Union has had to overcome. Third, Italian liberal democracy will be much safer in Continental European Union than it is in the traditional, purely nationalistic Italy. The same is true of Italian liberal Socialism. In Italy alone, liberal Socialism is weak because of the flirting of the major Italian Socialist leaders with the Communists. Combined, however, with the major French liberal party—the Socialists under Guy Mollet's leadership—and the strengthened liberal Socialists of Belgium under M. Spaak, and with the liberal Dutch, Luxembourg and West German Socialists, the liberal Socialists would carry a weight in Italy not to be dismissed lightly by the Left-Wing Socialists there. Furthermore, in such able and influential company, the liberal Italian Socialists, led by MM. Saragat and Spinelli, might win many Socialists in Italy away from collaboration with the Communists. This would provide the two possible liberal governmental coalitions which, as the previous chapter noted, Italian liberal democracy so badly needs.

But quantity is not everything. Quality also matters; and, viewed qualitatively, the living-law norms of the three largest parties in the Continental Community are truly European, rather than chauvinistically provincial. These norms have been specified in part in earlier chapters. It is well, however, to record them again and in more detail from the standpoint of the Continental Community as a whole.

The Christian Democratic party rests on two basic norms: it is Christian, and it is liberally democratic. The two reinforce each other, making its Christianity Protestant as well as Catholic, even though the Roman Catholics are in the majority. Its liberal democracy derives from two sources. The first is the Stoic Roman continental code type of law, which explains the recurrent emphasis upon "the rule of law" in the treaties constituting the Schuman Plan, the Pleven Plan and the European Political Community. The second source is the liberalism of modern Continental Rationalistic philosophy—from which continental European liberalism derives, just as modern American and British liberalism is born of modern British Empirical philosophy.

It is to be recalled that continental philosophical liberalism was initiated by the French Roman Catholic Descartes and Malebranche, was carried forward by the Jewish Spinoza in the Netherlands and came to completion in the moral and legal philosophy of the German Protestant Leibniz and Kant. In short, the democratic liberalism of the continental Europeans is the joint creation of Christians and Jews, Catholics and Protestants, and Frenchmen, Netherlanders and Germans. For this reason Christian Democratic statesmen like Robert Schuman, Georges Bidault and Pierre-Henri Teitgen of France, Gaston F. Eyskens and Paul van Zeeland of Belgium, L. J. M. Beel and F. J. F. M. van Thiel of the Netherlands, Pierre Dupong and Joseph Bech of Luxembourg, Prime Ministers Giuseppe Pella, Alcide de Gasperi and Mario Scelba of Italy, and President Heuss, Chancellor Konrad Adenauer and Heinrich von Brentano of West Germany believe that they can work together and trust one another in building a supranational European Community that will keep both the Communist dictators of the Left and the chauvinistic Gaullist, Nazi and Fascist dictators of the Right under the control of Christian, Roman legal and modern liberal Continental Rationalistic democratic principles. For this reason also Protestant leaders like Queen Juliana and the Protestant Working Group of the Socialist party of the Netherlands, and Bishop Dibelius, Propst Asmussen and President Heuss of West Germany have worked shoulder to shoulder with the Roman Catholics in the Christian Democratic party to bring Continental European Union into being. The popular support of 33.66 per cent of the Continental Europeans—the largest for any Continental European Community party—shows that these Protestant and Catholic Christian Democratic statesmen have a basis for their trust.

The norms of the liberal Socialists also are liberal democratic and continental European rather than chauvinistically national in their content and quantitative support. Like the Christian Democrats, the liberal Socialist leaders have attended the European lycées and gymnasia—institutions which immerse their students in modern British empirical economic and political thought as well as modern Continental Rationalistic philosophy. Both traditions are normatively liberal. Bergsonian intuitionism and the sociology and socialism of Comte and Proudhon form part of the intellectual background and spiritual equipment of educated Continental Europeans.

It is not an accident that the more recent empiricism (*die reine Beschreibung*) of the Jewish German Husserl stems from the more rationalistic, mathematical physicist's way of knowing anything in terms of universal laws of Descartes, Leibniz and Kant rather than from the more purely inductive natural history scientists' sensed way of knowing of Bacon and Hume. Nor is it an accident that the Continental European mode of legal thinking is that of the rationalistic neo-Kantian Kelsen rather than that of the more inductive case-study type of law of the British empirical Austin and Bentham or the American pragmatically minded Holmes. It is from the more formal, rationalistic theoretical way of thinking about modern economic and political institutions and controls, instituted by the Continental Rationalistic philosophers and filled in with content by the Continental European sociologists and socialists, that the norms and the policies of the liberal Socialist parties of the six continental European nations take their common direction and their spiritual inspiration. Clearly, a supranational Continental European Community in which its second largest political party is based on such indigenous common values is not artificial, born of foreign dangers of the moment or mere economic advantage. Instead, it has common spiritual roots, nurtured over the centuries.

The third largest normative liberal political group is similar. We have called it the Liberal party. In France its largest member is the Radical Socialist party, whose radicalism is Pickwickian and derives from opposition to the King at the time of the French Revolution. In its economic norms it is similar to the Democratic and Republican parties in the United States. Its two contemporary French leaders are Edouard Herriot, the dean of living French statesmen and early protagonist of European collaboration, and René Pleven, the instigator of the European Defense Community and Minister of Defense in the Laniel government of 1953–1954. Normatively, its philosophy and political policy can be stated very simply: Its legal thinking, like that of all other Continental Europeans, is Stoic Roman as expressed in the French continental code. Its economic and political concept of liberty is rooted, like those of Great Britain, the Scandinavian nations and the United States, in British empirical, philosophical, economic and political thinkers and in Rousseau, all of whom at one time were considered to be revolutionists. This is the source of its "radicalism." Its concept of fraternity and justice, however, following the Socialist Proudhon (hence its "socialism"), is rooted in the moral and legal philosophy of Kant. As has been noted, French Radical Socialism is British empirical in its concept of liberty and Franco-German Rationalistic in its concept of fraternity and justice and in its emphasis on the rule of universal law. The Italian Liberal party, led after World War II by the philosopher Croce, affirms the same principles, as do the Belgian and Dutch Liberals and West German Free Democrats. Being in opposition to the Church as well as the King in the French Revolution, the Radical Socialist French liberals are intensely anticlerical, as was Proudhon, and thereby similar to the Protestant Liberal parties in the Netherlands and Germany. Clearly, there are common norms in the third largest political group in the supranational Continental European Community.

But there is even more common living law in the Continental European Community, viewed in its unity, than the common qualitative norms of the Christian Democratic parties, the Socialist parties and the Liberal parties of the six member nations exhibit independently. Between these three major liberal Continental European parties there are norms in common also, which have already been indicated and only need to be brought together: (1) the pluralistic theory of political and religious sovereignty; (2) the Stoic Roman, continental code, type of law and legal thinking; (3) secular Continental Rationalistic philosophical liberalism; (4) political anticlericism; and (5) the Christian personal religious faith.

It is important to note that the first, third and fourth of these basic normative principles for ordering the relations of men in society hold as much for the Roman Catholic leaders of the Christian Democratic party as for its Protestant leaders or for the leaders of the liberal Socialist and the Liberal parties. The identical Roman legal and secular modern Continental Rationalistic education of the Christian Democratic MM. Schuman, Adenauer and de Gasperi was noted in the previous chapter. The education of M. Spaak, the head of Belgium's Socialist party, is similar. Such an educational experience required all four to study Stoic Roman law and modern Continental Rationalistic philosophy, and every educated modern European has been steeped in both.

The practical significance of this, as previously noted, is that, although the major leaders of the Christian Democratic party are Roman Catholic in their personal living-law religious faith, they are secular and anticlerical in their legal and political philosophy and in their political conduct. This is why Chancellor Adenauer made it a condition for collaboration with the Christian Democratic leaders of the other five nations that they stand unequivocally for religious as well as political pluralism and so formulate their Christian democracy that Protestants as well as Roman Catholics would feel at home in it.

Nor is this attitude true only of Chancellor Adenauer among Christian Democratic leaders or due solely to his natural desire to have Protestants as well as Roman Catholics support his party's policy. It is just as true of the Italian people generally, who are almost entirely Roman Catholic, and of Alcide de Gasperi, the leader of the Italian Christian Democratic party, who has nothing to gain politically in Italy by appealing to Protestants. He commands the respect of liberal democratic leaders throughout Continental Europe, regardless of party affiliation, because his deeds conform to his liberal democratic convictions. Notwithstanding the fact that his Christian Democratic party unaided had a majority in the 1948 Italian election, he insisted upon bringing liberal Socialists, Republicans and Liberals into his government. Such are the ways in which the norms common to the three major, otherwise differing, liberal parties of Continental Europe bind the majority living law of this Community into a common living-law unity.

Table IV

THE RELIGIOUS NORMS OF THE
CONTINENTAL EUROPEAN COMMUNITY

Country	Population	Roman Catholics Number	%	Protestants et al. Number	%
Belgium	8,757,691	8,696,387	99.3	35,031	0.4
France	42,400,000	41,340,000	97.5	1,060,000	2.5
Italy	47,020,536	46,832,434	99.6	188,082	.4
Luxembourg	301,500	295,470	98.0	3,015	1.0
Netherlands	10,434,979	4,017,467	38.5	4,622,695	44.3
West Germany	48,478,000	21,912,056	45.2	24,578,346	50.7
	157,392,706	123,093,814	78.2	30,487,169	19.3

These figures have been computed from information in the *Information Please Almanac, 1954,* and the *Britannica Book of the Year, 1953.* The figures for Belgium are based on the number of clergy as no religious census is now taken. The figures for the Netherlands are those of the 1947 census.

The religious living law of the Continental European Community, when seen collectively, is equally important. Table IV expresses it in quantitative terms.

Table IV shows that at least three-quarters of the 157,000,000 people of the Continental European Community are Roman Catholics. As noted in Chapter 7, Roman Catholics probably now outnumber Protestants in the Netherlands. If they do, the Roman Catholic religious living-law majority in the Continental European Community is now more than 78 per cent. It is to be noted, also, that the Belgian religious statistics in the table are estimated.

We saw in Chapter 7 that Protestants and Catholics in West Germany and the Netherlands—the only countries of the Continental Community with large Protestant living-law religious groups—are collaborating in a major way in both the Christian Democratic and the Socialist parties. The resulting bond of unity in common political as well as Christian principles supplements the strong Roman Catholic religious living law that is common to the six nations; and it is quantitatively significant. Thus religious as well as political factors give the Continental European Community a common living law.

Only in West Germany, if the unofficial report of the increase in Roman Catholics in the Netherlands is correct, is the majority support of the religious norms slightly more Protestant than Roman Catholic; but never since Bismarck have Germans of the Roman Catholic faith formed so large a part of the population. This is why West Germany's largest political party is that of the Christian Democrats, whose leader and a majority of whose members are Roman Catholic in their personal religious faith. Also, as the foregoing examination of their political norms has shown, these West German Christian Democrats are secularly and liberally democratic in their legal thinking and in their political philosophy.

The practical significance of this religious and secular normative fact has not received the attention it merits. It means that in living law, as well as geographically, this is not the Germany of World Wars I and II. It is a new Germany—drawing its major moral, spiritual and political support and the political leadership of its largest party from the Roman Rhineland and Bavaria of western and southern Germany rather than from a secular Berlin-centered, Junker East Prussian Germany. This is what Chancellor Adenauer and his associates undoubtedly mean when they believe—as reported by M. S. Handler from Bonn—"that only by reorienting their historic trends will the German people avoid such great disasters as befell them in two world wars." [7] This is also what *The Economist* of London notes when it describes the norms of the Christian Democratic parties of Continental Europe as follows:

[Their] philosophy is distinct and moderate and probably, because of its religious bias, little understood in this country. Its Christian basis makes it an enemy to extreme nationalism and has undoubtedly strengthened its federal leanings. In economic affairs it is conservative, favouring private enterprise and fearing excessive state control; yet a strongly marked social philosophy makes it sympathetic to the claims of the trade unions to influence and status—as in Germany—to the need for social services—as in France—and not averse to some measure of radical change, such as the proposed land reform in Italy. . . .

These parties cannot be called clerical, for in the main they represent the activities of Catholic laymen in the political field and not the direct influence of ecclesiastical authority. This distinction can be most clearly seen in Italy where Signor de Gasperi has attempted, throughout his seven years of office, to govern in conjunction with a coalition of other moderate parties, including the small right wing of the Socialists. . . .[8]

Later, in 1953, this British periodical, with its customary objectivity, summarized the practical achievements and importance of Chancellor Adenauer and the Christian Democratic coalition in the statement that he had used his office

in a determined effort to change the whole trend of Germany's development from a nationalist, predatory, *eastward-looking power, dominated by Prussia*, and without a real friend in the world, into a firm base for a free, federated Western Europe.[9]

The Economist has noted also that Chancellor Adenauer has implemented his professions with deeds.[10]

Only such a westward-looking Germany, guided by (1) the Continental Roman legal mentality, (2) a politically influential Christian religious faith under secular leadership that is Roman Catholic in its majority support, yet Protestant also, and (3) modern secular Continental Rationalistic philosophical, political and fraternal thinking, can be effectively married to the French and the other Continental European peoples in a supranational Continental European Economic, Defense and Political Community. In short, it is because the Yalta Treaty and the later division of Germany have given the present free Germany major religious and secular living-law norms and political parties that are similar qualitatively and, in considerable part, quantitatively to those of the other five peoples in this Community, that Continental European Union has the necessary common spiritual basis and normative unity from within to be a practical venture in contemporary supranational statesmanship.

Once more, *The Economist* has analyzed the German problem in its relation to the European Defense Community and suggested the correct conclusion when it states:

The middle-aged men whose minds were formed in the Hitlerite era, and the Protestants who look towards Eastern Germany and are traditionally bound to a national state, are not very likely to produce a European leader who would tie Germany so closely to the western community. . . .

The time and the man are therefore at hand for forming a Germany that will not prove a menace to the world again. But the present constellation will never recur. If . . . the European army does not take practical shape, Germany may secure a national army with the aid of America, and so fall under the influence of the old-time militarists; and if the goal of political and economic federation does not offer the younger Germans an ideal and an opportunity for working off their dynamic energies, the drive to secure Germany's lost lands in the east will grow dangerously. . . . The timid will be tempted to take fright at Western Germany's strength. Before they are led into silly mistakes, let them ask themselves whether Germany's growing power—which is a fact—is better deployed on the side of European unity or better left to develop in nationalist ways of its own.[11]

It appears, therefore, that common living-law factors of both a religious and a political nature are present in West Germany and the other five Continental nations which, if given political expression by a sociologically realistic statesmanship, instead of left dormant, make the supranational Continental European Community both practical and wise.

Why, then, the recent French fears? Why, then, did the French, who first proposed the European Defense Community and who led in the installation of the European Coal and Steel Community, of a sudden in October 1952 attack both the European Defense Community and the foreign policy of the United States? And, why, two months later with the fall of the Pinay government, did the French dismiss from office Robert Schuman, who would participate in no government which did not stand for both EDC and Franco-American collaboration?

The attack upon the foreign policy of the United States as well as upon EDC suggests a possible answer. Could something have happened to the foreign policy of the United States in the latter half of 1952 which threatened to make the Continental European Community unrealistic from a living-law standpoint and hence both impractical and unwise? To answer this question, we must examine recent United States foreign policy.

Chapter 9

The Effect of U.S. Foreign Policy on Continental European Union

The importance of Continental European Union for United States foreign policy with respect to Communist expansion in both Europe and Asia was noted in Chapter 2. There is a converse effect of American foreign policy upon the practicality and wisdom of the Continental European Community which has not received the attention it deserves.

A reason for the adverse influence becomes evident when one discovers the questions that arise in the different countries when Continental European Union is proposed. The basic American query is, What effect will the European Defense Community have on containing or rolling back the Communist Russians? This expresses the fact that for Americans the major concern is military with respect to Communist Russia. The six Continental European nations can contain or roll back Communist Russia more effectively if they have a single army under a joint command, including German divisions, than if they act unilaterally or without the German divisions. Therefore, to Americans, the advisability of the European Community is obvious; and American statesmen—whether Democrats or Republicans—find it difficult to understand why any Continental Europeans hesitate. To refuse to unite seems to amount to an insistence upon being ineffective and inefficient.

To the Continental Europeans, however, the crucial questions are quite different. Moreover, the questions they ask differ from one

people to another. For the Italians there are two practical concerns:
(1) What effect will membership in the European Defense Community have upon Italy's overpopulation with respect to relatively
scarce raw materials and natural resources? (2) What effect will
membership have upon Italy's relations to Yugoslavia, and upon
Italian claims to Trieste and the related British-American election
promises of 1948. Of the two, the first question is the more fundamental and has the longer range; the second is the more volatile and
has the greater immediate popular appeal.

The first of these Italian questions points up a crucial considera-
tion that counts also for the other Continental European nations. It
is the essential connection between the European Defense Com-
munity, its Coal and Steel Community and the Political Community.
Italy's interest in the European Defense Community is secondary.
The Alps isolate her from a sudden attack by Soviet Russia. The
Italian army alone is likely to be capable of taking care of Marshal
Tito's army, particularly with the Adriatic between. Should Soviet
Russia move in North Europe, the Italians probably believe that
Britain, the United States and the five other Continental European
nations would stop her even if Italy were not a member of the Defense Community. Italy's main practical long-range reason for entering the European Defense Community is, therefore, to create a single
European economic and political community which will open the
whole of the Continental European Community to Italian workers,
thereby in considerable part at least solving Italy's pressing unem-
ployment and population problem. One of the younger, yet highly
influential, members of Premier de Gasperi's coalition government
summed up the matter to me in October 1952 as follows: "If Italians
have the duty to give their lives to defend Europe on the Rhine in
time of war, they have the right to employment there in times of
peace."

For this to occur, immigration barriers as well as tariff walls be-
tween the six Continental European Union nations must be removed.
Common European political action and hence a common Continental
European Political Community as well as a common Continental

European Economic Community will be required. An informed United States foreign policy with respect to Italy will give primary emphasis to the Political and Economic Communities of Continental European Union, making the European Defense Community secondary and incidental to the Economic and Political Community.

The Trieste affair and United States and British policy with respect to Yugoslavia raise a different concern in Italian minds. There is no point to Italian entrance into the Continental European Defense Community if the result would be to send Italian soldiers to the Rhine or East Prussia to contain or roll back some distant potential danger, leaving Italy defenseless before a nearer danger at home in Trieste and Yugoslavia. The European Defense Community is tied, by the very treaty which specifies its powers, to NATO, and hence to the foreign policy of Great Britain and the United States; and it follows that if Italy is to trust Continental European Union with respect to Yugoslavia and Trieste, it must be able to trust Great Britain and the United States on these matters.

The handling of the Trieste affair does not encourage such trust. In the 1948 Italian elections, Great Britain and the United States, guided by vote-catching considerations of power-politics expediency with respect to Soviet Russia, made certain promises to Italy regarding Trieste. The election having been won, they forthwith forgot about the promises and instead offered similar power-politics lures to Yugoslavia. This, as we have noted, undoubtedly contributed to Italy's lukewarm or negative reaction to the European Defense Community in the 1953 elections.

The major question which the European Defense Community raises in the minds of West Germans is different from that of the Americans or the Italians: What effect will membership in the Community have upon the 18,000,000 Germans in the Russian sector? Will German membership mean betraying them to a Communist dictatorship and perhaps consigning them to Soviet labor camps? In 1952, the second largest party in West Germany—the Socialist party —answered the latter in the affirmative. The Protestant leader, Pastor Niemöller, agreed, though for different reasons. Chancellor Adenauer's Protestant and Roman Catholic Christian Democratic coalition answered in the negative. When I was in Germany talking to Protestant and Roman Catholic religious leaders and the major party leaders, during five weeks of November and December 1952, it would have taken a brave prophet to predict the outcome. Apparently the spontaneous uprising of the laborers in East Berlin before the 1953 elections turned the scales in favor of the Christian Democratic coalition.

The almost terrifying, key question for the French is, What effect will the European Defense and Political Communities have on Franco-German relations? For the French, unlike the Americans, the basic European problem is something more than the Communist threat: it includes Germany, especially since the remarkable political and economic recovery of West Germany. The Soviet Russians are distant; the Germans are next door. I recall a conversation some two or three years ago with a former Assistant Secretary of State in President Hoover's administration, who had just returned by night plane from Paris. Two nights before, he had been walking with a member of the French Foreign Office on the Rue de Rivoli, opposite the Tuileries. As they neared the Place de la Concorde the Frenchman pointed out a ring fastened to a wall, saying, "Russian officers once tethered their horses there." He paused. "Yes! If the Russians are here today, they will be gone tomorrow. If the Germans are not here today, they will be back tomorrow." This is the way realistic Frenchmen tend to read history. For them the German problem is perhaps even more serious than the Communist Russian problem. West Germany's tremendous economic recovery has strengthened the feeling. On November 7, 1953, *The Economist* reported that "there is a growing belief on the Continent that the German is becoming a more urgent problem than the Russian." [1]

The Economist was quick to note, however, that this did not mean that France must reject the European Defense Community. It meant instead that French approval of the EDC will depend upon the wisdom of British and American foreign policy with respect to Germany.[2] It meant also that France must choose whether (a) to make

West Germany share the cost of the military defense of Western Europe, thereby bringing the West German economy more into equality with the French, and to encourage that nation to return to Luxembourg and Paris as one among six collaborators in the Continental European Community, or (b) to let West Germany rearm unilaterally and become a rival in a chauvinistic power-politics Europe.

The foregoing differences over Continental European Union prove two points: the primary United States interest in it is as an instrument within NATO for containing or rolling back Communism; the European peoples tend to be more interested in it as it affects matters nearer home. To the extent, therefore, that American foreign policy arouses fear that the United States will use EDC in ways opposed to their primary interest in it, the French and other Europeans become inclined to reject what they initially proposed and in part instituted, and what they would otherwise accept.

There is a second reason why a United States foreign policy which rests upon, and even insists upon, a European Defense Community within Continental European Union might none the less prevent its creation. Chapter 2 noted that a clause in the Treaty of May 27, 1952, which constituted the European Defense Community, was implemented by an accompanying NATO Protocol, and that the Protocol placed EDC within and under the command of NATO, which is focused on the United States rather than Europe. The Continental Europeans know also that, because of the heavier American military contributions, NATO's military authority, SHAPE, has been continuously commanded by a general from the United States.

This means that before the French, the Italians or any other of the six Continental European peoples can commit themselves to EDC they must be sure of two matters: First, that a supranational Continental European Community is realistic and practical from an inner, purely Continental European common living-law standpoint. This, the majority of Continental Europeans believed to be true, for the objective living-law reasons given in the previous chapter. Second, they must trust what the United States will do with EDC, particularly with respect to Tito and the Germans, through its domination of NATO and SHAPE.

Incidentally, certainty on both points, not merely for the present but also for the next fifty years, is as important to Dr. Adenauer and his Christian Democratic coalition vis-à-vis the German Socialists, Communists and Nazi Right, as to the other peoples in the Continental European Community. Should United States use of EDC in NATO be such as to bring the chauvinistic Nazi Right to power, the aims of Chancellor Adenauer and his majority following will suffer. Not only will Western Europe be in serious danger, but the liberal forces in Germany will be destroyed also.

These considerations show why the principles upon which American foreign policy rests need to be clear and dependable. There can be no serious conflict of opinion among Americans over foreign policy and United States use of NATO if the Europeans—Chancellor Adenauer's liberal Germans included—are to transfer sovereign national powers for fifty years to the supranational Continental European Community. Consequently, it is not only correct, as Secretary of State Dulles pointed out to the French in Paris on December 14, 1953, that failure of the French Parliament to authorize EDC would force a "painful reappraisal" of the foreign policy of the United States, but equally evident, as the French and other Europeans noted in the fall of 1952 and 1953, that any uncertainty or change in the basic principles of United States foreign policy forces Europeans to reappraise their initial judgment of the practicality and wisdom of EDC.

Once this is recognized, the simultaneous events in Continental Europe and in the United States, in and after the autumn of 1952, take on a new significance. Two points were noted in Chapters 1 and 2: (1) Continental European Union (in particular its Schuman and Pleven Plans) was initiated by Frenchmen and was carried forward step by step by the Europeans themselves, in the face of initial lukewarm support, if not positive opposition, by the British Labor and Conservative governments. (2) In the fourteen French governments from January 29, 1946, to December 22, 1952, Robert Schuman—

who would participate in no government which did not stand for Franco-German and Franco-American collaboration—was either Premier or Foreign Minister. Therefore every French government was of the same mind on foreign policy. This disposes of the notion prevalent outside of France that the French hesitations concerning EDC and Franco-American collaboration which began in the fall of 1952 are due to the incapacity of the French to agree long politically about anything. Every one of the fourteen French governments up to December of 1952 fell over differences on domestic policy; all fourteen were in complete agreement on foreign policy, including even the fourteenth, the Pinay government of March 8 to December 22, 1952—otherwise, M. Schuman would not have been its Foreign Minister.

Nor did the frequent government resignations over domestic policy suggest any serious turn against liberal democracy. As Chapter 8 shows, the French supply of liberal democratic coalitions is overgenerous rather than scanty; hence, the frequent shifts from one to another. Table II indicates that the popular support of liberal democracy outweighs that of Communist Left and Gaullist Right combined by the ratio of 51.4 to 48.3; and the poll in the summer of 1952 by the French Institute of Public Opinion, described in Chapter 1, showed that the majority of Frenchmen definitely favored defending Europe with a European army, and that "61 per cent believed the danger was less if German troops were incorporated into an international army." Moreover, 46 per cent of those voting favored EDC; only 22 per cent opposed it, the remainder being at the time undecided.[3] Such was the French and, it may be added, the European mind in June of 1952.

Only two or three weeks later, on the evening of July 11th, Dwight D. Eisenhower accepted the nomination by the Republican National Convention for the Presidency of the United States, stating his positive purpose as follows:

You have summoned me on behalf of millions of your fellow Americans to lead a great crusade—for freedom in America and freedom in the world. I know something of the solemn responsibility of leading a crusade. I have led one. . . . I will lead this crusade.[4]

Thus was born the Republican conception of United States domestic and foreign policy as a crusade. Mr. Eisenhower's next paragraphs specified the aims of the crusade, beginning: "To sweep from office an Administration which has fastened on every one of us . . . the bitter fruit of a party too long in power. . . . To achieve these aims we must have total victory." To this end he added that more Republicans must be placed in every branch of government.

Did this "total victory," sweeping all Democrats from office, mean that the bipartisan foreign policy of the Truman administration was to be either thrown aside or not implemented with the appointment of leading Democrats to high posts in its administration? Here was a question which arose immediately in European statesmen's minds. The frequent emphasis upon a "crusade" caused them to shudder a bit, especially following Senator McCarthy's and General MacArthur's speeches to the convention but a few days before arguing that the United States should drop collaboration with her allies for a go-it-alone foreign policy both in Europe and across the Yalu in Asia.

Mr. Eisenhower's next paragraph was not too reassuring: "Today is the first day of this great battle. The road that leads to November 4th is a fighting road. In that fight I will keep nothing in reserve." Did this mean that the Republican candidate might now send into battle Senator McCarthy's, General MacArthur's, and Senator Taft's conceptions of foreign policy? Then to the dropping of influential Democrats from key posts in the implementation of United States foreign policy would be added a lack of collaboration between Democrats and Republicans at home and lack of consultation with allies abroad. Were decisions affecting Europe to be made the football of domestic American politics, instead of being treated objectively, in a bipartisan manner through allied collaboration, in terms of the living-law realities of the European situation, then European collaboration with the United States in the U.N. with respect to

Asia and in NATO with regard to Europe and the rearming of the Germans in EDC within NATO would take on an entirely new light.

Mr. Eisenhower's speech in Chicago on July 11, 1952, raised every one of these queries in the minds of Europe's statesmen. To imagine otherwise would be completely to underestimate their acuteness, realism and intelligence. Europeans followed every major address in the election campaign with the closest attention. I was in their midst at the time. Furthermore, the interest was not that of disinterested spectators; it was that of people who felt that their fate, more even than that of the Americans who were not so near Germany and Moscow, depended on the result.

Would Mr. Eisenhower, if he came to power, follow the Truman policy and implement foreign policy with Democrats as well as Republicans so that, regardless of domestic politics, Americans generally could agree on foreign policy, and Europeans could therefore count on it for the twenty-five years they were committed to NATO and perhaps even the fifty years to which membership in EDC would commit them? Or would the Republican party, coming to power, accept, or be neutralized by, its two midwestern (Taft-Jenner-Bricker isolationist and MacArthur-McCarthy military showdown) go-it-alone wings? In that case, would United States foreign policy decisions affecting Europe and Asia be made unilaterally or perhaps, even worse, hang fire to be set off by some sudden act of a President Rhee or some passionate outburst of the moment? Such a situation would, through the tie of EDC to NATO, take the rearmed Germans in EDC not merely out of French, but out of European, hands.

The answers to these European queries soon began to come in, and they were not too reassuring. Instead of waiting for the defeated candidate to offer congratulations upon the victory, as is customary, the victorious Republican candidate at Chicago called upon Senator Taft. The late Senator was the epitome, in European minds at least, of isolationism and a go-it-alone foreign policy. A few weeks later there was the famous breakfast with the Ohio Senator on Morningside Heights.

Gradually, to Europeans at the time, the pattern was becoming clear, which Americans did not see until the Stevens affair in 1954. Paul Hoffman, who helped launch the Eisenhower boom, and Senator Henry C. Lodge, who won the nomination for Mr. Eisenhower at Chicago, ceased to appear in the campaign pictures of the candidate, and Senators Taft, Jenner and McCarthy took their place. Clearly, for the purpose of winning the election at least, the nominee was disassociating himself from Republicans who stood for collaboration with allies in foreign policy and was associating himself instead with the midwestern Republicans who stood for a go-it-alone foreign policy.

Meantime Senator McCarthy was becoming a more vocal Republican campaign orator. Not only had he charged the previous administration with naming traitors to high posts in the Department of State but he branded Mr. Eisenhower's revered colleague, General Marshall, with being one also. To the junior Senator from Wisconsin at least, Mr. Eisenhower's "crusade" and "total victory" over the Democrats meant not merely a rejection of collaboration of the United States with her allies but also the sabotage of the bipartisan foreign policy upon which Europeans could depend. As W. H. Lawrence, the Washington political correspondent, noted in *The New York Times* of February 28, 1954, the crucial, initial showdown had come in Peoria, Illinois, on October 2, 1952. General Eisenhower was about to enter the state of Wisconsin. He had in his pocket a speech already written, to be delivered at Milwaukee, which combined an endorsement of Senator McCarthy "with an attack upon Senator McCarthy's methods" and "a glowing endorsement of his old friend, General of the Army George C. Marshall." Furthermore, that evening in Peoria, when General Eisenhower, Senator McCarthy and the Republican National Chairman, Arthur E. Summerfield, were closeted together about an hour, "some of Eisenhower's exuberant aides were telling newsmen through the night that the nominee had a first-rate speech for Milwaukee which included the high praise to Marshall as a direct rebuke to Senator McCarthy." [5]

Suffice it to say that when the Republican candidate for President delivered the address the paragraph in praise of his good friend General Marshall was not in it. Mr. Lawrence concluded later that "it was General Eisenhower, not Senator McCarthy, who gave ground," that "from that time on, McCarthy had little fear of Dwight Eisenhower," and that "Senator McCarthy has gone on from there to one victory after another over the Eisenhower Administration," culminating in February 1954 when Secretary of the Army Stevens failed to receive the support from the White House necessary for maintaining his initial stand against the Senator with respect to the latter's treatment of General Zwicker.

European statesmen were unaware in 1952 of the behind-the-scenes meeting in Peoria or of the fruits of the meeting which were to show themselves in 1953 and 1954. Nevertheless, observation of the nominee's association with the go-it-alone wings of the Republican party during the election campaign made them uneasy about rearming the Germans in a European Defense Community that was tied through NATO to the foreign policy of the United States. This showed in increasing neutralism and anti-Americanism in Europe. The first dramatic official reaction came in France on October 17, 1952, when the pioneer of European and allied collaboration, Edouard Herriot, reversed the position on European Union he had maintained since 1930, by attacking both the European Defense Community and French collaboration with the United States in foreign policy generally. His tying the two together was significant. It showed that French change of mind about the rearming of the Germans in EDC was essentially connected with a similar change of mind concerning the dependability of the foreign policy of the United States.

During the American election campaign one other thing was happening. Mr. John Foster Dulles, whose name was linked with that of Mr. Eisenhower as his likely Secretary of State, was attacking the Truman policy of containing Communism as merely negative and defensive, and was outlining a dynamic roll-back policy that made European statesmen shiver even more than Mr. Eisenhower's earlier militant crusade. Add together McCarthyism and MacArthurism and the militant crusade and the dynamic roll-back, and one had the Continental European mind which was developing in the last four months of 1952. As the experienced European observer C. L. Sulzberger reported in *The New York Times* of April 18, 1954:

To Europe the name Dulles a year ago meant "rollback" and "liberation." These in turn implied determination to push the imperial realm of communism back inside the 1939 borders of the U.S.S.R.—regardless of the risk of war. Europeans were terrified at this prospect and feared that an effort to compress the Soviet empire was going to precipitate another conflict.[6]

Why did the "Dulles dynamism," as Europe called it, have this deleterious effect upon both the European Defense Community and European collaboration with the United States in foreign policy? Was not Mr. Dulles, fresh from the National Council of the Churches of Christ, a morally principled and responsible man? Was it not an essential part of his and Mr. Eisenhower's conception of foreign policy that it must be morally principled and something definite, not shifting about with every flurry of the moment, upon which both the American people and America's friends abroad could count? Had not both he and his superior asserted that opportunism was to be replaced with integrity and constancy of purpose?

The reason usually given for the Europeans' negative reaction to the Eisenhower crusade and the Dulles roll-back dynamism is McCarthyism. That this was a factor, and a most serious one, is not to be doubted. However, it was not the only factor or the major one.

Europeans knew very well that the junior Senator from Wisconsin did not represent the Democrats, the Taft-Bricker isolationist Republicans or the Eastern internationalist Republicans, and that as a consequence, for all the noise he made, he spoke at best only for a minority of Americans. Not so with the Republican Presidential candidate and his likely Secretary of State. Not only might they express the mandate of tomorrow's majority, but the sober, moral, conservative, Christian, rather than merely chauvinist demagogic, voice of America seemed to be speaking in Mr. Dulles and in Mr. Eisenhower. Hence anything that these men said which was disturbing to Europeans left a far greater impression upon them than did even Senator McCarthy, bad as his effect was.

Near the end of the summer of 1952, Mr. Eisenhower gave a major address on foreign policy. The *Listener* of London, on September 4, 1952, reported the European reaction as follows:

> Commentators in western Europe, for the most part, were critical of Mr. Eisenhower's speech. . . . This disapproval centred on the fact that the western nations were united under the Atlantic Pact to resist Soviet imperialism in a military *defensive* alliance, and not one committed to the liberation of the enslaved nations by war. Other commentators pointed out that Mr. Eisenhower was not advocating their liberation by war, but that his policy—if put into operation and not considered as merely electioneering—would seem to involve the risk of war. Many commentators, therefore, gave a more favourable reception to Mr. Stevenson's speech. As the conservative *Le Figaro* was quoted as saying:
> "The language used by Stevenson tends to recognize that Europe has a right to decide what policy it is to pursue towards the Soviet Union. The Atlantic Pact is an instrument for the containment of Communism, and cannot become an instrument for pushing it back." [7]

The key to the above European reaction to Mr. Eisenhower's conception of United States foreign policy is to be found in the word "*defensive*," which the British editor put in italics. It points up the fact that the NATO Treaty, both in its literal purposes and in the de facto commitments which it places upon its members, is a defensive, not an offensive, alliance. Clearly, therefore, if Mr. Eisenhower were to determine foreign policy, collaboration with the United States would involve much more than Europeans had agreed to at Washington, D.C., on April 4, 1949, in signing the NATO Treaty.

But Mr. Eisenhower's major election campaign speech on foreign policy was even more disturbing to Europeans. It also was incompatible with Article 8 of the NATO Treaty. This is what *Le Figaro* meant when it said that the Atlantic Pact "cannot" be turned from a defensive into an offensive alliance.

Article 8, reading,

Each Party declares that none of the international engagements now in force between it and any other of the Parties or any third state is in conflict with the provisions of this Treaty, and undertakes not to enter into any international engagement in conflict with this Treaty,[8]

was put in the NATO Treaty for two reasons: (1) Many people in free Europe feared that NATO would generate a Soviet attack, rather than defend the West from such a danger. The creators of NATO saw that these criticisms would be valid if NATO were offensive, because Russia then would be justified in self-defense in meeting an offensive from the West with an offensive against the West. (2) Europeans were also mindful of Germany. As a consequence, Great Britain and France had, and still have, mutual defense pacts with the Soviet Union protecting the three nations from the risk of a revived Nazi Germany. Having just gone through a debilitating war to rid themselves of such a menace, Great Britain and France naturally did not want the NATO defense against possible Russian aggression to be at the cost of defense against the possible revived Nazi German aggression which their defensive pacts with the Soviet Union provided. Both of these would be possible so long as NATO remained purely defensive; hence, Article 8 of the NATO Treaty.

At the time the NATO Treaty was signed the French Foreign Minister, Robert Schuman, made a public speech, pointing out to Soviet Russia, to the people of France and to the rest of free Europe that, because the Treaty was explicit in being merely defensive, it in no way threatened Russia and hence in no way increased the grounds for, or the danger of, an attack from Russia and was therefore quite compatible with the similar treaties of mutual defense between Great Britain, France and the Soviet Union which gave protection against a revived Nazi Germany.[9]

Commitment through collaboration in a NATO alliance led, even dominated, by a United States under the Truman administration whose foreign policy with respect to Communism was containment and whose aims for NATO therefore were strictly defensive was one thing—a thing which Europeans had accepted gladly and were hoping to continue. The proposal of the Republican Presidential candidate to turn NATO from a merely defensive organization into a Dullesian dynamic offensive alliance was, however, a radically different thing, which made further collaboration with the United States questionable. Incompatible with Article 8 of the NATO Treaty, it would threaten Russia, thereby (a) justifying a Russian attack in self-defense and (b) destroying the French-British-Russian mutual defense pacts, so that the three nations would lose their protection against the dangers of a remilitarized Nazi Germany.

Similarly, for the French to rearm the Germans in an EDC tied through the NATO Protocol of May 27, 1952, to a purely defensive United States foreign policy with respect to Communism was one thing—the thing the French had in mind when they proposed EDC and introduced the Schuman Plan and Franco-German collaboration generally. To rearm the Germans, however, in an EDC which was tied through NATO to an offensive United States foreign policy with respect to Russia, and which would therefore destroy the French-Russian mutual defense pact against the danger of a rearmed Germany, was quite a different thing. Such a price was perhaps too great to pay for Franco-German and Franco-American collaboration.

The French response was almost instantaneous. A few weeks after Mr. Eisenhower's major election campaign speech on foreign policy, the French, no doubt agonizingly, had reappraised their position on both EDC and Franco-American collaboration in foreign policy generally. The dean of French statesmen, M. Herriot, arose and attacked both. Forthwith, neutralism and anti-Americanism increased continuously in intensity in Europe.

Temporarily in October of 1952, Franco-German collaboration in Continental Europe and Franco-American collaboration in the

United Nations to police the peace of the world against Communist aggression in both Europe and Asia were saved by an ultimatum to the Pinay government from the Christian Democratic party in its coalition. It informed Premier Pinay that if he wanted Christian Democratic support for the Pinay-Herriot domestic policy of his government, he must keep the Christian Democrat Robert Schuman in the Foreign Office and pursue the latter's foreign policy. After the Eisenhower election victory, however, so great became the neutralism and anti-Americanism in France that the Pinay government fell on December 22, 1952, and M. Schuman left the Foreign Office. The Mayer and the Laniel governments which followed in 1953 and 1954 could obtain a majority only by including Gaullists; and, although M. Bidault, a believer in both Franco-German and Franco-American collaboration, was Foreign Minister, loss of the Gaullist support would have brought their fall had they attempted to act as Mr. Bidault felt. Furthermore, in the weeks between the fall of the Mayer government and the establishment of the Laniel government, when no proposed coalition could obtain a majority, one attempt to form a government, committed to collaboration with the Communists on foreign policy, missed a parliamentary majority by only a few votes. M. Mendes-France was its head.

Prime Minister Churchill, reacting similarily to the Eisenhower foreign policy, pointed out in 1953 that if war was to be avoided it was as necessary to allay Russian fears of an attack from the rearmed Germans and the West as it was to allay the fears of Dr. Adenauer's liberal Germans and of the other liberals of the West of an offensive attack from the Russians.[10] Chancellor Adenauer agreed. Even as late as January of 1954, the Chancellor emphasized that: "The entire structure of EDC is designed to make it a purely defensive organization. . . . This limitation . . . constitutes an essential security factor for the Eastern neighbors of the Defense Community." [11] Through June of 1952 the Truman policy of containment, combined with Article 8 of the NATO Treaty, which made both NATO and EDC strictly defensive, and the British-Russian, French-Russian mutual security pacts, had gone far to allay both of these fears and to make possible the rearming of the Germans in EDC without too great danger. The Eisenhower and Dulles' pronouncements intensified both Russian and Western European fears and made the rearming of the Germans in EDC more dangerous.

It may be thought that this widespread European reaction was premature and based upon superficial evidence—the superficial evidence resulting from taking Mr. Eisenhower's and Mr. Dulles' campaign statements, made for domestic political purposes, as expressions of what they proposed to do in fact if given positions of responsibility with respect to the foreign policy of the United States. Much European opinion came to this interpretation late in 1953 and especially after Mr. Dulles' conciliatory attitude toward Mr. Molotov at Berlin in February of 1954. For example, *The Economist* of London, on October 31, 1953, and also on January 23, 1954, reported that Mr. Dulles had gone a considerable way to restoring in the European mind the damage done to European-American collaboration by his dynamism.[12] Nevertheless, the damage was done. Furthermore, Mr. Eisenhower's behavior in the Presidential campaign of 1952 and his first deeds upon taking office do not fit the theory that his fascination with the word "crusade" and Mr. Dulles' dynamic roll-back language were designed merely to catch Republican votes.

Mr. Walter Lippmann pointed out in the Republican *New York Herald Tribune* of September 5, 1950, that there are two opposing Republican traditions in foreign policy. The earlier tradition was that of President Theodore Roosevelt. It was dynamic, affirming the need to carry a "big stick" which would permit the United States to act on its own unilaterally, with no need of conferring with other nations. Instead, it told them what to do and had the military strength to implement its telling as guided by purely American considerations. Mr. Lippmann noted also that it had a touch of imperialism, as Theodore Roosevelt's methods of acquiring the Panama Canal and pursuing America's destiny in the Philippines suggest.[13] General MacArthur and Senator McCarthy, and probably also Senator Knowland and Vice President Nixon, derive from this tradition in foreign policy.

The other Republican tradition in foreign policy, Mr. Lippmann noted, took its inspiration from the Ohio Republican machine of the Harding era. Initiated in the 1920's by President Harding and carried on by Presidents Coolidge and Hoover, it was not merely anti-imperialistic, but stood for doing even less abroad than President Woodrow Wilson attempted through the League of Nations and President Truman accomplished through the United Nations in Korea. Thus it was that Senator Taft of Ohio thought it had been a mistake to send American boys to Korea in 1950. From the same tradition came Senator Bricker, with his Constitutional amendment to curb the President's power in foreign affairs. In the same tradition also are Herbert Hoover and all the Republicans who would balance the budget and freeze the national debt, regardless of the Communist danger and military needs abroad. They are quite consistent, being isolationists in foreign policy; for them there are no military needs abroad—at least not until it may be too late.

When the Republican General Eisenhower returned to civilian life after World War II, with many urgings to run for President, he chose to make his residence neither in his childhood state of Kansas nor in Ohio, but in New York, and to associate himself with the Republican tradition of that state. John Foster Dulles comes from the Theodore Roosevelt New York Republican tradition; not from the Ohio one.

For Theodore Roosevelt, as for his protégé General MacArthur, not merely the destiny but even the Western military frontier of the United States was in the Philippines and Asia. When, therefore, General MacArthur attempted, as United Nations Commander in Korea, to revive the dynamic Asian foreign policy of his model, the dramatic Teddy Roosevelt, he met two embarrassments. One, everyone has noticed: the recall by President Truman, which was required by the go-it-together-with-one's-allies U.N. containment policy and the purely defensive character of the NATO Treaty. The other embarrassment seems to have been noticed only by Walter Lippmann, in the *New York Herald Tribune* article already cited: "One of his embarrassments is that the old guard Republican leaders in Congress are political survivors and heirs of the three isolationist

Presidents [Harding, Coolidge and Hoover] who disarmed in the western Pacific and withdrew to Hawaii."

Notwithstanding this incompatibility, the Republican foreign policies of the Taft-Bricker-Jenner-Hoover Ohio tradition and of the McCarthy-MacArthur-Roosevelt New York tradition have one thing in common: each is a go-it-alone policy. They correspond in short to the foreign policies of the Right-wing parties in the Continental European nations, which we have noted. This is why both the Taft-Bricker-Jenner group and the group including General MacArthur, the Bull Moose, and Senator McCarthy are opposed to a go-it-together-with-one's-allies foreign policy; and because of it Senator Taft had the wholehearted support of Senator McCarthy and General MacArthur at the 1952 Republican convention in Chicago.

But whereas the Taft-Bricker-Jenner-Hoover Republicans of the Ohio tradition would do less than the Truman administration had done, withdrawing behind Hawaii, leaving Koreans, Chinese, French and Germans to themselves and keeping American boys at home during breaches of the peace in Europe or Asia, the MacArthur-Knowland-McCarthy Republicans, acting equally unilaterally, would do more abroad than the Truman administration with its go-it-to-gether-with-one's-allies *defensive* foreign policy. These Teddy Roosevelt Republicans would not merely have kept in Korea the boys sent there by President Truman; they would also have sent more after them in bombers flying across the Yalu into China.

Senator Taft reconciled his Harding-era Republican tradition with the contradictory Theodore Roosevelt Republican position of General MacArthur by saying that, while he thought sending American boys to Korea to protect President Rhee and the South Koreans from aggression had been an error, the Korean affair should now be fought through to a military victory as General MacArthur affirmed. The important thing to be noted is that both the late Senator Taft and General MacArthur, while self-contradictory, agreed in their unilateral nationalism and in the rejection of a go-it-together-with-one's-allies foreign policy and agreed also about what should be done in Korea once President Truman had ordered General MacArthur there. They differed only over whether American soldiers should have been sent to South Korea in the first place and whether the United States should establish military outposts in Asia and Europe (as General MacArthur affirmed), or keep American boys at home, relying for defense largely on a bomb-carrying air force (as Senator Taft and former President Hoover maintained).

Their agreement upon a war to the finish in Korea made European-American collaboration in EDC, NATO and the United Nations an exceedingly dangerous thing, in the opinion of Europeans. Europeans noted also that, once the Korean affair was settled or stalemated, the Taft-Hoover Republican foreign policy would, on the other hand, destroy both NATO and an effective U.N. by forbidding any further commitment of American troops to either Asia or Europe. (This, in fact, was the point of the later Bricker amendment.) European statesmen saw all these conflicts in Republican foreign policy in 1952. When the Republican Presidential nominee rejected the MacArthur position for Korea, at least by announcing that he would go to Korea himself and do everything in his power to get the boys home from there "with honor," Europe had to reckon with the possibility that the Taft-Hoover isolationist Republican foreign policy would triumph and that the United States would let down the United Nations and NATO as it had let down the League of Nations in the era of Presidents Harding, Coolidge and Hoover. Were this to occur, rearming the Germans in EDC would also take on a new and ominous light.

Mr. Eisenhower's position with respect to United States foreign policy, like that of the Eastern Republicans who had won the nomination for him at Chicago, and *The New York Times* which supported him, corresponded neither to that of Senators Taft and Bricker and Mr. Hoover nor to that of General MacArthur and Senator McCarthy, and of course the Europeans knew it. But even if he should be elected he would have the support of no more than a third of his party in his personal foreign policy of collaboration with the rest of the free world in NATO, SHAPE and the UN to police Communist aggression anywhere. Two-thirds of his party— the two-thirds with the senior committee posts in the House of Representatives and the Senate—would be against him. Can a President lead, or be depended upon, in foreign policy who has but a third of his party on his side and must depend upon the majority in the opposition party for Congressional support? This is difficult under the best of circumstances. It would be especially difficult for a man who had committed himself in his speech accepting the Republican nomination to crusade as unreservedly against Democrats as against Communists, and who had located the ills of his countrymen in foreign affairs in the "negative," merely defensive foreign policy of the opposition party.

The situation was made even worse on November 4. Then Mr. Eisenhower's and Campaign Manager Brownell's earlier unfortunate decision at Chicago and Peoria to disassociate themselves in public from Paul Hoffman and Henry Cabot Lodge and to associate with the midwestern go-it-alone Senators Taft, Jenner and McCarthy bore its tragic fruit. An incredible thing happened—so incredible that it has not received the attention it deserves: Senator Lodge, who had won the Republican nomination for Mr. Eisenhower at Chicago, was defeated for reelection in the Commonwealth of Massachusetts, leaving no Republican member of the United States Senate with seniority who stood with the President elect for collaboration in foreign policy with the Democrats at home and with allies abroad. Thanks to Senator Lodge, Mr. Eisenhower had won the Republican nomination at Chicago; but, thanks to the defeat of Senator Lodge, the midwestern go-it-alone foreign policies had won the election and the control of Congress. Dwight D. Eisenhower was the leader of the Republican party in name but not in fact.

Mr. Lodge, the one Republican Senator with seniority on the crucial committees, who had voted beside the Democrats against the midwestern go-it-alone Republicans to approve the Marshall Plan, the NATO Treaty, the Korean action, a strong air force and allied collaboration generally, was not in the Senate to provide senior support for the President's version of foreign policy. With one exception, the midwestern Republican machine Senators, who opposed (1) collaboration with our allies, (2) the foreign policy of President Eisenhower the individual, and (3) the Democrats, held the chairmanship of every major committee in the Senate. Moreover, Senator Lodge's defeat in Massachusetts meant that the go-it-together-with-allies portion of the Massachusetts Republican machine, symbolized by him and Senator Saltonstall, was smashed, and that the Taft wing represented by Representative Joseph Martin had won. Mr. Martin was to be the Speaker of the House of Representatives.

European statesmen saw these facts and their implications on November 5, 1952, even if most Americans did not. Although Europeans believed in President Eisenhower, could they believe in what his Republican Congress and Senator McCarthy would permit him to do?

President Eisenhower's acts on taking office did little to reassure them. Without consulting either the United Nations or the European allies, he first ordered the withdrawal of the United States Fleet from the Straits of Formosa and permitted Chiang Kai-shek on Formosa to attack the Chinese mainland. This fitted the MacArthur-McCarthy version of United States foreign policy rather than the Eastern Republican, go-it-together-with-allies, supposedly Eisenhower policy. Immediately a storm broke loose in the British Parliament. Public opinion was so aroused that in order to maintain their hold on their own parties, the two arch-champions of British-American collaboration, former Prime Minister Attlee and Prime Minister Churchill, found it necessary to attack the United States openly on the floor of the House of Commons.

Another early act of President Eisenhower was to replace General Omar N. Bradley with Admiral Arthur W. Radford as Chairman of the Joint Chiefs of Staff. On military grounds, General Bradley had opposed treating the action of the United States and the United Nations in Korea as anything more than a defensive containment policy. Speaking in Hong Kong as a private citizen some few weeks before, Admiral Radford had expressed opinions more in accord with General MacArthur's and Senator McCarthy's foreign policy.[14]

On January 27, 1953, Secretary of State Dulles said in a radio and television address: "President Eisenhower has often used a phrase, which I would like to pick up here, the phrase is 'enlightened self-interest.' That is going to be our guide in the making of our foreign policy." These words suggested that the previous administration had based its policy too much on what other nations wanted, and that the new administration was going to make the interests of the United States alone its guiding principle. To be sure Mr. Dulles added in a later paragraph: "In our own interest we have to pay close attention to what is going on in the rest of the world and we need to have friends and allies." [15] None the less, the implementation of the words was not reassuring.

Two facts in particular disturbed the Europeans. The first was the failure of President Eisenhower and Secretary of State Dulles to implement their "bipartisan foreign policy" by appointing outstanding Democrats to key posts in the administration after the manner in which President Truman had implemented the previous bipartisan foreign policy by appointing such Republicans as Henry L. Stimson, Robert A. Lovett, Paul Hoffman, Senator Warren Austin, John J. McCloy and even John Foster Dulles and Mr. Eisenhower himself. This showed that, however bipartisan the foreign policy of the Eisenhower administration might be verbally, and in dependence on Democratic votes for passage, it was not to be bipartisan, and hence above domestic politics, in implementation. Only Republicans were to implement it.

The second disturbing fact was the refusal to appoint the distinguished career diplomat George F. Kennan to even a minor ambassadorial post, notwithstanding the Europeans' high estimation of his ability, his knowledge and understanding of both the theory and the practice of Communism and his dramatically demonstrated, publicly expressed opposition to its ways. Moreover, President Eisenhower's Secretary of State made it clear that the resignation of Mr. Kennan was accepted because of speeches in which he had pointed out the dangers, both to allied collaboration and to the peace of the world, of turning the collaboration from a defensive into an offensive instrument. Europeans could hardly interpret this as anything other than a determination upon the part of President Eisenhower and Secretary Dulles to proceed with their dynamic roll-back crusade.

Whether the Europeans judged all the foregoing facts correctly is a secondary concern. The important thing is the fact that during these times neutralism and anti-Americanism increased continuously throughout the whole of Europe, embracing Great Britain as well as the Continent.

Perhaps the most disturbing deed of all was the speech by President Eisenhower early in his administration threatening to tear up the Yalta Agreement. To most Americans this probably did not seem to be very upsetting. When they think of this proposal, the release of the Czechoslovakians and the fulfillment of allied promises made in World War II to the Poles come to mind. To every informed citizen and realistic statesman in Europe, something quite different comes to mind. The following experience will make this clear.

In the fall of 1952, interviewing the major political and religious leaders of Europe on the social and cultural foundations of Continental European Union, I was struck again and again in the different capitals by the impressive effect that the release of the German foreign-trade statistics (mentioned earlier) was having on European statesmen. The remarkable recovery which the figures showed made Europeans realize that, economic strength being potential military strength, Germany would no longer be a secondary power in Western Europe. As *The Listener* of London noted a year later, following Chancellor Adenauer's smashing victory in the German federal election of September 6, 1953, "Germany has come to control the destinies of Europe." [16]

To marry such a Germany in the European Defense Community was disturbing enough to France. Even so, with Saar coal tied to Lorraine steel, as it would be under the Schuman Plan, France could hope to carry sufficient weight along with Belgium and the Netherlands to prevent West Germany from becoming the dominant economic factor in the Continental European Community. Imagine the consternation of the French and all other Europeans when President Eisenhower suggested tearing up the Yalta Agreement. This meant that the *aim* of EDC as used by the United States through NATO would be not merely the unification of Germany to include the Russian sector west of the Oder-Neisse upon which all Europeans were agreed, but also the addition of East Prussia and the restoration of the old Germany. Certainly no one can be so naïve as to suppose that German troops in the EDC would release the East Prussian Germans, the Czechs and the Poles east of the Oder-Neisse only to turn the East Prussians over to the Czechs and the Poles. But if this did not occur the effect of the aim of United States foreign policy, even though accomplished peacefully, as Secretary Dulles tried to assure the Europeans, would be to add East Prussia and Silesia to the economic strength of West Germany, creating a Germany which would dominate the Continental European Community economically, politically and militarily, instead of being merely a coequal partner with the other members.

Even worse, it would result in Prussia and East Prussia dominating Germany as well. Thus, the effect of President Eisenhower's threat to tear up the Yalta Agreement and of Mr. Dulles' dynamism, even if the aims of both were achieved peacefully, would be to restore the old Germany with the traditional East Prussian-Nazi leadership. The living law of such a Germany would not be that of the other five Continental European nations and would not, therefore, sustain Continental European Union. Consequently, it would destroy the present liberal democratic German leadership and be as fatal for the German people as for the rest of the free world.

Furthermore, no European believes that the result would be freedom for the Czechoslovakians and the Poles. Instead, it would merely shift them from domination by the Russians to domination by the East Prussian Junkers and the Nazis, thereby returning Europe to the point at which it found itself in 1939 when World War II had to be fought.

The heart of the matter was expressed to me on October 30, 1952, but five days before Mr. Eisenhower was elected President of the

United States. The place was the national headquarters in Paris of the largest French liberal party.

In the outer reception office was displayed a huge statement in letters four or five inches high to the following effect: "Any statesman who is unwilling to transfer specified sovereignty from his own nation to the European Community is incompetent to lead in the Twentieth Century." Beneath this statement was the word "Blum." Léon Blum, it will be recalled, was one of the four Honorary Presidents who launched the European Movement immediately following its meeting at the Hague in May of 1948. These words would hardly have been there if Guy Mollet, his successor as the leader of the liberal Socialist party of France, had not shared the thought. Let it also be recalled that M. Mollet delivered practically en masse the 105 Socialist votes in the French Parliamentary vote on the Schuman Plan.

A few minutes after I had read the words, M. Mollet spoke approximately as follows: "My fear of a rearmed Germany—and I believe I speak here for the majority of my countrymen and of Europeans—is not that for a fourth time in a period of one hundred years the Germans will attack France. I believe that both the Germans and the French have had enough of fighting and destroying each other in every generation. My fear, instead, is that the Germans, pushed on from behind in the name of the American way of life and Christian civilization, will pull the rest of Europe, through EDC, into a holy crusade, nominally to release the satellites, but actually to win back East Prussia, thereby restoring the East Prussian Junker Nazis to power. Most of the people of free Europe are willing to lay down their lives to defend the present free nations of Europe; but very few are willing to give their lives to a foreign policy which they believe will have the practical effect of restoring the former Nazi Germany to power."

The crucial reason for this prevalent European judgment of the conditions under which collaboration of France with Germany and with the United States is practicable appeared in an earlier remark by M. Mollet, already noted, to the effect that, whereas its economic and military advantages in stopping Communism can be occasions for and by-products of Continental European Union, they cannot be its basis: the basis must be common living-law beliefs and norms.

The previous chapters have shown that the common political and religious norms, with approximately similar quantitative support, that are essential for an effective supranational Continental European Defense and Political Community, exist in the present West Germany and the other five Continental European nations. The norms and their quantitative support would not be too greatly disturbed by the addition of the eighteen million Germans in the Russian sector. It is upon these common norms that the statesmen of the six nations have based their faith in the practicality of this supranational community.

Moreover, the majority of Frenchmen are prepared to marry the present West Germany with its present qualitative and quantitative religious and political normative controls. This, the French and the other Europeans were willing to do because West Germany, from 1946 through early 1954 at least, was made westward-looking by the majority Roman Catholic religious living law and the Roman Stoic and Continental Rationalistic secular norms of its largest party. Neither the French nor anyone else in Europe will, however, marry an eastward-looking Germany in the European Defense Community.

The reason why Europe went first neutralist and then anti-American, losing even its momentum toward Continental European Union, should therefore now be clear. The shift in United States foreign policy from containing Communism to rolling it back, announced in the fall of 1952, would have, in the opinion of Europeans, the practical effect of turning the Germans from a westward-minded to an eastward-minded people. The Germans with such a mind are the old Germans, a majority of whom put the arbitrary demands of the chauvinistic will of the German *Volk* above law-abiding reason and Continental European values.

As *The Economist* of London pointed out on August 16, 1952:

Without the efforts of M. Schuman, Dr Adenauer and Signor de Gasperi, the Schuman Plan would have remained a planners' blueprint, and for the future the staying power of the three men and of the parties they represent is the key to any further federal advance. . . . [Also] if votes given to [the] nationalistic Right were seriously to undermine the Catholic Center, no alternative constitutional coalition could be created rather further to the Left in order to continue the programme of European federation.[17]

It is because East Prussia is heavily Protestant and the East Prussians have been traditionally associated with German chauvinism and imperialism that C. L. Sulzberger of *The New York Times* was correct when he reported from Paris that "the domination of Chancellor Konrad Adenauer's largely Catholic coalition also would fade with the addition of the primarily Protestant East." [18] With this, therefore, also would vanish the possibility of an effective supranational Continental European Community. With the Catholic and Latin Roman living law of southern and western Germany thus reduced to a minor rôle in German politics, the common qualitative and quantitative living-law norms necessary for any effective collaboration between the Germans and their Latin neighbors to the West would not exist.

This is why the previous chapters concentrated on the religious as well as the political living-law norms of the six Continental European nations. An influential Roman Catholic living law under Roman Stoic and Continental Rationalistic secular leadership is the *sine qua non* for Chancellor Adenauer's leadership in Germany and for French trust in EDC. To see more specifically why this is so, it is necessary to consider the ideological content of German Protestantism.

Like any other Protestantism it tends to oppose any transfer of sovereignty from one's own nation to a supranation. The Council of Europe clearly demonstrates this fact, as does the United States. Among the nations in the Council of Europe, none with a Protestant majority or whose major party is not heavily Roman Catholic is willing to make any such transfer. One can hardly imagine the present Senate of the United States doing it. Only those nations on the continent of Europe with political parties in common and majorities that are Roman Catholic in their living law or, like West Germany, with the largest political party under Roman Catholic leadership, were willing to transfer national sovereignty to the supranational community.

But German Protestantism differs from Protestantism elsewhere in that it is predominantly Lutheran. The German Lutheran Church has a unique theory of the independence of Church and State. Whereas Protestantism elsewhere interprets that independence as still permitting the Church to subject its secular statesmen continuously to moral judgment and criticism, German Lutheranism tends to interpret the independence of Church and State as forbidding any criticism of the Church by secular officials and any criticism of secular officials by the Church, except when one or the other party violates this rule. This showed dramatically in the case of Pastor Niemöller's opposition to Hitler. The pastor was very careful, avoiding any moral indignation over what Hitler did in incinerators and concentration camps, to base his opposition solely on the fact that Hitler had violated the basic concordat between the Lutheran Church and the State when he tried to put a pastor of his own choice over a Lutheran church. The practical effects of this basic normative principle of German Lutheran Protestantism are obvious. It leaves the political chauvinist completely free from religious and moral control, and may perhaps explain why the German people are such religious and moral folk individually yet so passive with respect to a violation of moral and religious values by their politicians. Undoubtedly the Kantian theory of ethics as autonomous, with its sharp separation between empirical facts and values, contributes also to this state of mind.

Whatever may be the vices of Latin European Roman Catholicism, they are not these. Men like Robert Schuman, Konrad Adenauer and Alcide de Gasperi have deep and sincere religious conviction and forthright moral integrity. Moreover, they believe that religious and moral principles, European in their universality, yet liberal and secular in their application, must control political action. Moreover, they are as serious in their belief that the state should be kept secular as they are in their Roman Catholic religious and moral Latin European convictions; they combine for Germany and Continental Europe generally the saving virtues of Roman and European universalism with modern secular philosophical and political liberalism.

In any event, the ideological content of German Lutheran Protestantism is the reason why Germany must be kept at least for a considerable period of time under the leadership politically of its southern and western portion. This is what the Yalta Agreement, Article 8 in the NATO Treaty and a United States defensive policy toward Communism insures. It is because President Eisenhower and Secretary of State Dulles threatened to tear up the Yalta Agreement and reject Article 8 of the NATO Treaty by turning United States foreign policy toward Communism from the defensive to the offensive that both French interest in EDC and European-American collaboration went into a decline, with neutralism and anti-Americanism increasing from the late summer of 1952 through 1953. In short, Europeans found themselves confronted not merely with the Russian problem and the German problem, but also with the American problem. Moreover, what made the American problem so dangerous in their minds was that it intensified the German problem.

Under such circumstances there is always the temptation to Europeans, of which Mr. Molotov was not unmindful at Berlin in February 1954, to drop the NATO Treaty with the United States and strengthen the older treaty with Soviet Russia. This means that the American problem is a problem for Americans as well as for Europeans and makes it imperative that we examine it more closely.

As we turn to do so, one point about all the foregoing evidence is to be noted. The important factors are not what Senator McCarthy said or did, irresponsible and reckless as this was. What most disturbed the Europeans were the statements and deeds of Candidate and President Eisenhower and his Secretary of State, John Foster Dulles. Thus even if there had been no Senator McCarthy, the European reaction would have been what the foregoing facts indicate that it was. This is why in January 1954 *The Economist* spoke of the "still suspended judgment" of Europeans, concerning President Eisenhower's leadership of the free world, because of his "false beginnings" and added:

A year ago the advent of the Republicans was awaited with considerable apprehension throughout the free world. This was . . . because the Republicans, during the campaign, had declared themselves just as determined to change the Democrats' foreign policy where it was good as where it was bad. There was to be a complete re-shuffle, and America's allies could not help feeling frightened about what might be lost in the process. Mr Dulles himself had been saying things that sent shivers down the European spine.[19]

Senator McCarthy merely made the European neutralism and anti-Americanism worse. He intensified, but President Eisenhower and Secretary Dulles created, the American problem.

Chapter 10

The American Problem

The American problem came into the open in Europe in the
spring of 1953 after a series of unilateral actions by the United States
had raised the question in every European parliament as to whether
further collaboration with the United States would not engulf each
European people in dangerous situations and policies about which it
had never been consulted and to which it had never committed
itself. Prime Minister Churchill's and Mr. Attlee's attacks upon the
United States in the House of Commons have already been noted.
The failure of the De Gasperi coalition to obtain 50 per cent of the
official popular vote in the Italian elections was of similar significance. For weeks during 1953 the French Parliament was unable
to form a government. This arose from the fact that France, on the
one hand, needed United States financial aid until it could negotiate peace in Indo-China and, on the other hand, was unwilling to
rearm the Germans in an EDC subject to a NATO directed by a
United States whose foreign policy toward Russia had shifted from
the defensive to the offensive. In June, 1953, *The New York Times*
ran a two-column headline over a report from its correspondent in
Paris which read as follows:

The political complexion of Europe is beginning to change in a manner
that can be considered only as unfavorable to the policy and interests of
the United States.
This is the lesson to be deduced from the Italian election results announced today, from the inferences to be drawn from certain aspects of

169

the French political crisis, and from certain implications of the Soviet "peace offensive" as it perseveres on this continent. . . . Unless this trend can be checked it bodes ill for the entire political and strategic policy of the United States and the North Atlantic Treaty Organization.[1]

Prime Minister Churchill saw the seriousness of the situation, and the need for immediate action to prevent the Communists from destroying the unity of the free world in both Europe and Asia. Obviously, what was needed was a meeting of the heads of the French, American and British governments which would cause the United States (1) to confront the reasons for the fears of the French and other Europeans and (2) to make changes in foreign policy that would allay the fears and permit immediate ratification of EDC by the French Parliament, thereby restoring allied unity. Only then could the West forestall Moscow from dividing the free world and negotiate effectively over Korea and in Berlin from a position of unity and strength. Consequently Mr. Churchill, at the urgent request of the French, invited President Eisenhower in May 1953 to meet him at Bermuda. The response of the President was lukewarm.[1a] Ill health partially saved the Prime Minister from diplomatic embarrassment, and the conference was called off a few weeks later.

In June, before the cancellation, Anne O'Hare McCormick reported from Rome in *The New York Times* the "rather gloomy" outlook of Middle and Far Eastern leaders en route home from the "joyous" coronation ceremonies and the British Commonwealth gathering in London. They regarded the Bermuda meeting as "the first stage of a power struggle within a power struggle" between Great Britain and the United States.[2] Four days later a Paris dispatch in *The New York Times* reported that "extremely intelligent diplomats" contended that "the great division in the West is now between Britain and the United States," with Sir Winston forced to "steal the thunder" of the Left wing British Bevanites by embracing the neutralists who "enthusiastically" supported his moves. The result was "a growth of something verging on neutralism in France and the rest of Western Europe" which threatened the Schuman

Plan, the European army plan and the unity of the free world generally.[3]

Following Sir Winston's invitation *The Economist* carried a leading editorial of unprecedented length and urgency, which citizens of the United States will do well to take seriously: both before and since it was written, there has been no more continuous and loyal supporter of American foreign policy in the world than this sober and objective British periodical. Five years before, in 1948, a shorter editorial had stated:

Men lose their capacity for astonishment very easily. Let a thing be mentioned often enough and they begin to accept it as a normal unsensational fact. Few things have been mentioned more persistently in the last ten months than . . . the Marshall Plan. Insensibly, people have grown used to it. Its fabulous quality has been stripped away. But this week, since the Plan is . . . a concrete reality—an Act approved by Congress and signed by the President, . . . it is fitting that the peoples of Western Europe should attempt to renew their capacity for wonder, so that they can return to the United States a gratitude in some way commensurate with the aid they are about to receive. . . . [The Plan must be] seen for what it is—an act without peer in history. . . . And search back as one may through the annals of the United States or of any other Power, there is no record of a comparable act of inspired and generous diplomacy.[4]

The 1953 editorial began:

The diplomacy of the western powers has fallen behind the march of events. . . . It is clearly no longer the case that the free and allied powers are working together on an agreed plan and bending events to their purpose. They rather seem to be proceeding by expedient on divergent courses to a goal that is in doubt. . . . The Bermuda meeting was originally proposed for domestic reasons by a desperate French Prime Minister; but it has grown into something more. It is, or ought to be, an attempt to reconstruct a policy. . . . Perhaps the best way of seeing clearly what has gone wrong is to go back to the last time the western powers can be said to have had a consistent policy which they were pursuing in unison. That was in the days of Mr Acheson and Mr Bevin. For all their difficulties and their mistakes, they were operating an effective alliance with a working agreement on the policy of containment. The name has, for inevitable reasons of domestic politics, been much abused. But there can be even less doubt now than there was at the start that it was the right policy or that it has been on balance successful. Revolutionary aggressive Communism has been contained, without a world war.[5]

The editorial went on to specify how domestic politics had corrupted allied collaboration:

In America, the Republicans attacked the Democrats for being weak and gullible in their handling of Communism, with the result that they took away from Mr Acheson all his freedom of movement and that Mr Eisenhower must at all costs prove himself to be firm and incredulous. In Britain, Sir Winston Churchill was attacked as a warmonger, with the result that the Conservatives are determined to prove themselves the peace party. The gap thus opened up has been enlarged by the impact of the "new look" in Moscow. . . . The result is that . . . Europeans are encouraged to believe that there is a hand outstretched from Moscow which has only to be grasped for the cold war to be over, [whereas] Americans are encouraged to believe that, with firmness producing such results, the obvious need is for more firmness. In these circumstances, the major task of statesmanship is in the field of psychology. To work out an agreed policy may not be too difficult. . . . What is more urgently needed is to rebuild for the agreed policy the necessary foundation of public support.[6]

What should the urgently needed, agreed policy be? The editorial concluded that it could not be either the Churchill or the Eisenhower policy. Neither had worked, and neither stood "any chance of working."[7] The Prime Minister's power-politics appeal to neutralism based on appeasement would fail. The "American policy has been losing friends," thereby becoming self-defeating.[8] There was "much danger" and "little prospect of success"

either in the "open challenge" policy towards which domestic political pressure is constantly pushing the American Government, or in the "negotiated settlement" policy towards which so much wishful thinking in Britain and Western Europe is inclining. Imperfect and incomplete though it may be, the policy of containment is more practical than these.[9]

The editorial concludes, therefore, that the "task of Bermuda" would be for the President and the Prime Minister to take counsel together how they can rekindle in the peoples of the West the confidence in the policy that domestic politics—in each country, though in different directions—has so largely undermined.[10]

The day before this editorial appeared, an event occurred in the United States which showed the diagnosis and prognosis of *The Economist* to be as important for the Republican party and the harmony of the American people as for Continental European Union and allied unity before the Communist successes in Europe and Asia. The event was a speech in New York City by Alexander Wiley of Wisconsin, the chairman of the Senate Committee on Foreign Relations. Speaking of his own Republican party, the senior Senator from Wisconsin said that "a sizable group" was "effectively trying to sabotage" the administration's foreign policy. He added immediately that the group was likely to succeed "if the sabotage effort is regarded complacently by the party itself." [11] Among the cornerstones of foreign policy which the President and the administration were pledged to the American people to fulfill, the chairman of the Senate Committee on Foreign Relations listed two: "cooperation between the Republican majority and the Democratic minority on the basic issues of our international relations," and "cooperating with our allies." [12]

The foreign policy of the majority of the Democrats in Congress was the policy of containment of the Truman administration and the Democratic nominee, Adlai Stevenson. Because the Democrats were divided only with respect to domestic policy and were in agreement on foreign policy, this meant that the 27,000,000 voters who cast their ballots for Mr. Stevenson were for the policy of containment. Mr. Eisenhower was represented to the American people in the election, at least by the Republican *New York Herald Tribune* and the independent *New York Times* that supported him, as being against the go-it-alone foreign policy of both the Taft-Bricker isolationists and the MacArthur-McCarthy interventionists. In fact these papers asserted that there was no issue between the two presidential nominees on the aim of American foreign policy.

If this be true, as many Republicans, independents and Democrats who voted the Republican ticket believed, then it would appear that not merely the 27,000,000 Americans who voted for Mr. Stevenson, but also at least one-third of the Republicans who voted for Mr. Eisenhower did so because they favored a go-it-together-with-allies foreign policy toward the Communist world that would contain it by strictly defensive means. One-third of Mr. Eisenhower's total is 11,000,000, which, added to the 27,000,000, makes 38,000,000, almost two-thirds of the total popular vote of 61,000,000. If therefore, as Senator Wiley suggested, the President had an obligation to pursue the bipartisan foreign policy which expressed the will of the majority of the American people, then the policy for which he must stand is containment.

Certainly, as Vice President Nixon pointed out later in 1953, the majority of the American people believed that President Truman had been right when he ordered General MacArthur to Korea with American troops immediately following the North Korean aggression.[13] It should be added also that the majority of Americans believed President Truman had been right in not leaving this order in the status of a unilateral decision upon the part of the United States. Instead, he had immediately processed it through Congress —where it received one of the few almost unanimous votes ever given such a Presidential message—and through the United Nations, thereby making the United States action in Korea a U.N. police action authorized by the world community rather than a war. It is equally certain that the majority of Americans in the 1952 election did not believe in throwing additional boys across the Yalu into China. Proof of this is to be found in the popularity of Mr. Eisenhower's election campaign promise to go to Korea himself and get the boys home from there "with honor."

In any event Senator Wiley spoke the truth on the evening of June 26, 1953, when he said:

There is an obligation on all of us—on the President, on the White House staff, on the Executive Branch and on the Legislative Branch and it is this: not to ignore schismatic conditions, particularly on foreign policy, and not to regard their provokers complacently. . . . Why? Because such schisms can destroy not only the Republican party but can make a shambles of the Eisenhower Administration.[14]

President Eisenhower was reported to have personally approved the speech. Officially, however, he did nothing to implement the approval. Senator McCarthy's sabotage was allowed to continue, and no concern was shown over the cancellation of the mid-1953 Bermuda conference.

The fruits in Europe were immediate. Neutralism and anti-Americanism intensified. M. S. Handler reported to *The New York Times* from Bonn that the peoples of Europe outside Germany were "riddled with neutralism, defeatism and anti-Americanism." [15] A report from Stewart Alsop in Bonn to the *New York Herald Tribune* indicated that not merely the Europeans but also "Americans here are . . . rapidly losing their confidence in themselves and their country." [16] Two detectives named Cohn and Schine, representing Senator McCarthy in the Legislative Branch of the American government and Scott McLeod in the Executive Branch, in what Mr. Alsop described as a "reign of stupidity," had spied upon a party "attended by High Commissioner James B. Conant," thereby making the United States "look ridiculous" in European eyes, and had succeeded in getting top men in the foreign service removed from their posts—men whom the Germans, as well as their American superiors, regarded as very able in defeating Communist aims in Germany. This had created an atmosphere in which "a past error of political judgment can be interpreted as disloyalty" and "saying nothing becomes, obviously, the better part of wisdom." Secretary of State Dulles later showed the correctness of the report when he found it necessary in early 1954 to appoint a commission, including former career diplomats, in order to restore the morale of the foreign service. Need one wonder that during the summer of 1953, when American diplomats abroad lost confidence in themselves and their country, the Europeans' confidence in the United States as an ally reached an unprecedented low also?

Of this situation *The New York Times'* European correspondent wrote several months later:

In West Germany especially the seemingly brutal ousting of some of Washington's ablest representatives left a bad impression. What looked abroad like a "McCarthyist" purge of American diplomacy frightened many essentially friendly foreigners, and Mr. Dulles was held responsible.[17]

Thus it happened that neither the United States in Germany, nor the free world generally, was able to take advantage of the tremendous opportunity for immediate negotiation from strength with the Russians that the riots in East Berlin offered. Thus it was also that the shambles which Senator Wiley had predicted in New York would result if the President did not stop appeasing a minority wing of his party came true for the foreign service within two months after he spoke.

Let it be said, however, to the credit of both High Commissioner Conant and Secretary of State Dulles that they carried the defense of the morale of the United States foreign service in West Germany to the highest authority, where the issue was decided against them and in favor of Secretary Dulles' own assistant, Mr. McLeod, and Senator McCarthy. As in Mr. Stassen's reprimand earlier, following the Greek ship issue, and in Secretary of the Army Stevens' collapse when, later, the shambles technique was extended from the foreign service to the Army, the core of the American problem was shown to center not in a junior Senator in the Legislative Branch of the United States government, but in the head of its Executive Branch. In March 1954, after the tragic "Stevens affair," *The New York Times* commented that what was needed from the President, if the traditional American conception of the relation between the Legislative and Executive Branch of the government was to be preserved, was not merely words but also deeds.

An American columnist, speaking over the British Broadcasting Corporation, reached the same conclusion much earlier, in October 1953, when he said:

The inclination of the Congressional group of Republicans is nationalist. The inclination of Mr. Eisenhower, and also of those Republicans who made him President, is internationalist. . . . Thus, the ultimate direction of the Eisenhower Government in both foreign and domestic policy is going to be determined not by what has happened so far, or by what is in the mind of Mr. Eisenhower himself, but rather by what happens when the group of Congressional Republicans who supported Senator Taft seek to take and exercise the leadership in the American Government this winter. . . . Then we will learn whether the political man Eisenhower is going to be a presiding President of the United States or a prime-minister President.[18]

By a "presiding President" this commentator meant one who would not lead and who, like a good but completely transcendental deity, sits above the moral conflict, never committing himself on anything.

One man and one government were able, however, to take advantage of the East Berlin riots: Chancellor Adenauer and his Christian Democratic coalition. Using the June riots as proof that the Communists had no popular support from the Russian-zone Germans, taking unequivocally the position that German entry into EDC was merely defensive, even recognizing Soviet Russia's right to a guarantee against change of the Yalta Agreement by force, the Chancellor carried this sharp issue straight to all his Socialist, Communist and Nazi opponents and won a resounding victory. It took the Germans, of all people, to show that even for Germans the defensive foreign policy of allied collaboration with the aim of containment was not only the wisest but also the victorious policy.

This victory, and this victory alone, saved United States foreign policy and allied collaboration in Europe from catastrophe in 1953. By the stand that made it possible Dr. Adenauer and his coalition proved the genuineness of their loyalty to Continental European Union with triumphant deeds. Nor was this stand their only such demonstration of loyalty. In November, when the High Authority of the Coal and Steel Community at Luxembourg under its French President issued an order vitally affecting West German economic interests,[19] there was an immediate protest from powerful West German industrialists. Chancellor Adenauer without hesitation backed the decision of the Community. At another time chauvinistic Germans demanded that the West German government stop paying the reparations to Israel to which the government had committed itself. Again, without apology or temporizing, the Chancellor met his critics head on; with moral indignation, he not merely made it a matter of principle to fulfill the commitments but also referred to the disgrace which the Nazis had brought upon the German people. Before anyone charges that the loyalty of the present West German government to the Continental European Community, and of the people who supported it so decisively in the September elections of 1953, is not to be trusted he will do well to remember that Franco-German collaboration, Continental European Union and allied unity were then heading straight to catastrophe. Deeds count, and the German people's deeds in September 1953 were on the side of Europe and effective collaboration between the liberal nations of the free world.

Unfortunately, however, the deeds of the Germans alone are not enough. In fact, Chancellor Adenauer's victory, at a time when the French were so distrustful of American aims with respect to Germany, merely intensified French fears. The American problem, combined with the Chancellor's victory, made the German problem all the more terrifying not merely to the French but to other Europeans. Consequently in 1953 and during the period of the 1954 Berlin and Geneva conferences no government was possible in France without the participation of Gaullists, who opposed both the European Defense Community and the foreign policy of the United States.

At the same time French public opinion turned strongly toward a foreign policy of collaboration with Russia. The leading and most sober French newspaper is *Le Monde*. In October of 1953 its political correspondent, Jean-Jacques Servan-Schreiber, in a radio broadcast from London, described a by-election which had just taken place in a small agricultural district of France, its Conservative representative in the National Assembly having died. In the election eighteen months previously, this Conservative had received 1,500 votes; other liberal candidates, 1,000 votes; and the Communist candidate, but 800 votes. The Conservative nominated to fill the vacancy was well known and popular. Nevertheless he received only 1,300 votes to the 1,200 for the Communist, less than a majority. In the second ballot that had to be taken, one week later, the Conservative candidate received but 100 more votes, whereas the Communist increased his votes by 600 and was elected. Having described the results, the experienced French political observer commented:

> Those facts are momentous: first, that the Communist vote has increased more than double since 1951; second, that 600 people decided to vote Communist from one Sunday to the other. . . . It is considered in French political circles to be a disturbing symptom of a widespread phenomenon.[20]

M. Servan-Schreiber used these facts, however, to support a statement at the beginning of his broadcast:

> There lies a tragic misunderstanding between us and our allies, a misunderstanding that our governments should have cleared up a long time ago. . . . The misunderstanding can be put in simple terms. The French people have been told that we are fighting to preserve the integrity of our common world. But on the other hand our allies have been convinced that we are fighting in the name of the Anti-Communist Alliance to promote the independence of Indo-China. The men who fight are dying for the defence of the Union Française; but the guns they fight with have been given to us for an anti-communist crusade in Asia. . . . Suddenly it appears to many people that the Indo-Chinese people, who were supposedly on our side, are almost as anti-French as those we are fighting under communist leadership. . . . [Moreover,] it is now clear that in the name of that fight we are rather helping communism in Europe and in France. The conclusion, for a growing number of Frenchmen, is that we should take the first possible occasion to end the war in Indo-China by an armistice and negotiation. . . . Immediately after the Indo-Chinese problem, and closely linked to it, comes in France the problem of the European army.[21]

Did this mean that France wanted peace in Indo-China at any price and knew that Mr. Molotov would not allow President Mao to negotiate such a peace unless the French gave up collaboration both with Germany in EDC and with the United States in Europe and Asia for Franco-Russian collaboration? Although M. Servan-Schreiber did not say so explicitly, the point of his reference to the French by-election in October 1953 seemed to be that in his mind the answer was "Yes."

These events made the Bermuda meeting of December 4–7, 1953, which the French and Prime Minister Churchill finally persuaded President Eisenhower to attend, all the more crucial. To avoid intensification, by the Eisenhower roll-back crusade terminology in conjunction with Chancellor Adenauer's victory, of French fears of rearming the Germans in EDC, and to prevent Mr. Molotov from obtaining absolute strength at the Berlin Four Power conference as a result (1) of M. Bidault's mandate from his people to get peace in Indo-China at any price and (2) of the presence of Gaullists in the French government, it became imperative that Premier Laniel, Prime Minister Churchill and President Eisenhower at Bermuda face without evasion the factors in United States foreign policy that required change in order to secure in advance the passage of EDC by the French Parliament. Otherwise Mr. Molotov would be negotiating with three verbally united but in fact divided free nations, and the French people and Parliament would be neutral if not in considerable part on his side.

Imagine therefore Sir Winston's "hurt feelings," as reported by Roscoe Drummond,[22] at the opening of the Bermuda conference when the Secretary of State of the United States announced that the President would not be able to stay for the final day because he was flying to New York to make a speech before the United Nations. The changes in United States foreign policy necessary for the passage of EDC by the French Parliament were not to be faced. Instead, in a speech moving so far as its verbal propaganda effect throughout the world was concerned, the President spoke for peace and for international collaboration in the United Nations after running away from the changes in foreign policy necessary for implementing this ideal in the French Parliament and in Europe. Need one wonder that Sir Winston was reported to have returned to England pessimistic about the Western world, suggesting that the nations were committing all over again the isolationistic mistakes and the non-implementation of collaboration in Europe which destroyed the League of Nations and led straight to World War II?[23]

The Economist with its customary objectivity and insight had foreseen such an outcome and the consequences. Before the Bermuda conference of December 1953, it stated: "Sir Winston, faint yet pursuing, will talk with an American President who is bored but polite, and with a Prime Minister who is willing but powerless until it is known who France's next President will be." [24] On January 2, 1954, under the caption, "Berlin Prospects," it remarked:

Only six months ago Soviet policy in Germany was confronted with a dangerous failure. . . . Now, thanks largely to western errors of judgment, it is achieving a recovery worthy of Stalin himself. . . . There is to be a meeting of Foreign Ministers on the date [Mr. Molotov] wants, in the place he wants and on the subject he wants, and on the conditions that he has no intention of abandoning even though the western governments have not accepted them.[25]

In one short sentence, it then placed its finger on the key to Moscow's remarkable recovery from the Berlin riots and on the weakness in the West's position: "A consolidated Soviet position faces a not yet consolidated western position." [26] The Bermuda meeting, having left France wavering between (a) collaboration with the United States and the Germans in NATO and EDC, and (b) a power-politics-balancing alliance with Russia which would work to prevent German rearmament and at the same time get French boys home from Indo-China, gave Moscow no worries over the East Germans. And, to show that the West was so divided and weak and that the East Germans could do nothing about it, Moscow dared even to hold the Four Power conference of January 1954 on the very spot where the East Berlin riots had occurred.

One need hardly wonder, therefore, that Secretary Dulles brought back from Berlin little more than the absolute commitment on the part of the United States, demanded by the French, to allow the Communist Chinese to participate in a conference at Geneva two months later on peace in Indo-China. In return for this, Mr. Molotov had given nothing; and Mr. Dulles had not even the guarantee from the French that in return for the United States concession the French Parliament would vote on EDC before the Geneva conference occurred.

In justice, however, to Mr. Dulles at Berlin, the following must also be noted. President Eisenhower had failed to face the difficulties in the way of allied unity at the Bermuda conference, thereby putting Mr. Dulles, Mr. Eden and M. Bidault into a weak position, with no support from the French Parliament or government, as they entered the negotiations with Mr. Molotov at Berlin. Thereupon Mr. Dulles made the utmost of what was practically an impossible position, negotiating like his British and French colleagues from de facto allied division and weakness rather than from effective parliamentary unity and strength. With allowance for the fact that Mr. Molotov knew Mr. Bidault's professions of allied unity did not express the majority opinion of the French government, Mr. Dulles' diplomacy was outstanding. Europeans complimented him on his skill—*The Economist* saying that it was "diplomacy as it should be conducted." [27] It is to be noted also that these compliments from Europeans came not merely because of the skill which he exhibited, but also from the fact that his deeds at Berlin took United States foreign policy toward Communism away from an offensive position and back to a strictly defensive, and even a conciliatory, aim. *The Economist* warned, however, that the conciliation exhibited by the free world at Berlin "must not be allowed to interfere with the organisation of Western Europe and the reconciliation of France and Germany. These are things good in themselves, not to be bargained about." [28]

If therefore Secretary of State Dulles made any mistake at Berlin, it was not in the concessions he granted as representative of the United States but in the failure to make them and the Geneva conference itself conditional upon French parliamentary approval of

EDC before that conference. Then M. Bidault, Mr. Dulles and Mr. Eden could have gone to Geneva on April 26, 1954, speaking not merely for themselves personally but also for the French Parliament, the entire Continental European Community already assured as a fact, the whole of the NATO Community and the free world, to negotiate from a position of physical strength and living-law spiritual unity.

But to have obtained such approval Mr. Dulles would have had to make clear that not merely he and the President, but also the Congress of the United States, were through with undermining Article 8 of the NATO Treaty with Dulles dynamism and with McCarthyism, and would maintain, through the fifty years that EDC runs, a foreign policy restricting NATO, EDC and allied collaboration in Asia through the United Nations to a strictly defensive aim. Not having done this at Bermuda, or before Berlin, M. Bidault could give no such guarantee from his government or the French Parliament in return for Mr. Dulles' commitment at Berlin to invite Communist China to the Geneva conference. Consequently the Geneva conference was doomed instantly to be the Berlin conference all over again except that Mr. Molotov would have the Foreign Minister of Mao's China at his side. It would be a conference between the free West and a Molotov and a Mao who could keep everything they already had and gain more, because they knew full well that the French people wanted peace in Indo-China at almost any price and were likely to be opposed to German rearmament in the Continental European Community so long as their distrust of United States foreign policy continued. Again *The Economist* hit the nail on the head when it said:

So long as the Russians have the faintest hope that the western ranks can be divided on [EDC] . . . they will continue to represent the European Defence Community as the main obstacle to peace and German unity. That bluff must be called before any progress in negotiation can be made; and the way to call it is to press on with the political acts that are needed in France and Italy to bring the community into existence and the Bonn conventions into force.[29]

This requires, however, not merely action on the part of the French and Italian parliaments, but also on unequivocal constant truly bipartisan, go-it-together-with-allies U. S. foreign policy in which the French and Italians can have confidence because it is (1) above domestic American politics, (2) strictly defensive rather than offensive, and (3) bases its collaboratively determined decisions concerning Europe and Asia on the objective living-law realities of the peoples in these areas.

The British government saw the need for such collaboration, immediately following the Berlin conference. On March 12, 1954, Drew Middleton reported to *The New York Times* from London, "Britain is eager to arrange preliminary talks with the United States and France to provide a common front against an expected divisive diplomacy of the Soviet Union and Communist China at the Geneva conference." [30] Conditions in France showed the wisdom of this third British attempt to get the differences on foreign policy dividing Britain, the United States and France faced and removed before entering a conference with the Communists. On March 15th, a report from the Paris correspondents of *World* made two points: (1) "a secret survey ordered by French Premier Joseph Laniel" showed that enough members of the National Assembly wanted the vote on EDC postponed until after the Geneva conference to prevent its passage earlier; (2) six members of his cabinet—obviously the Gaullists—had informed Premier Laniel that they would resign, leaving France without a government, if he pressed for a vote.[31] Naturally the Communists were elated. This assured them that Messrs. Molotov and Mao would find at Geneva a divided West and a French Foreign Minister who knew that his people wanted their boys home from Indo-China. The article from Paris began:

The rice fields and jungles of Indo-China are today the crux of world politics. It is the West's failures in this vital area that the Sino-Soviet bloc is exploiting to achieve its double purpose: the international recognition of Communist China and the torpedoing of the West European defense structure. . . . The heavily censored press dispatches from Indo-China fail to reveal the full gravity of the military position. WORLD can flatly state . . . that the predicament of the French Union forces is *steadily growing worse.*[32]

It appears that for Europeans there is not merely the Communist problem but also the Asian problem, and that the two problems are entwined and cannot be solved without a simultaneous solution of the American problem. The Continental Europeans, even though their living law is favorable, cannot alone carry through Franco-German collaboration to establish EDC and the Continental European Community generally. British policy must also be favorable. In addition if French fears of German rearmament are not to drive the French away from collaboration with Germany and the United States into neutralism and even perhaps into the arms of the Communists in Europe and Asia, United States foreign policy with respect to Communism must revert to a strictly defensive aim.

Moreover, it would not be enough, even if President Eisenhower and Secretary of State Dulles officially and publicly announced such a shift, thereby (1) making NATO and the mutual security pacts between France and Britain and the Soviet Union compatible again, and (2) giving the French the protection from the East Prussian and Nazi Germans as well as from the Communist East which they want before they commit themselves to rearming the Germans in the European Defense Community. In addition, the President must show that this strictly defensive allied policy is that of the Congress of the United States. To this end, the foreign policy of the United States must be lifted above domestic politics. If this is to occur, it must be that of the Democrats as well as of the President and his Secretary of State and those Republicans like Senators Wiley and Saltonstall who want to follow the President in foreign affairs. For it to be thus in fact as well as word, above domestic politics, it must be discussed with the Democrats as well as the Republicans before it is decided upon, and it must be implemented afterward in the manner of the Truman administration with outstanding members of the opposition party in key administrative posts. Only then can the world know that United States foreign policy is an American foreign policy rather than merely the temporary foreign policy of the one of the three factions in the Republican party which the President and his Secretary of State happen to represent, and which may be tossed out tomorrow or neutralized by a sudden coalition of (a) the go-it-alone Taft-Bricker-Hoover Republican isolationists, and (b) the go-it-alone McCarthy-MacArthur Republican showdown interventionists, who together represent only a minority of the American people.

To see more explicitly that the popular support of these two groups is no more than this, recall the aforementioned 1952 election statistics. Give these groups two-thirds of President Eisenhower's votes. The result is 22,000,000 in a total electoral vote of 61,000,000. Again we see that the only genuinely American bipartisan foreign policy with respect to Communism which could possibly have had the support of the majority of the American people in the 1952 election is the go-it-together-with-allies foreign policy which keeps the aim of allied unity strictly defensive—midway between the go-it-alone Republican showdown policy at the one extreme and the stay-at-home Republican isolationist policy at the other extreme.

Fortunately this is the policy of our allies and even of Soviet Russia so far as she wants to protect herself against the danger of a resurgent East Prussian, Nazi Germany and so far as she needs her present mutual defense pacts with Britain and France in order to have such protection. Fortunately also this is the policy of Dr. Adenauer, which won him the resounding victory in the West German elections of 1953. Let it be recalled that he campaigned in this election on the twofold thesis (1) that the Soviet Union must have guarantees that the Yalta Agreement restricting Germany to the area west of the Oder-Neisse would not be forcibly altered by the free German government or by anyone else, and (2) that, just as the Russians needed such a guarantee from Germany and the free West generally, so Germany and the other Western free peoples needed the similar mutual Defense Community guarantee against a Russian tearing up of the Yalta Agreement which would extend Soviet Russia and her satellites west of the Oder-Neisse.

But even a United States foreign policy strictly defensive with respect to Communism, and bipartisan in the sense of being discussed by Democrats as well as Republicans before decisions are made, and administered by both afterwards, is not sufficient. The allies of the United States also must be treated in precisely the same way. The idea of the United States alone deciding upon those portions of its foreign policy which require cooperation from allies, and then confronting these allies with a *fait accompli* which they must accept "or else," is as self-defeating abroad as it is at home. This is demonstrated by the foregoing events in Europe and Indo-China.

Moreover, all the top administrative military posts should not go to United States commanders. It is just as stupid to insist that one's own nation must be at the head of everything as it is to assert that members of one's own party alone can be trusted in the foreign service. As Canada's Secretary of State for External Affairs, Lester B. Pearson, said in Washington on March 15, 1954, according to *The New York Times* of the next day, Canada's uneasiness about United States foreign policy has been determined in part by the

feeling that our [Canada's] destiny . . . may be decided, not by ourselves, but across our border "by means and at places not of our choosing"; to adapt a famous phrase. . . . This accounts for much of the uneasiness that enters into the minds of some Canadians as they look south, and realize that they are quite unable to escape the consequences of what you do—or don't do.[33]

However, Mr. Dulles pointed out in his news conference the next day, when questioned about Mr. Pearson's quotation from his January 12th speech on "the new look" in United States foreign policy, that although he had said the decision to pursue this policy, made "by the President with the advice of the National Security Council,"[34] was "to depend primarily upon a great capacity to retaliate, instantly, by means and at places of our choosing,"[35] this did not mean that collaboration or consultation with allies had been rejected. And he referred the reporters to his article in the April 1954 issue of *Foreign Affairs*, as a "somewhat more polished" restatement of the January 12th address.[36]

Examination of the article shows that it omits the phrase "at places and with means of its own choosing" which occurred in the January 12th address. However, it states that the decision to pursue the new policy was made by the President with the advice of the National Security Council and with supporting decisions by other departments of the Executive Branch of the government. One sentence reads: "It has been necessary to exchange views with Congressional leaders and our principal allies and to inform world opinion so that neither our friends nor our enemies abroad would misinterpret what we were doing." [37]

Even so the uneasiness of Canada and the European allies seems to be justified. An article of February 25, 1954, by Walter Millis, military and political expert of the Republican *New York Herald Tribune*, described what had happened as

one of the most far-reaching decisions in the power of government to make, of the kind which in the past no President would have dreamt of taking without submission to Congress and thorough argument and debate. . . . The Alsops . . . lend precision to Secretary Dulles' statement by saying that the "basic decision" flowed in fact from a council staff paper—NSC–162—worked out during the summer and "adopted" by the council itself on Oct. 7. But who or what is the council staff? It is headed by . . . [three men], but beyond that its membership is as anonymous as its papers are secret. . . . One comes down to the curious result that a decision . . . [is] taken on the basis of a staff paper worked out by an anonymous group of doubtless able young men hidden far beyond the control of what we normally think of as our policy-making agency. . . . It reveals the extent to which Congress, by its own chaos, division and incompetence, is losing the policy-making function and allowing it to pass to executive agencies who can at least chart a course, even if they are quite irresponsible to public control and unable to insure that the course is followed. . . . But, unfortunately, it also reveals the corresponding weakness in the executive.[38]

Similarly, the momentous decision was not submitted to NATO for discussion and approval—notwithstanding the sentence in the early part of Mr. Dulles' article in *Foreign Affairs*, "Without the coöperation of allies, we would not even be in a position to retaliate massively. . . ." [39] Need one wonder that the allies of the United States lacked confidence in anything tied by a treaty to her foreign policy, or that Canada's foreign minister felt that the time had come to be both frank and critical?

Mr. Pearson was also constructive, as when he said, "Collective action means collective consultation." [40] Professor Toynbee expressed the same principle, that must guide the foreign policy of any nation which keeps its allies, when he said, "No annihilation without representation." [41] An effective United States foreign policy must therefore not merely be bipartisan in discussion and administration, expressing the majority will above the issues of domestic politics; it must also be discussed in advance with our allies and administered jointly with them after it has taken form.

It appears, therefore, that there is a solution of the American problem which will remove French fears sufficiently to permit the Continental European Community to come into being, and which will restore allied unity for policing the peace of the world through EDC, NATO and the United Nations in Europe and Asia. The solution which alone will achieve these two purposes involves constructing a bipartisan United States foreign policy which will be strictly defensive toward Communism, and in which consultation between Republicans and Democrats and with allies will occur before important decisions are made.

Apparently Mr. Dulles realized this in early April of 1954, for he suddenly flew to London and to Paris to clarify the position of the United States and to secure greater agreement before entering the Geneva conference. The beneficent result was immediate. Not only did he obtain interest in a future allied security establishment in South Asia, but the press exhibited a temporary shift from the previous neutralism and anti-Americanism toward a renewed faith in the United States and in effective allied unity. Following his visit *The Times* of London commented, "One of the most admirable of Mr. Dulles' qualities has been his readiness to go out in search of first-hand information." [42] The *Daily Mail* remarked, "Our two countries are closer and stronger as the result of the useful and welcome visit of the Secretary of State." [43] In an article from Paris on France and Europe generally, C. L. Sulzberger referred to the purge of American diplomacy in Germany in the comment:

Now it seems to Europe that this nasty trend has ended, together with the strong talk of "rollback," Europeans are happy to forget those first impressions. The earlier picture of John Foster Dulles, etched in obdurate, unyielding lines and associated with ideas basically unpleasant on this side of the ocean, is being altered.[44]

Obviously, only a go-it-together-with-allies foreign policy which is implemented with deeds, so that the allies enter into the decisions, will work.

Will President Eisenhower and the Republicans in Congress learn this also? If they do not, the American people will have to return to the Democrats to obtain a foreign policy that expresses the will of the majority and to prevent the Communist successes in dividing the free world which have occurred since June 1952 from being followed by further Communist victories. In the light which they throw on this possibility, the November 1954 United States elections will be interesting.

In any event, a truly bipartisan go-it-together-with-allies foreign policy for the United States, implemented with consultations before decisions are made, is the only one which can succeed in Europe or Asia. The Stevens-McCarthy hearings and the Geneva conference have made it evident also that this is the only foreign policy which can succeed at home. On May 4, 1954, *The New York Times* carried front-page headlines reading: "Dulles Is Facing Heavy Criticism on Asian Policy—Accused of Exposing U.S. Leadership to a Serious Defeat." Beneath the headlines James Reston reported from Washington:

Secretary of State John Foster Dulles will face the most serious criticism of his long career tomorrow when he returns . . . to report to Congressional leaders of both parties . . . and to the Senate Foreign Relations Committee. . . . The criticisms being leveled against him . . . [include] these: . . . He went to London and Paris to press for adoption of [the "united action"] . . . policy on the eve of the Geneva Conference with the Communists on Indo-China and was met (a) with a public refusal by the British, and (b) with a French request for immediate United States air intervention in the war. The intervention was immediately refused by Washington. . . . The result of these things was a public demonstration, not of "united action" by the Western Powers, but of "disunited inaction," which greatly weakened the Western position at Geneva and exposed American leadership to its worst diplomatic defeat since the fall of Continental China. . . . Consequently, the questions that are now being asked . . . [in Washington] are these: . . . When the French defense of Indo-China began to deteriorate seriously, and the Administration felt obliged to consider the possibility of intervening there along with the British, French and others, why was so serious a move not explored more thoroughly with Congressional leaders! . . . Since the Administration had decided not to intervene in Indo-China without the British, French and others, why did Mr. Dulles not find out privately whether they would support a policy of "united action" before he announced it? . . . Finally, why was it necessary to dramatize such a gamble with a trip to London and Paris a few days before the Geneva Conference! [Mr. Reston added,] These questions imply certain inaccuracies. For example, Mr. Dulles did mention his "united action" speech to one or two of the Senators before he delivered it. However, he left out some of the top Republicans (including the chairman of the Senate Foreign Relations Committee, Alexander Wiley of Wisconsin) and all of the Democratic leaders.[45]

Clearly, the announcement of a major foreign policy decision before it has been agreed to by allies or even by the chairman of the Senate Foreign Relations Committee and a member of one's own party, does not work.

It appears also that the "shambles" (1) of the Republican party, (2) of the bipartisan foreign policy of the majority of the Republicans and Democrats in Congress and (3) of allied unity before the Communist threat abroad, which Senator Wiley predicted in mid-1953 unless the President unequivocally repudiated minority saboteurs to affirm the bipartisan go-it-together-with-allies foreign policy of the majority, had come to pass in Washington and at Geneva in May of 1954. Then, in the Stevens-McCarthy feud, the different factions of the Republican party were fighting each other, to what

Senator Mundt described as "the bitter end," in a degrading and disgraceful washing of Republican dirty linen before the eyes of the entire world, while the President sat in the background trying as usual to please both sides and hence standing for nothing. At the very same moment the Communists abroad were gleeful over the division of the free world thus achieved for them. Secretary of States Dulles' turning from a unilaterally announced take-it-or-leave-it United States foreign policy to a go-it-together-with-her-allies foreign policy, had come with too little too late.

It is to be noted also that only through a truly implemented bi-partisan go-it-together-with-allies foreign policy can the budget of the United States be balanced by keeping military expenditures at the minimum necessary to secure adequate protection against Communist ideological aims and practices. Obviously the allies are going to leave the financial cost and the loss of life involved in policing the peace of the world largely to the United States if the United States makes all the decisions, insists upon all the top administrative posts and talks continuously, through the only Administration voices that speak out unequivocally, about going it alone. The only effective foreign policy for the United States which can possibly be financially economical is one into which one's allies enter with enthusiasm. This they will not do unless it is their policy as much as it is the policy of the United States.

Such is the solution of the American problem. Were this solution in effect, French fears with respect to the European Defense Community probably would be dispelled. But even with these fears the Continental European Community has shown remarkable strength. To this we must now turn.

As we do so, events at Berlin and Geneva in 1954 have made one thing clear: The foreign policy of Candidate and President Eisenhower and his Administration has been a tragic failure. By dividing the United States from her allies and causing the French to change their minds about rearming the Germans in EDC, it enabled the Communists to recover within six months from the East Berlin riots and to name their own terms in Southeast Asia.

Chapter 11

The Persisting Power
of the European Idea

Notwithstanding the obstacles from without and within that the European idea faced from July 1952 through the Bermuda Conference in December 1953 and afterward, it showed in 1954 that it still had to be reckoned with. The living law of Continental Europe was still alive.

Dramatically, on March 12, 1954, the Senate of Belgium by a vote of 125 to 40 approved the European Defense Community, thereby committing Belgium to it. The lower house of the Belgian Parliament had given its approval by a three-to-one vote on November 26, 1953. The circumstances were such, however, as to indicate that something deeply moving, and out of the ordinary, had happened in the Senate debate. *The New York Times* reported the event as follows:

Contrary to custom in Belgian political life, the Senators, except the three Communists, disregarded party discipline in the vote and in the debate preceding the vote. . . . Irrespective of party, the treaty supporters drew cheers from fellow supporters belonging to the Social Christian, Liberal and Socialist parties. . . . The scene when Paul van Zeeland, the Foreign Minister, and Eugene de Greef, the Defense Minister, both speaking in support of the treaty, were cheered by the Opposition was a rare one in Belgian parliamentary history.[1]

The similar approval by the Netherlands and Germany of entry into EDC has already been noted. In Italy after the fall of the De Gasperi and the Pella coalition governments another such government was formed with Signor Scelba as Premier and with the Right-wing Socialist, Giuseppe Saragat and three other liberal Social Democrats in the Cabinet. Like the two former governments, it is Christian Democratic in its leadership and Right-wing Socialist in its major additional support. But, what is most important, with Socialist Vice Premier Saragat's unqualified approval, it stands like its two predecessors for Italian entry into the European Defense Community. In March of 1954 Premier Scelba announced in the Italian Chamber his intention to present the EDC Treaty for ratification at an early date. On April 7, the Luxembourg Parliament ratified that treaty in a unanimous vote, except for four Communist members who dissented.

Everything depended, therefore, upon France. As has been noted, the Laniel government in 1953 and 1954 did not have a majority in favor of EDC and collaboration with the United States because it contained Gaullists who threatened to resign following the Berlin Four Power conference if EDC were brought to a vote. In the earlier debates, in November of 1953, the Socialist M. Jaquet reaffirmed the position of the French Socialist party leader as previously expressed by Guy Mollet at Strasbourg: that the French Socialists would vote to ratify the European army plan if the supra-national political community were simultaneously produced and if "Britain should be closely bound to the Community." [2] Of French fear of the Germans, M. Jaquet said, "It is a funny sort of patriotism, this inferiority complex!" [3] Again later in the debate Guy Mollet repeated the Socialist position. This, as we have previously noted, meant that, provided the two conditions were met, the Socialists could replace the Gaullists in the Laniel governmental majority so far as the Continental European Community was concerned, thereby insuring a majority for it.

From London, Drew Middleton reported in *The New York Times* of February 23, 1954:

British official support for German rearmament under the defense community rather than under NATO has grown noticeably stronger during recent months. . . . The British Government is prepared to make public at an appropriate time the draft of a treaty linking the United Kingdom politically and militarily to the European Defense Community, under which West Germany is to be armed.[4]

On April 14th in London the text of such a treaty between Great Britain and the six nations in the European Defense Community was revealed. It provides not merely for the most intimate collaboration between British military forces and the military command of the EDC army, but may include the placing of some British units under that command.[5] Because French fears apply far more to the military portion of the Continental European Community than to its economic and political portions, this meeting of the French Socialists' second condition should go far to allay those fears.

Two days later, on April 16, 1954, from Augusta, Georgia, President Eisenhower sent a message to the Premiers of the six European Defense Community nations, stating:

> The United States will continue to maintain in Europe, including Germany, such units of its armed forces as may be necessary and appropriate to contribute its fair share of the forces needed for the joint defense of the North Atlantic area while a threat to that area exists. . . . The United States will consult with its fellow signatories to the North Atlantic Treaty and with the European Defense Community. . . . The United States will encourage the closest possible integration between the European Defense Community forces . . . and the United States. . . . In consonance with its policy of full and continuing support for the maintenance of the integrity and unity of the European Defense Community, the United States will regard any action from whatever quarter which threatens that integrity or unity as a threat to the security of the United States.[6]

Notwithstanding the President's commitment to "consult," protest came from Republicans such as Senator Saltonstall on the Armed Services Committee and Democrats such as Senator Mansfield on the Foreign Relations Committee because they had not been consulted on this Presidential message. The implementation of words concerning consultation seems to be difficult for President Eisenhower and his Administration.

On September 14, 1953, the Socialist leader of the Netherlands, Marinus van der Goes van Naters developed a plan for the Europeanization of the Saar. About the same time a report came from West Germany that Chancellor Adenauer was willing to accept M. van der Goes van Naters' proposal, if the French accepted the European Defense Community and the Saar became a member of the Continental European Community. *The New York Times* of November 6, 1953, reported from Saarbrücken that 75 to 85 per cent of the Saar people favored becoming "European." This removed a third condition that certain French statesmen had said would have to be satisfied before they accepted EDC. The thing to note about M. van der Goes van Naters' solution is that the existence of the Continental European Community was a condition also for the Europeanization of the Saar. The two must come into being together.

On May 5, 1954, a dispatch from Paris on page 9 of *The New York Times* reported that the foreign ministers of the six countries in the European Defense Community had just agreed that the Community's assembly "should be elected by universal suffrage":

> With this action it is hoped the French Socialists' demand for democratic control over the defense community has been met and that a large number will support the European army treaty when it is presented for ratification in the French National Assembly.

The final factor which had led many Frenchmen to refuse to vote on EDC was their feeling that the treaty should be ratified only after every effort had been made to negotiate with Moscow. At the Four Power Berlin conference such negotiation occurred, and failed to achieve any agreement with Russia on the solution of the German problem. On September 19, 1953, a French statesman said that if peace talks failed, he was for rearming the Germans within Continental European Union; and he described Dr. Adenauer as a "man of high conscience, courage and sincerity." The French statesman was the Speaker of the National Assembly and the President of the Radical Socialist party—the very same Edouard

Herriot who a year previously made the first French public attack on EDC and Franco-American collaboration in foreign policy generally.[7] In March of 1954 an important local election occurred in a strongly Communist suburban area of Paris. The issue was sharply drawn between the Christian Democratic party's candidate, Mme. Peyrole who was an outspoken advocate of EDC, and the Communist's candidate who attacked EDC. In a total vote 12 per cent larger than normal, Mme. Peyrole won.[8] Clearly the European idea and the Continental European living law still have some life left in them.

But even if Continental European Union does not come into being, its lasting accomplishments are considerable. Our comparison of its positive and living law with that of the Council of Europe, and the greater success of the Continental European Community in achieving a transfer of sovereignty from the nation to the "supranation" gives us an insight into the factors upon which the bringing of disputes between nations under the rule of law depends, which otherwise we should not have. More specifically, the European Movement enables us to see when federation between nations is possible, and when only confederation is likely to be practicable.

The Continental European Community illustrates federation. The Council of Europe instances confederation. In federation there is a real transfer of specified sovereign powers from the nation to the legal institutions of the international body. In a confederation there is no such transfer of economic, political and other social norms which govern the relations between men in the community. In a federation the executive body has legally specified power which the member states cannot veto. In a confederation this is not the case with respect to economic and political social norms. It can be the case for a Bill of Rights applying to persons qua persons, as the Convention for the Protection of Human Rights and Fundamental Freedoms of the Council of Europe demonstrates. In a federation there is a popularly elected legislative body with initiatory power to legislate and binding power for its statutes. In a confederation the legislative body is appointed by the member state governments and is merely consultative, with none of its legislation binding on the member states except in the aforementioned case of a Bill of personal rights and in one other case to be noted in the sequel.

The crucial and novel lesson which the experiment in sociological jurisprudence that is Continental European Union has to teach us is that federalism requires common social norms, and hence common political parties, for ordering social relations economically and politically in the member states, whereas confederation does not. Common living-law social norms and parties, the nations in the Continental European Community possess, not merely qualitatively but also to a remarkable degree quantitatively. This is why realistic statesmen of its six nations believed a genuine transfer of sovereignty to the legally instituted supranational community was practicable.

The nations in the Council of Europe do not have a common living law, or common political parties, for the economic and political ordering of the social relations of their citizens. This is why the positive law of the Council of Europe did not achieve a transfer of sovereignty from the nations to the legal institutions of the international body, even as a mere positive constitutional proposal. For the same reason Great Britain and the United States can associate themselves by treaty with the Continental European Community but cannot become members of it.

The hesitation of the French with respect to the Germans in the European Defense Community has its roots likewise in living-law considerations. The nation among the six whose qualitative religious and political living-law norms deviate most in quantitative support from that which they have in the other five in the Continental European Community is West Germany. This is true even when West Germany is restricted to the area west of the Oder-Neisse, and even, to a lesser extent, when it is restricted to the latter area without the Russian sector. Our comparative quantitative analysis showed, however, that the quantitative difference is not great enough to make West Germany's loyalty to the Community unlikely, if Germany is restricted to the area west of the Oder-Neisse. The chance that Franco-German collaboration will break down is even more unlikely if West Germany does not include the Russian sector. The reasons for these conclusions are that the qualitative norms are such that the two parties in West Germany with the largest quantitative support are liberal democratic parties, equally opposed to the East Prussian Junkers and to the Nazis, and that the larger of the two has leadership and additional norms which bind it religiously to Roman Catholic Europe and secular Latin Europe rather than to Lutheran East Prussia.

The living-law statistics would indicate to anyone from Mars, knowing sociological jurisprudence and the tables in Chapter 9 but knowing nothing of what has happened in Europe in fact, that Italy was the other possible questionable case in the Continental European Community. Needless to say, events in Europe in 1953–1954 show this to be the case. The living law of Italy cannot, however, be entirely blamed for the events. Foreign diplomatic errors had much to do with the situation.

The implications for the United Nations are obvious: at the very least, the only practical and effective program for the immediate future is world confederation, not world federalism. The Council of Europe, with its fourteen nations in a limited geographical region, could not achieve federalism. It is hardly likely, therefore, that the eighty-odd nations of the world can do so. The greater diversity in living-law social norms among all the nations in the world, as compared with the nations in the Council of Europe, tells us why this is so.

This does not mean, however, that the United Nations and the Council of Europe cannot achieve a real transfer of sovereignty of one specific kind—if they base the international law and treaty between their members on one principle. The principle clearly must be that of living-law pluralism in economic, political and philosophical norms for ordering communal relations in the member nations. This follows because, as we have just noted, the religious and political living-law norms for ordering the communal relations between men differ from nation to nation throughout the world, even more than among the nations in the Council of Europe.

However, a Council of Europe, or United Nations, based on the principle of living-law pluralism can achieve one specific transfer of sovereignty from the member nations to its supranational community which will be effective—namely, the transfer of the right to have the unique living-law norms of each state and people *protected and policed* by the international community in return for the correlative responsibility to contribute troops automatically to the international police force which is necessary to make the right of protection mean anything. This, the nations of the Council of Europe, with the United States included, have done in NATO, even though, as our study of their living law has shown, they do not possess common religious, economic and political norms for ordering communal relations. In other words, NATO, of which the Council of Europe is a part, is an empirical confirmation of the thesis expressed in 1952 in *The Taming of the Nations*, that a world confederation can be made effective if (1) it is grounded in the objective fact of the pluralism of the living-law economic, political, religious and philosophical norms which the world's nations use in ordering their respective domestic social institutions, and (2) it is implemented by the automatic responsibility of each nation to contribute to any police action authorized by the world community. This, let it be noted, is precisely what the Council of Europe through NATO affirms and has achieved.

This specific type of transfer of sovereignty from the nation to the supranational confederation in the case of nations with diverse living-law communal norms and political parties is but the extension of the pluralistic principle of religious, economic and political sovereignty from the domestic to the international field. It can be made effective because, being the only all-embracing international positive legal principle for the world that is in accord with the world's many different cultures, living religions and de facto political parties, it has living-law support.

It is to be emphasized that under law and under morals no one can make a demand on the community without a balancing contribution to the furtherance of the community. Similarly, no member nation can make a demand on the United Nations or a protest in the name of its Charter against an act of another member without just as vigorous a performance of duties to the larger body. To demand rights from the United Nations without participating in its police actions is like demanding the right to draw upon a joint checking account in a bank without ever depositing anything. This is what the wise liberal Spaniard de Madariaga meant in the days of the League of Nations when he pointed out that its members were better at consuming peace and collective security than at contributing to it. Until each nation's contribution to the disagreeable work of the United Nations, such as the loss of life in its police actions, matches that nation's demands from it there will be no peace: there are no moral rights which are not built out of moral responsibilities.

This principle has important implications for the foreign policy of any nation. It means, as President Truman noted in the 1952 election campaign, that any use of force by the United Nations to stop or prevent aggression must be treated as, and called, a police action; it must never be called a war. The difference between a police action and a war is basic and cuts to the roots of both domestic and international morality. The difference has nothing to do with the number of people killed. A police action is a peace-making enterprise. A war is a war-making enterprise. A policeman is good. War is evil. The moral difference between the two is this: Evil, or war, is the use of force on one's own unilaterally declared decision concerning what one does. Goodness or peace everywhere, short perhaps of Heaven, is the community-authorized use of force to put down unilaterally initiated use of force.

For the nations of the world generally as well as the United States, the only good and the only effective international policy therefore must base the use of force to police aggression on legally constituted and processed community decisions, not on the self-interest of any one nation, however enlightened. A unilaterally authorized use of a nation's force is evil even if it is enlightened. Only community-authorized use of force is good. This, it may be added, is precisely the difference between a private citizen who kills another man and a policeman who kills a man in the pursuit of his legal duty. The former killing is murder, an evil thing; the latter killing is peacemaking, a good thing.

The difference in society between evil killing and a good use of force which may involve the death of many people is the difference between a unilaterally authorized and a community-authorized action. A unilaterally declared decision not to contribute to a community-authorized police action is just as immoral as a unilaterally authorized decision to use national forces to stop aggression. Any member of a legally authorized community, whose legal rules he has accepted in signing its charter, is therefore just as irresponsible when he goes-it-alone to set up his own unilaterally declared definition of peacemaking by refusing, after the manner of the United States in the League of Nations or India in the United Nations, to contribute to a community-authorized decision to police the peace, as is the member nation which, acting unilaterally, would break away from the community-authorized rules for policing the peace to insist on going it alone in a bombing expedition across the Yalu.

Whatever may be the weaknesses of the Council of Europe and of NATO, their member nations are not guilty of such irresponsibility. This is shown by the fact that the NATO Treaty makes any violation of the rights of any member carry automatic responsibility for police action upon the part of every other member.

This principle, that a nation's foreign policy with respect to other nations is good only when it is community-authorized, throws important light upon the difficult question confronting the United States in April of 1954 when it was faced with the possibility of the defeat of the French in Indo-China and the fall of perhaps the whole of South Asia to the Communists. The correct stand to take is that policing the peace of the world anywhere is the responsibility not merely of the larger community in that area but of the entire world community. This means negatively that each and every nation has the responsibility to act. It is completely immoral for any nation to allow the situation to go by default. It means positively that the problem is a problem of the world community.

Furthermore, there is no reason whatever why there should not be a Council of South and Southeast Asia with its PATO just as there is a Council of Europe with its NATO. Furthermore, there are other peoples in Southeastern Asia than the people of India. The wishes and rights of the people of Thailand and of the Philippines and of Formosa are as worthy of consideration as the wishes and rights of any other people in the area. The Asians are rightly indignant over the determination of what happens in their area by Westerners. The cure for this evil is for the Asians themselves to assume the responsibility in a community-authorized policing of the area. The people of the United States and France will be more than happy to avoid contributing their sons to a community-authorized policing of the peace in Asia, *provided the community-authorized policing is done.* The time has come for the Americans and the French and the other Europeans to say to the Asians that the Western nations are through with doing the dirty work, and assuming the major share of the loss of life, involved in the world community's responsibility to police the world's peace, only to be charged with imperialism and with war-making. The time has come also for each and every Western nation to assert with equal firmness that it is through with unilaterally declared, or bilaterally arranged, power-politics-motivated policies internationally, and that it stands unequivocally for world-community-authorized policing of the peace and will accept the automatic responsibility to contribute its fair proportion of the policemen necessary for any community-authorized police action. The time has come to put responsibilities first, and the insistence upon rights second, in foreign policy and in world affairs. Unless money is first deposited in the bank, there is nothing upon which anyone can draw.

It will be said that such an attempt to extend—from the Council of Europe and NATO to the entire world community and a reformed United Nations—the pluralistic principle of political and religious sovereignty with the responsibility of every member to contribute automatically to any community-authorized police action will not work because the domestic positive-law, and in some cases even the living-law norms, of nations such as Franco's Spain, Communist China, Soviet Russia and Tito's Yugoslavia contradict this principle, affirming as they do the monistic principle of political and religious sovereignty. That these nations do hold the monistic principle is true; but the inference drawn from the fact does not follow. Even in domestic communities where law is effective there are always groups of individuals, even strong groups of individuals, who, apart from the positive law, do not hold or practice the living-law norms of the community as a whole. This shows that there can be effective law internationally for the world as a whole based on the pluralistic theory of positive- and living-law sovereignty even though the living and positive-law beliefs and habits of certain nations in the world community do not conform to this principle. If the majority of the groups in any community accept the living and positive-law norms of the community as a whole, the public opinion and morale necessary to prevent others from breaking its peace are forthcoming.

It appears that this is the case for the world as a whole. An overwhelming majority of the nations of the world have a plurality of normative groupings in their domestic living law and respect and police the positive pluralistic principle of political and religious sovereignty to which this living-law fact gives rise, after the manner of the nations in the Council of Europe and in NATO. This is true also of Pakistan, India, the Philippines and practically all the Latin American republics. Thus the creation of a supranational confederation in which each member nation has the automatic responsibility to contribute to the police force, which has been accomplished in the Council of Europe and its wider military instrument NATO, can be extended to the entire world community, notwithstanding the fact that a certain minority of the world's nations have living and positive legal norms which do not respect the global fact of living-law pluralism and its positive constitutional pluralistic principle of political and religious sovereignty.

All that needs, therefore, to be done in the forthcoming proposed revision of the United Nations Charter is to base it unequivocally on the pluralistic principle of living-law sovereignty and upon the second principle that there is never, under moral law or under community law, a right without a correlative duty. This entails that if one has the right to appeal to the United Nations to protect one's own nation or any other from aggression, then one has the correlative corresponding automatic duty to contribute to the police force necessary to make effective such a right with respect to one's own nation or any other. The pluralistic principle of living-law sovereignty also permits one to define aggression. Aggression is any violation by one nation of the pluralistic principle of living-law sovereignty with respect to another nation. This occurs when any nation tries to impose the norms of its own positive-law ideology or living law upon the different living-law norms and positive-law majority choices on another nation.

The experience of the Council of Europe suggests also that it is not wise to attempt to create a standing police force of the world community in the United Nations after the manner of the permanent standing army in the Continental European Community. Such a standing supranational army may be appropriate only for a supranational federation, but not for a supranational confederation.

The Continental European Community makes it clear, however, that a supranational federation with its own army is possible and can be effective in any international community in which the member nations have common economic and political norms for ordering their citizens socially. Then also there can be a standing police force. As the introduction of the Schuman Plan shows, such a community can also order its economic life supranationally, because the norms of the different political parties in all the member nations for ordering the economic life are the same. The Continental European Community shows also that where nations joining an international community have common economic and political norms they can have a common, directly and popularly elected parliament which is more than consultative. The people of the member states will trust their fate to such supranational legislatures and leaders because, their living laws being identical, they know the larger community will respect their separate living-law values and norms. This is also the reason why the Frenchmen, Germans, Luxembourgers, Netherlanders, Belgians and Italians at Luxembourg under M. Monnet can have a common mind—not any common mind, but the common mind that is peculiar to the Continental European mentality.

The consultation with the statesmen in the Continental European Union nations in 1952 and the foregoing study of the living law of this Community have made abundantly clear that one other principle must govern international relations and the foreign policy of any nation if they are to be effective. An international or foreign policy that is to be effective can be based neither on power politics nor on economic aid. As Socialist and Christian Democratic leaders alike in different Continental European nations told me, military and economic advantages can both lead to and result from Continental European Union; but they cannot be its basis. The basis of any economic or political community must be in common domestic living-law norms. Power cannot be pooled to balance other power unless the nations pooling their power have enough norms in common to trust one another. Our analysis of the Franco-German problem and the manner in which the loss of trust of the Europeans in the foreign policy of the United States has threatened the pooling of power in EDC, in NATO and in the United Nations makes this abundantly clear.

There is another reason why power politics is self-defeating as a basis of foreign policy, especially in the world today. As every statesman has made clear, no foreign policy can succeed without allies. This is especially true in an atomic age. Power, being neutral with respect to ethics and morality, is neutral with respect to moral responsibility and to community responsibility, and hence generates neutralism rather than allies. If a nation is to have allies, other nations must be prepared to share responsibility for its foreign policy.

Since only moral principles can generate responsibility, it follows that only a morally based foreign policy can generate the responsibility necessary to insure allies.

The reason why men as morally sensitive as George F. Kennan turned to a power-politics theory is also clear. Previous attempts at a morally based foreign policy were founded on the living-law norms of one nation. Instead of producing peace, this tends to generate a moral crusade. Then the existence of but two nations with traditional morally based foreign policies is enough to increase rather than decrease the chances of war.

The cure for this mistake is not to make foreign policy neutral with respect to ethical norms, thereby generating neutralism and a self-defeating foreign policy. It is instead to base foreign policy morally on the international cultural and moral fact that different nations have different living laws. This means that while one people chooses the norms of its own living law as the guiding principle for its own social institutions, it respects similarly the right of other peoples to build their institutions in the light of their own living-law political parties, cultural traditions and domestic choices.

Economic aid while necessary, just as power is necessary to police the peace of the world, cannot be the basis of an effective foreign and international policy. Experience in Europe with the Marshall Plan and in Asia with Truman Point Four aid has made this evident. *The New York Times'* informed correspondent in India, Robert Trumbull, wrote in 1953, near the end of Mr. Bowles', otherwise successful, ambassadorship: "United States standing in India has happened . . . to diminish in inverse proportion to the amount of American economic assistance being given to that country." [9] Speaking about the same time before a foreign affairs conference in Washington, held by the Johns Hopkins University School of Advanced International Studies, the Frenchman A. Rossi referred to "the limited return from the Marshall Plan" so far as the aims of the United States in Western Europe were concerned.[10] *The New York Times* on March 18, 1954, reported from Rome that former Premier de Gasperi had said that the economic "reforms had not helped in the fight against communism as had been hoped," the reason being that "Communist propaganda urges them to demand more." [11] In explaining the inadequacy of economic aid as a basis for U. S. foreign policy in Europe, M. Rossi stated that

the United States perhaps placed too much confidence in economics and the autonomism thereof. Actually, struggles fought in the field of economics require, in order to be truly won, a transmutation of their economic results into political results; the contests engaged in may be economic, but the points measuring success or failure are tallied on a political "computing machine." [12]

Our study of the living law of Continental Europe reveals why this is the case. The word "economic" is exceedingly ambiguous. It becomes significant socially only when a group of people in a given nation or society have a given normative theory for ordering their relations to one another economically. The Communist theory specifies one normative ordering for effective economic aid, the liberal Socialist of the Continental European nations specifies a different normative ordering, the Radical Socialists a still different one and so on. Consequently, there is no effective economic aid in a given society apart from its living-law norms; and these, to be effective, must express themselves politically.

It is clear that the Continental European Community and the Council of Europe, in their relations through NATO to United States foreign policy, have important lessons to teach to every statesman, citizen and student of international law and relations who is concerned—as every senstive person in an atomic age must be—with bringing the relations between nations more and more under the rule of idealistically motivated and realistically grounded legal procedures and institutions. There are spiritual living-law resources in the world, and in the hearts, minds and customs of men, which—if we will but study objectively what they are, and then harness our national foreign policies and our positive international legal institutions to them—will take this fearful and troubled world nearer to community-policed international peace than our predecessors, for all their achievements in policing the domestic peace, ever brought mankind.

In international law and foreign policy, as in transportation, what has been does not have to be. When moral and spiritual resources are at hand unused, which can permit men to do, as the Continental Europeans have done, what never was done before, history is a poor instructor, as Henry Ford saw. The frequent wars of yesterday do not have to be tomorrow.

In the realm of the world's cultures and of man-made institutions, man not only receives from the past but he also creates what is and what is to be. Ideas matter, especially when embodied in untapped strata of the living law. To have helped us see this is the lasting achievement of the realistic statesmen who, at The Hague in May of 1948, trusted in the living, constructive, unifying power of the European idea. In six brief years, making themselves its instruments, they transformed the rigid habits of one of the most conservative cultures in the world to create the confederation which is the Council of Europe and the federation which is the High Authority of the Continental European Community. By having faith in, and by drawing upon, the deepest philosophical foundations of classical, Christian and modern Europe's living law, these contemporary statesmen reformed its secondary outmoded positive forms to meet present needs. And in doing this, whether they be followed or not, they have shown the world the way to peace. For every people with a rich cultural tradition have their underlying living law.

Regardless, therefore, of what others may do with their handiwork, they have served their countrymen and mankind well. They have given the lie to those who say that contemporary Western man has mastered the instruments of life but is morally bankrupt with respect to the values which are necessary to direct those instruments to good ends. A Europe that can do this is not dead. Nor is a world which includes such a Europe doomed to an atomic Armageddon. If mankind, profiting by the European Movement's example, leaves the scorner's seat by the side of the road to take to the world's highway to become a friend and community-authorized protector of man, even our age can face its future calmly, confidently and without fear.

Asia and Islam also have their contributions to make; but this is another story, and their achievements are for a later day. Today's celebration is for Europe.

At the end of an essay on "The Place of the Classics in Education" Whitehead wrote:

Roman Law embodies the secret of Roman greatness in its Stoic respect for intimate rights of human nature within an iron framework of empire. Europe is always flying apart because of the diverse explosive character of its inheritance, and coming together because it can never shake off that impress of unity it has received from Rome.[13]

Here lie the secret, the difficulties, and the power of Continental European Union. In these elements also lies its present originality. Only by combining the liberalizing effect of its Protestant Reformation and of its modern British Empirical and Continental Rationalistic philosophy with its Roman Catholic religious, and Stoic Roman secular, concept of moral man as universal man, rather than nationalistic tribal man, can Europe substitute for its traditional inclination toward the chauvinistic iron framework of empire a liberally democratic supranational community and achieve the Stoic respect for intimate rights of human nature, which the pluralistic principle of religious and political sovereignty expresses, thereby turning into a positive political reality that impress of unity which is its genius.

In this contemporary creative attempt to bring its traditional diverse and often conflicting living-law elements together into a novel economic, military and political synthesis is to be found the profound meaning of the remarkable phenomenon which is the experiment in sociological jurisprudence that is European Union. Only by objectively understanding, contributing to and profiting from this great experiment can the United States find a foreign policy that serves both its own values and the peace of the World, thereby in part repairing the dangerous situation, deteriorating fast toward World War III, into which the tragic errors and failures of the foreign policy of Candidate and President Eisenhower and his Administration have brought the free nations in Europe and in Southeast Asia. Such is the significance, the one for the other, of European Union and United States foreign policy.

NOTES

CHAPTER 1

1. *European Movement and the Council of Europe*, with Forewords by Winston S. Churchill and Paul-Henri Spaak, published on behalf of The European Movement, Hutchinson & Co., London, 1949, p. 11.

2. *Ibid.*, p. 38.

3. *Ibid.*, pp. 42 43.

4. *Ibid.*, p. 43.

5. *Ibid.*, p. 52.

6. *Ibid.*, p. 53.

7. *Ibid.* See also "Britain and Europe," special issue of *European and Atlantic Digest*, published in cooperation with the United Europe Movement, edited by Elma Dangerfield and Howard Russell, London, May, 1952.

8. Herriot, Edouard, *The United States of Europe*, transl. by Reginald J. Dingle, Viking, New York, 1930.

9. *European Movement, etc.*, p. 56.

10. *Concise Handbook of the Council of Europe*, Directorate of Information of the Council of Europe, Strasbourg, 1951, p. v.

11. Spaak, Paul-Henri, "England Tiptoes into Europe," *United Nations World*, Vol. 7, No. 4 (April 1953), p. 18.

12. *Ibid.*

13. *Ibid.*

14. McCormick, Anne O'Hare, "Abroad," *The New York Times*, Jan. 14, 1952, p. 18, col. 5.

15. Schuman, Robert, "Europe Will Go Forward to Unity," *The New York Times Magazine*, Sept. 27, 1953, p. 28.

16. McCormick, Anne O'Hare, "American Policy and France's Decision on E.D.C.," *The New York Times*, Dec. 16, 1953, p. 34, col. 5.

17. "Up E.D.C.," *The New York Times*, Sept. 13, 1953, p. 1E, col. 2.

18. Cortesi, Arnaldo, "Italy's Election Leaves Large Problems in Wake," *The New York Times*, June 14, 1953, p. E1, col. 8.

CHAPTER 2

1. *The Statesman's Year-Book, 1953*, S. H. Steinberg, ed., St. Martin's Press, New York, 1953, p. 36.

2. *Ibid.*, Article 9.

3. *Ibid.*, pp. 35–38.

4. *The Annual Register*, 1949, Longmans, Green and Co., London, 1950, p. 214.

5. "Text of Eisenhower's First Annual Report to NATO As Commander of West's Forces," *The New York Times*, April 2, 1952, p. 14, col. 8.

6. *The World Almanac, 1953*, New York World-Telegram Corporation, New York, 1953, pp. 354–355.

7. *Ibid.*, p. 355.

8. *Council of Europe, Consultative Assembly, Official Report of Debates*, Vol. 7, Strasbourg, 1951, p. 1004.

9. The Convention on Relations Between the Three Powers and the Federal Republic of Germany, *Senate Executive Documents Q & R*, 82nd Congress, 1952, p. 9.

10. Treaty Constituting the European Defense Community, Protocol Concerning Relations Between the European Defense Community and the North Atlantic Treaty Organization, *Senate Executive Documents Q & R*, 82nd Congress, 1952, p. 226.

11. Protocol to the North Atlantic Treaty on Guarantees Given by the Parties to the North Atlantic Treaty to the Members of the European Defence Community, *Senate Executive Documents Q & R*, 82nd Congress, 1952, p. 23.

12. *Ibid.*

13. *The New York Times*, Feb. 21, 1954, p. E5, col. 4.

14. *The New York Times*, Feb. 22, 1954, p. 1, col. 1.

15. White, William S., "Republicans Tell Dulles of Doubts on Geneva Parley," *The New York Times*, Feb. 23, 1954, p. 2, col. 2.

16. *The New York Times*, Feb. 23, 1954, p. 3, col. 3.

17. Warburg, James P., *Germany: Key to Peace*, Harvard University Press, Cambridge, 1953. See also his "Policy for Germany," *The New York Times*, Aug. 23, 1953, p. E8, col. 5.

18. Lippmann, Walter, "Into Molotov's Hands," *New York Herald Tribune*, March 30, 1954, p. 18, col. 3. See also quotations from Mr. Lippmann in Warburg, *op. cit.*, pp. 136, 147–148 and 276.

19. Middleton, Drew, "British Laborites Split on Germany," *The New York Times*, Feb. 24, 1954, p. 8, col. 3.

20. Handler, M. S., "West German Problems Rendered More Acute," *The New York Times*, Feb. 21, 1954, p. E5, col. 2.

21. "To Meet the President," *The Economist*, Vol. CLXIX, p. 638 (Nov. 28, 1953).

CHAPTER 3

1. Ehrlich, Eugen, *Fundamental Principles of the Sociology of Law*, transl. by Walter L. Moll, Harvard University Press, Cambridge, 1936.

2. Moore, Underhill, and Charles C. Callahan, *Law and Learning Theory: A Study in Legal Control*, Yale Law Journal Co., New Haven, 1943; Moore and Hope, "An Institutional Approach to the Law of Commercial Banking," *Yale Law Journal*, Vol. 38 (1929), p. 703.

3. Northrop, F. S. C. "Underhill Moore's Legal Science: Its Nature and Significance," *Yale Law Journal*, vol. 59 (1950), pp. 196–213.

4. Kroeber, A. L., "Concluding Review" in *An Appraisal of Anthropology Today*, edited by Sol Tax, University of Chicago Press, Chicago, 1953, p. 372.

5. Northrop, F. S. C. *The Taming of the Nations*, Macmillan, New York, 1952, pp. 108–148.

CHAPTER 4

1. *Concise Handbook of the Council of Europe.*
2. *European Movement and the Council of Europe,* p. 129. See also Northrop, *The Taming of the Nations,* Chaps. 10 and 11.
3. *European Movement, etc.,* p. 170.
4. *Ibid.,* p. 173.
5. *Ibid.,* p. 175.
6. *Concise Handbook of the Council of Europe,* p. 8.
7. *Ibid.*
8. *Ibid.,* p. 11.
9. *European Movement, etc.,* p. 48.
10. *The European Convention on Human Rights,* Directorate of Information of the Council of Europe, Strasbourg, 1952, p. 39.
11. *Ibid.,* Art. 21, pp. 46–47.
12. *Ibid.,* Art. 22 (1), p. 47.
13. *Ibid.,* Art. 27, p. 48.
14. *Ibid.,* Art. 31 (3), p. 50.
15. *Ibid.,* Art. 31 (2), p. 50.
16. *Ibid.,* Art. 32 (2), p. 50.
17. *Ibid.,* Art. 32 (3), p. 50.
18. *Ibid.,* Art. 38, p. 51.
19. *Ibid.,* Art. 39 (1), p. 51.
20. *Ibid.,* Art. 40 (1), p. 51.
21. *Ibid.,* Art. 41, p. 52.
22. *Ibid.,* Art. 43, p. 52.
23. *Ibid.,* Art. 46 (1), p. 53.
24. *Ibid.,* Protocol, p. 59.

CHAPTER 5

1. Treaty Constituting the European Coal and Steel Community, Annexes and Protocols, *Senate Executive Documents Q & R,* 82nd Congress, 1952, p. 256.
2. *The Council of Europe and the Schuman Plan,* Directorate of Information of the Council of Europe, Strasbourg, 1952, p. 23.
3. *Ibid.,* p. 24.
4. *Ibid.*
5. *Ibid.,* p. 25.
6. Treaty Constituting the European Coal and Steel Community, Annexes and Protocols, p. 309.
7. *The Council of Europe and the Schuman Plan,* chart opposite p. 16.
8. Bebr, Gerhard, "The European Coal and Steel Community: A Political and Legal Innovation," *The Yale Law Journal,* Vol. 63, pp. 1–43 (Nov. 1953).
9. *The Statesman's Year-Book, 1953,* p. 35, and *The World Almanac, 1953,* p. 279.
10. Warren, Lansing, "Monnet Tells Pool to Think European," *The New York Times,* Jan. 14, 1953, p. 12, col. 2.
11. McCormick, Anne O'Hare, "On Hearing the Voice of the New Europe," *The New York Times,* April 21, 1952, p. 20, col. 5.

12. Hoffman, Michael L., "European Steel Pool Found Still Far From Single Market," *The New York Times*, June 23, 1953, pp. 1 and 15.

13. Hoffman, Michael L., "Belgium and Italy Are Tests of Pool," *The New York Times*, June 24, 1953, p. 13, col. 6.

14. Matthews, Kenneth, "The European Coal and Steel Community," *The Listener*, Feb. 5, 1953, p. 206.

15. Callender, Harold, "Single Market Is Step Toward Goal of Unity," *The New York Times*, Feb. 15, 1953, p. E12, col. 4.

16. The Convention on Relations Between the Three Powers and the Federal Republic of Germany, *Senate Executive Documents Q & R*, 82nd Congress, 1952, p. 9.

17. Treaty Constituting the European Defense Community, etc., p. 167.

18. *Ibid.*, Art. 9, p. 169.

19. *Ibid.*

20. *Ibid.*

21. *Ibid.*, Art. 10, Secs. 1 and 3, p. 169.

22. *Ibid.*, Art. 11, p. 170.

23. *Ibid.*, Art. 15, Sec. 2, p. 171.

24. *Ibid.*, Art. 18, pp. 171–172.

25. *Ibid.*, Art. 20, Sec. 1, p. 172.

26. *Ibid.*, Art. 20, Sec. 2, p. 173.

27. *Ibid.*, Art. 21, Sec. 1, p. 173.

28. *Ibid.*, Art. 21, Sec. 2, p. 173.

29. *Ibid.*, Art. 21, Sec. 3, p. 173.

30. *Ibid.*, Art. 21, Sec. 4, p. 173.

31. *Ibid.*, Art. 25, Sec. 1, p. 174.

32. *Ibid.*, Art. 25 and Art. 25 Bis, p. 174.

33. *Ibid.*, Art. 25, Sec. 1, p. 174.

34. *Ibid.*, Art. 26, Sec. 1, p. 174.

35. *Ibid.*

36. *Ibid.*, Art. 26, Sec. 2, p. 175.

37. *Ibid.*, Art. 31, Sec. 1, p. 176.

38. *Ibid.*, Art. 33, Sec. 1, p. 176.

39. *Ibid.*, Art. 34, p. 177.

40. *Ibid.*, Art. 40, p. 179.

41. *Ibid.*, Art. 39, Sec. 1, p. 178.

42. *Ibid.*, Art. 39, Sec. 2, p. 178.

43. *Ibid.*, Arts. 51–67, pp. 181–184.

44. Callender, Harold, "France to Ratify a European Army, Its Advocates Say," *The New York Times*, Sept. 27, 1953, p. 1, col. 5.

45. Middleton, Drew, "Britain to Offer Pact to Aid E.D.C.," *The New York Times*, Feb. 23, 1954, p. 1, col. 6.

46. Treaty Constituting the European Defense Community, etc., Art. 38, Secs. (1a) and (2), p. 178.

47. *Ibid.*

48. *Ibid.*, Art. 38, Sec. (1c), p. 178.

49. Draft Treaty embodying the Statute of the European Community adopted by the ad hoc Assembly instructed to work out a draft treaty setting up a European Political Community (hereinafter cited as EPC Treaty), *Inter-Parliamentary Union, Constitutional and Parliamentary Information*, published

by the Autonomous Section of Secretaries General of Parliaments, Geneva, 3rd Series, No. 14, April 1, 1953, p. 52.

50. *Ibid.*, Art. 9, p. 54.
51. *Ibid.*, Art. 11, p. 54.
52. *Ibid.*, Art. 17, p. 55.
53. *Ibid.*, Art. 11, p. 54.
54. *Ibid.*, Art. 15, p. 55. Also Robert R. Bowie and Carl J. Friedrich, "Statute of the European Community," in *European Union: A Survey of Progress*, vol. III (American Committee on United Europe, New York, 1953), p. 22.
55. Bowie and Friedrich, *op. cit.*, p. 23.
56. EPC Treaty, Art. 52, p. 63.
57. *Ibid.*, Art. 52, Sec. 4, p. 63.
58. *Ibid.*, Art. 53, p. 63.
59. *Ibid.*, Art. 28, Sec. 1, p. 57.
60. *Ibid.*, Art. 28, Sec. 2, p. 57.
61. Bowie and Friedrich, *loc. cit.*
62. EPC Treaty, Art. 29, p. 58.
63. *Ibid.*, Art. 30, Sec. 1, p. 58.
64. *Ibid.*, Art. 31, Sec. 2, p. 58.
65. *Ibid.*, Art. 31, Sec. 3, p. 58.
66. *Ibid.*
67. *Ibid.*, Art. 31, Secs. 4 and 5, pp. 58–59.
68. *Ibid.*, Art. 35, p. 59.
69. *Ibid.*, Art. 36, p. 60.
70. *Ibid.*, Art. 37, p. 60.
71. *Ibid.*, Art. 38. Sec. 2, p. 60.
72. *Ibid.*, Art. 38, Sec. 1, p. 60.
73. *Ibid.*, Art. 39, Sec. 1, p. 60.
74. *Ibid.*
75. *Ibid.*, Art. 39, Secs. 1 and 3, p. 60.
76. *Ibid.*, Art. 45, pp. 61–62.
77. *Ibid.*, Art. 50, p. 62.
78. *Ibid.*, Art. 51, pp. 62–63.
79. *Ibid.*, Art. 55, p. 64.
80. *Ibid.*, Art. 64, Sec. 2, p. 66.
81. *Ibid.*, Art. 78, Sec. 1, p. 69.
82. Bowie and Friedrich, *op. cit.*, p. 25.
83. EPC Treaty, Art. 67, pp. 66–67.
84. *Ibid.*, Art. 70, Sec. 3, p. 67.
85. *Ibid.*
86. *Ibid.*, Art. 82, p. 69.
87. *Ibid.*, Art. 84, Secs. 2 and 3, p. 70.

CHAPTER 6

1. *Statesman's Year-Book, 1953*, p. 1132.
2. Churchill, Sir Winston S., "Triumph and Tragedy" (*Memoirs*, Vol. VI), as published in *Life*, Nov. 9, 1953, pp. 71–72.
3. Fauvet, Jacques, *Les Forces Politiques en France, de Thorez à de Gaulle*, Editions "Le Monde," Paris, 1951.

4. *The Statesman's Year-Book, 1953*, p. 960.

5. Lindsay, Alexander Dunlop (Lord Lindsay of Birker), *Religion, Science, and Society in the Modern World*, Yale University Press, New Haven, 1943, and "The Philosophy of the British Labour Government," in *Ideological Differences and World Order*, ed. F. S. C. Northrop, Yale University Press, 1949, pp. 250–268.

CHAPTER 7

1. *Information Please Almanac, 1954*, The Macmillan Co., New York, 1953. See also Table III in Chapter 8, following.

2. *The Statesman's Year-Book, 1953.*

3. Mozer, Alfred, "Netherlands Labour Party Becomes Strongest Party," mimeographed report circularized by the Partij van de Arbeid, Holland.

4. *Ibid.*, and "Programme of Principles of the Dutch Labour Party," mimeographed, distributed by the Partij van de Arbeid.

5. Mozer, *op. cit.*

6. "Programme of Principles of the Dutch Labour Party."

7. Mozer, *op. cit.*

8. *New York Herald Tribune*, April 23, 1954, p. 2, col. 4.

9. As quoted by Anne O'Hare McCormick in *The New York Times*, April 9, 1952. For further information see Geyl, Pieter, "Holland: Today and Yesterday," *The Atlantic*, April 1954, pp. 101–104.

10. Warburg, James P., *Germany: Key to Peace.*

11. Holborn, Hajo, "Germany," in *The Americana Annual, 1954*, Americana Corp., Chicago, 1954, p. 282. Also *American Foreign Policy and European Integration in World Politics*, Vol. VI, 1953. pp. 1–30.

12. *The Statesman's Year-Book, 1953*, p. 1049.

13. Office of the U.S. High Commissioner for Germany, *Elections and Political Parties in Germany, 1945–1952*, 1952, p. 37.

14. *Ibid.*, pp. 40 ff.

15. *Ibid.*

16. "Up E.D.C.," *The New York Times*, Sept. 13, 1953, p. E1, col. 2.

17. *Ibid.*

18. Office of the U.S. High Commissioner for Germany, *op. cit.*, p. 18.

19. *Ibid.*, p. 19.

20. "Dr. Adenauer and the Parties," *The Economist*, Vol. CLXVII, p. 644 (June 6, 1953).

21. *Ibid.*, p. 645.

22. Handler, M. S., "Old and New Nazis Take a Hand in Election," *The New York Times*, Aug. 30, 1953, p. E4, col. 6.

23. Office of the U.S. High Commissioner for Germany, *op. cit.*, p. 19.

24. Bullock, Alan, "Germany and the Future of Europe," *The Listener*, Vol. 1, p. 448 (Sept. 17, 1953).

25. Sulzberger, C. L., "Italy Still Split by Clerical Issue," *The New York Times*, March 16, 1954, p. 4, col. 3, and "Dilemma for Europe's Socialists," *The Economist*, Vol. CLXX, p. 847 (March 20, 1954).

26. *The New York Times*, June 14, 1953, p. E1, col. 8.

27. *Ibid.* See also McCormick, Anne O'Hare, "Italy Is Neither 'Safe' Nor in Dire Danger," *The New York Times*, March 8, 1954, p. 26, col. 5.

28. Office of the U.S. High Commissioner for Germany, *op. cit.*, p. 19.
29. Brown, John L., "Paris Letter," *Renascence*, Vol. IV (1952), p. 158.

CHAPTER 8

1. Northrop, *The Taming of the Nations*, chaps. 13 and 14.
2. Office of the U.S. High Commissioner for Germany, *op. cit.*, pp. 7–9.
3. Prittie, Terence, "The Frustration of German Social Democracy," *The Listener*, Vol. L, p. 1108 (Dec. 31, 1953).
4. Noyes, Crosby S., "Extremist Reactions on EDC Issue Pose Threat of Rebellion in France," *New Haven Evening Register*, April 20, 1954, p. 15, col. 1. See also *World*, Vol. 1, p. 1.
5. *World*, Vol. 1, No. 12 (April 15, 1954), p. 2.
6. "Belgian Shift," *The New York Times*, April 18, 1954, p. E2, col. 8.
7. Handler, M. S., "Germans Look to Future," *The New York Times*, Aug. 9, 1953.
8. "Champions of European Unity," *The Economist*, Vol. CLXIV, p. 375 (Aug. 16, 1952).
9. "Dr Adenauer and the Parties," *The Economist*, Vol. CLXVII, p. 644 (June 6, 1953). The italics are mine.
10. *Ibid.*
11. "A New Germany," *The Economist*, Vol. CLXVIII, Sept. 12, 1953, p. 678.

CHAPTER 9

1. "Paris on the Red River," *The Economist*, Vol. CLXIX, p. 400 (Nov. 7, 1953).
2. *Ibid.*
3. McCormick, Anne O'Hare, "American Policy and France's Decision on E.D.C.," *The New York Times*, Dec. 16, 1953, p. 34, col. 5.
4. "Acceptance Speech of Dwight D. Eisenhower for the G.O.P. Presidential Nomination" as distributed through the Press Secretary at the White House.
5. Lawrence, W. H., "McCarthy vs. Eisenhower: Showdown Again Off," *The New York Times*, Feb. 28, 1954, p. E3, col. 3.
6. Sulzberger, C. L., "Secretary Dulles' Trip as Viewed in Europe," *The New York Times*, April 18, 1954, p. E3, col. 7.
7. "What They Are Saying," *The Listener*, Sept. 4, 1952, p. 370.
8. "North Atlantic Treaty," *Treaties and Other International Acts Series 1964*, Department of State Publication 3635, Washington, D.C., 1950, p. 6.
9. See *Keesing's Contemporary Archives*, Vol. VII (1948–1950), p. 9901.
10. "Magnificent—but Is It Policy?" *The Economist*, Vol. CLXVII, pp. 417–419 (May 16, 1953).
11. Herald, George W., "Adenauer on the Berlin Conference," *World*, Feb. 1, 1954, p. 16.
12. "Firepower for Manpower?" *The Economist*, Vol. CLXIX, pp. 332–333 (Oct. 31, 1953), and "The President's Late Start," *The Economist*, Vol. CLXX, pp. 213–214 (Jan. 23, 1954).
13. Lippmann, Walter, "Policy and the Parties," *New York Herald Tribune*, Sept. 5, 1950, p. 17, col. 1.

14. Reston, James, "Asians Await Possible Shift of U.S. Policy Under Radford—His Strong Views on Pacific Defense Go Beyond Limited-Commitment Attitude," *The New York Times*, Aug. 13, 1953, p. 3, col. 2.

15. Department of State, Press Release No. 46, Jan. 27, 1953.

16. Bartlett, Vernon, "The New Look in Europe," *The Listener*, Vol. L, p. 284 (Aug. 20, 1953). See also Prittie, Terence, "Germany as a Trade Competitor," *The Listener*, Vol. LI, pp. 125–126 (Jan. 21, 1954).

17. "Champions of European Unity," *The Economist*, Vol. CLXIX, pp. 374–375 (Aug. 16, 1952).

18. Sulzberger, C. L., "Indo-China Settlement Vital to West Europe's Defense," *The New York Times*, July 2, 1953, p. 3, col. 6.

19. "The President's Late Start," *The Economist*, Vol. CLXX, p. 213 (Jan. 23, 1954).

CHAPTER 10

1. Sulzberger, C. L., "Trend in European Politics Held Inimical to U.S. Aims," *The New York Times*, June 11, 1953, p. 11, col. 3.

1a. Foreign Policy Briefs, Vol. II, No. 22, May 22 & June 23, 1953 and Vol. III, No. 11, Dec. 18, 1953.

2. McCormick, Anne O'Hare, "The Revolt in East Germany Will Be Felt in Bermuda," *The New York Times*, June 24, 1953, p. 24, col. 5.

3. Callender, Harold, "Diplomats in West Europe Relieved by Bermuda Delay," *The New York Times*, June 28, 1953, p. 4, col. 2.

4. "Unsordid Act," *The Economist*, Vol. CLIV, p. 569 (April 10, 1948).

5. "The Reconstruction of Policy," *The Economist*, Vol. CLXVII, p. 879 (June 27, 1953).

6. *Ibid.*, pp. 879–880.

7. *Ibid.*, p. 880.

8. *Ibid.*

9. *Ibid.*, p. 881.

10. *Ibid.*, p. 882.

11. "Excerpts from Wiley's Foreign Policy Talk," *The New York Times*, June 27, 1953, p. 4, col. 4.

12. *Ibid.*

13. King, Seth S., "Nixon Calls Truman Right on Going into Korean War," *The New York Times*, Sept. 1, 1953, p. 1, col. 6.

14. "Excerpts from Wiley's Foreign Policy Talk," *loc. cit.*

15. Handler, M. S., "Germans Look to Future," *The New York Times*, Aug. 9, 1953, p. E3, col. 5.

16. Alsop, Stewart, "Matter of Fact," *New York Herald Tribune*, Aug. 5, 1953, p. 17, col. 7.

17. Sulzberger, C. L., "Secretary Dulles' Trip as Viewed in Europe," *loc. cit.*

18. Harsch, Joseph, "A Turning Point for President Eisenhower," *The Listener*, Vol. L, p. 568 (Oct. 8, 1953).

19. *The New York Times*, Nov. 14, 1953, p. 2, col. 8.

20. Servan-Schreiber, Jean-Jacques, "France, Indo-China, and Communism," *The Listener*, Vol. L, p. 712 (Oct. 29, 1953).

21. *Ibid.*, pp. 711–712. See also Cadett, Thomas, "France Seeks Peace in Indo-China," *The Listener*, Vol. L, pp. 753–754 (Nov. 5, 1953).

22. Drummond, Roscoe, "Washington: Behind the President's U.N. Speech," *New York Herald Tribune*, Dec. 9, 1953, p. 3, col. 3.

23. *Ibid.*

24. "An Idea for Bermuda," *The Economist*, Vol. CLXIX, p. 467 (Nov. 14, 1953).

25. "Berlin Prospects," *The Economist*, Vol. CLXX, p. 3 (Jan. 2, 1954).

26. *Ibid.*, p. 4.

27. "Berlin to Geneva," *The Economist*, Vol. CLXX, p. 588 (Feb. 27, 1954).

28. *Ibid.*

29. "The Adenauer Way," *The Economist*, Vol. CLXVIII, p. 760 (Sept. 19, 1953).

30. Middleton, Drew, "British Want Allies in Pre-Geneva Talks," *The New York Times*, March 13, 1954, p. 1, col. 1.

31. *World*, mid-monthly supplement, March 15, 1954 (Vol. 1, No. 10), p. 1.

32. *Ibid.*

33. Schmidt, Dana Adams, "Canada Cautions U.S. on 'New Look,'" *The New York Times*, March 16, 1954, p. 12, col. 6.

34. "Text of Magazine Article by Dulles on Present Defense Policy," *The New York Times*, March 17, 1954, p. 4, col. 7.

35. "Transcript of Secretary Dulles' Remarks on Defense at His New Conference," *The New York Times*, March 17, 1954, p. 5, col. 2.

36. *Ibid.*, col. 3.

37. "Text of Magazine Article by Dulles on Present Defense Policy," *loc. cit.*

38. Millis, Walter, "Arms and Men," *New York Herald Tribune*, Feb. 25, 1954, p. 18, col. 7.

39. "Text of Magazine Article by Dulles on Present Defense Policy," col. 4.

40. Schmidt, *op. cit.*, col. 5.

41. Speech at Chatham House, London, Feb. 15, 1951, on "Politics, Opinion and Feeling in America in the Present Crisis."

42. As quoted by Sulzberger, C. L., in "Secretary Dulles' Trip as Viewed in Europe," *The New York Times*, April 18, 1954, p. E3, col. 8.

43. *Ibid.*

44. *Ibid.*

45. Reston, James, "Dulles Facing Heavy Criticism on Asian Policy," *The New York Times*, May 4, 1954, p. 1, col. 8, and p. 4, col. 3.

CHAPTER 11

1. "Belgium Becomes Third Nation to Approve E.D.C. Treaty," *The New York Times*, March 13, 1954, p. 1, col. 3.

2. "French Assembly Debates E.D.C.," *Europe Today and Tomorrow* (International Bulletin of the European Movement), No. 34, Jan. 1954, p. 7.

3. *Ibid.*

4. Middleton, Drew, "Britain to Offer Pact to Aid E.D.C.," *The New York Times*, Feb. 23, 1954, pp. 3 and 1.

5. "Texts of British Documents on Link with a European Army," *The New York Times*, April 15, 1954, p. 4, col. 3.

6. "Text of President's Message," *The New York Times*, April 17, 1954, p. 2, col. 2.

220   *European Union and United States Foreign Policy*

7. Callender, Harold, "Herriot for Union If Peace Talks Fail," *The New York Times*, Sept. 20, 1953, p. 22, col. 3. See also "Notes of the Week," *The Economist*, Vol. CLXX, p. 935 (March 27, 1954), and Goold-Adams, Richard, "Two Questions of Sovereignty," *The Listener*, Vol. LI, p. 556 (April 1, 1954).

8. "Notes of the Week," *The Economist*, Vol. CLXX, p. 852 (March 20, 1954). See also *The New York Times* editorial, "A Victory for E.D.C." March 16, 1954.

9. Trumbull, Robert, "U.S.-India Relations Strained by U.N. Debate over Korea," *The New York Times*, Aug. 30, 1953, p. E5, col. 7.

10. Rossi, A., "Soviet-Communist Pressures on Western Europe," in *The Threat of Soviet Imperialism*, edited by C. Grove Haines, The Johns Hopkins Press, Baltimore, 1954, p. 236.

11. Sulzberger, C. L., "Italian Reds Gain in Stricken South," *The New York Times*, March 18, 1954, p. 8, col. 2. See also Olivetti, Adriano, "How US Aid Boomeranged in Italy," *World*, Vol. 1, November 1953, pp. 60–62.

12. Rossi, *loc. cit.*

13. Whitehead, A. N., *The Aims of Education and Other Essays*, The Macmillan Co., New York, 1929, p. 115.

Index